MODERN
BULGARIA

TODOR ZHIVKOV

MODERN BULGARIA

Problems and Tasks in Building
an Advanced Socialist Society

TODOR ZHIVKOV

INTERNATIONAL PUBLISHERS, New York

Library of Congress Cataloging in Publication Data

Zhivkov, Todor.
Modern Bulgaria: problems and tasks in
building an advanced socialist society.
Collection of writings and speeches, 1958-1974.
Includes bibliographical references.
1. Communism—Bulgaria.   I. Title.
HX362.Z38 1974   335.43'4'094977   74-23868
ISBN 0-7178-0456-9
ISBN 0-7178-0457-7 pbk.

Contents

Editor's Note

All the footnotes in this volume were prepared by the editor. All quotations from Marx and Lenin conform to available English language editions of their works.

Foreword

Within a very brief period in terms of history, Bulgaria has gone through a revolutionary transition. Measured in years, the social and economic progress of the last 30 years outstrips the previous 1,300 years of Bulgaria's existence.

In these last 30 years Bulgaria has transformed itself from a backward country of misery, poverty, illiteracy and oppression into a land of modern industry and agriculture, maintaining one of the fastest growth rates of any country in the world. In 30 years it has wiped out the 1,300 years of poverty and illiteracy. From a country of backwardness, Bulgaria now stands in the front ranks of countries with modern systems of education, social security and medical care. There is no unemployment. There are no slums. In place of the mud huts and the slums there are beautiful new apartment complexes. There is stable economic growth. The Bulgarian people do not know the word "inflation." High rents and high taxes are foreign to them. The new Bulgaria has industry that in technology and science matches most other countries.

How is this possible? Bulgaria is a small country. It is not rich in natural resources. And yet in 30 years it has eclipsed 1,300 years of its past history. Of course the workers and the people of Bulgaria have worked hard. But they also worked hard during the previous 1,300 years. What, then, makes the differnce? The difference is Socialism.

For 1,300 years the people of Bulgaria worked like slaves for the slavemasters, the feudal lords, the capitalist who owned the factories and the mines. Now, because of Socialism, they work for themselves.

That is what this book is all about. It is about building a social and economic system without bosses, without exploitaition by corporations or banks. It is a system without private profits. It is a system in which the people are the bosses. It is their system. Whatever they produce goes into wages, social services and the expansion of their industry and agriculture, the products of which again go into raising the standard of living.

Only a Socialist system could have given Bulgaria that great thrust forward. Socialism is the high-powered booster rocket of social progress.

During the previous 1,300 years Bulgaria was the victim of wars and oppression. Its independent development was stymied. It was the victim of Bulgarian and foreign oppressors. Socialism put an end to both forms of oppression.

One of the important factors that has made it possible for Bulgaria to make such great strides forward is the fact that it is surrounded by a number of Socialist neighbors. The Soviet Union has made the most significant contributions to Bulgarian economic and social development.

Georgi Dimitrov, that great Marxist-Leninist leader of the Communist Party of Bulgaria and of the world revolutionary movement, laid the foundation for these relationships right from the beginning:

The people's democratic state is built and developed in cooperation and friendship with the Soviet Union, the land of Socialism. Just as our country's liberation from imperialism and the creation of our people's democratic state were possible only thanks to the Soviet Union's assistance and its liberating mission in the war against fascist Germany and its allies, the continued edvelopment of our people's democracy requires retention and atrengthening of close relations and sincere cooperation, mutual assistance and friendship between our country and the great Soviet Union.

The people's democtatic state belongs in the democratic, anti-imperialist camp.

Only by participating in the united democratic, anti-imperialist camp headed by the powerful Soviet Union, can each people's democracy uphold its independence, sovereignty and security against imperialist aggression." (From Central Committee Report to 5th Congress, Bulgarian Workers' Party, December 19, 1948.)

The 30 years of Bulgarian Socialism is proof that there need not be any contradiction between building Socialism in one's own country while fulfilling the needs of the world revolutionary movement. Bulgaria stands as a witness to the great gains that come from the close alliance made up of the family of Socialist countries.

The Communist leaders of Bulgaria have always rejected as opportunistic and false to seek for a contradiction where there in none. The Communist leaders of Bulgaria have always rejected the concept of getting small concessions from world imperialism in payment for weakening the forces of the world revolutionary movement by policies of division and disruption.

Lenin once observed: "Not a single class in history has achieved power without producing its political leaders, its prominent representatives, able to organize a movement and lead it." The working class of Bulgaria has certainly produced such leaders. The name Georgi Dimitrov is a household name the world over.

Todor Zhivkov is such a working class Marxist-Leninist revolutionary leader.

This book contains only some brief excerpts from the writings, speeches and reports of Comrade Zhivkov. But what comes through is his deep insight into the processes and forces that are the propellents for the building of Socialism. What comes through is that Socialism is a people's power, that above all else it is concerned with the welfare of all the people. What comes through is that Socialism is solely motivated and propelled by the desire to make life easier and more interesting, more humane and more just for all of the people. What comes through is Todor Zhivkov's deep understanding, his total commitment, his adherence to matters of principle, and his down-to-earth flexibility about secondary questions. What comes through is that Todor Zhivkov is a working class revolutionary leader in the mold of Marx, Lenin and Dimitrov.

This is a book about the experiences and problems of building Socialism in Bulgaria. But there are great lessons. It is a book of great significance to the world revolutionary movement. This is a book of great interest to the working class and the revolutionary movement in the United States.

GUS HALL
General Secretary, Communist Party, U.S.A.

Todor Zhivkov

First Secretary of the Central Committee of the Bulgarian Communist Party and President of the State Council of the People's Republic of Bulgaria.

Todor Zhivkov was born in the village of Pravets, Sofia District, on September 7, 1911. He joined the Young Communist League in 1928. He has been a member of the Bulgarian Communist Party (BCP) since 1932.

In the period of 1934-1941 Todor Zhivkov headed various Party Districts in Sofia. During those years he was also a member of the Sofia Regional Committee of the Bulgarian Communist Party. Between 1941 and 1944 he was one of the leaders of the Sofia Party Organization taking an active part in organizing the struggle against the Hitlerite occupiers and their Bulgarian lackeys. In 1943 Todor Zhivkov was one of the organizers of the partisan underground movement in the First (Sofia) Partisan Military Operation Zone.

In the September 1944 the Party entrusted him with the task of commanding the partisan regiments and battle groups, stationed in and around Sofia, which on the night of September 8th launched the main drive against the fascist regime and secured the victory of the armed anti-fascist uprising in Bulgaria.

After the People's Government came to power Todor Zhivkov was called upon to carry out responsible Party and Government functions. In the period of 1948-1949 he was First Secretary of the City Committee of the Bulgarian Communist Party in Sofia, Chairman of the Sofia Committee of the Fatherland Front and Chairman of the City People's Council of Sofia.

Todor Zhivkov was elected alternate member of the Central Committee of the Bulgarian Communist Party at its Eighth Plenary Meeting in 1945. He was elected full member of the Central Committee at the Fifth Congress of the Party in 1948. In 1950 he was elected alternate member of the Politbureau and Secretary of the Central Committee of the Party. He was also concurrently Secretary of the Sofia City and District Committees of the Party. In 1951 he was elected to full membership in the Politbureau of the Central Committee. At the Sixth Congress of the BCP, held in 1954, he was elected First Secretary of the Party Central Committee, and still retains this post.

Todor Zhivkov has emerged as a consistent Marxist-Leninist, an outstanding theoretician and organizer in the struggle to build up the socialist society in the People's Republic of Bulgaria, particularly so after the April Plenary Meeting of the Central Committee in 1956, which was of historical significance for the Bulgarian Communist Party.

Todor Zhivkov has been a Member of the National Assembly since 1945.

In November 1962 Zhivkov was elected Chairman of the Council of Ministers of the People's Republic of Bulgaria. The first session of the Sixth National Assembley, which met in July 1971, elected Todor Zhivkov President of the State Council of the People's Republic of Bulgaria.

The Tenth Congress of the Bulgarian Communist Party, held in April 1971, adopted a Program of the Bulgarian Communist Party and approved a Draft Constitution of the People's Republic of Bulgaria. Both of these historical documents for the Party and the State were prepared under the direct leadership and participation of Todor Zhivkov.

For his active part in the fight against fascism and capitalism, and in the construction of socialism, Todor Zhivkov was awarded the distinction of "Hero of Socialist Labor." He was also repeatedly awarded the "Order of Georgi Dimitrov," as well as other high State citations.

Todor Zhivkov has visited the Soviet Union on numerous occasions. He headed the Bulgarian Communist Party delegations to the 21st, 22nd, 23rd and 24th Congresses of the Communist Party of the Soviet Union, as well as to the Moscow conferences of the representatives of the communist and workers' parties in 1957, 1960 and 1969. He also headed the Party and Government delegation of the People's Republic of Bulgaria in 1957 and 1964, including the Bulgarian delegations to the conferences of the first secretaries of the Central Committees of the communist and workers' parties and heads of governments of the member states of the Council for Mutual Economic Assistance (CMEA) and the Warsaw Treaty.

In 1971, on his 60th anniversary, for his exceptional services to the Bulgarian people and the BCP he was awarded the highest distinction—"Hero of the People's Republic of Bulgaria." The Presidium of the Supreme Soviet of the Union of the Soviet Socialist Republics bestowed on Todor Zhivkov the "Order of Lenin" for his service rendered to the development of the deep friendship and co-operation between the peoples of the Soviet Union and Bulgaria, for the consolidation of peace and socialism, and for his long years of outstanding participation in the world communist movement.

Todor Zhivkov, 1944 as a member
of the People's Militia
General Staff

With Georgi Dimitrov

Greeting the Chavdar Partisan Brigade
on Victory Day, September 9, 1944

At an exhibit of the Union
of Bulgarian Artists

At an agricultural exhibit

Dedicating a petrochemical
plant at Pleven

With Young Pioneers

With Fidel Castro

With Leonid I. Brezhnev

With Indira Ghandi

With Charles De Gaulle

◆ With Yumjaagiin Tsedenbal, President of the Mongolian Peoples Republic

◆ With Romesh Chandra, Secretary of the World Peace Council

◆ With Erich Honecker, First Secretary of the Socialist Unity Party (SED), German Democratic Republic

◆ At a Paris interview with French and Bulgarian journalists

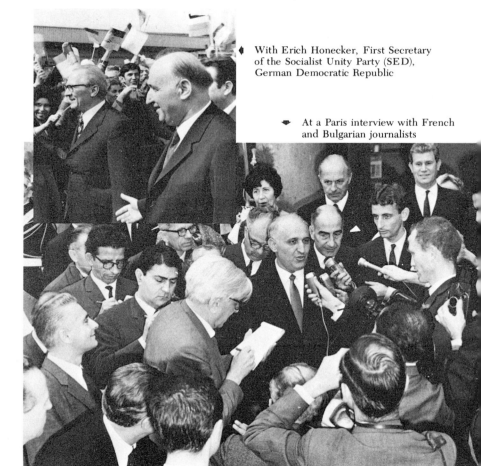

MODERN
BULGARIA

1

Problems of Our Revolution and the Fundamental Laws of Social Development

Excerpts from the Report of the Central Committee
of the Bulgarian Communist Party (BCP) to the
7th Congress of the BCP, July 2, 1958

During the past few years some problems of great importance have come to the fore in the work of our Party and in the development of the world communist and working class movement. They are especially significant for the theoretical and practical work of our Party, for its cadres and organizations. It is therefore our intention to dwell on these problems.

In the report of the Central Committee of the Party to the Fifth

Congress, (1948), Georgi Dimitrov[1] defined the September 9th People's Armed Uprising in 1944 as an important historic turning point in the development of our country. The nature of this change opened up the road for the construction of socialism in Bulgaria.

"Although the September 9th People's Uprising," says Dimitrov, "set out to solve immediate democratic tasks; *it could not, however, but shake the capitalist system in our country from top to bottom and go beyond the framework of bourgeois democracy.*

"Therein lies the *main* characteristic of our September 9th Uprising."

The Central Committee of the Bulgarian Communist Party has always considered that the Bulgarian revolution, popular and democratic in form, was from the very outset and in its laws of development a repetition of the basic content of the great October Socialist Revolution. It was a continuation of the same cause under our specific conditions, a part of the great world transition from capitalism to socialism that began with the socialist revolution of the Russian workers and peasants in October 1917.

Our own victory was the natural result of the revolutionary struggle of the Bulgarian working class, in alliance with the working people from town and country, against fascism and capitalism and with the decisive help of the Soviet Army.

The merger during World War II of the revolutionary struggle of the Bulgarian working class against capitalism with the struggle of the whole people against fascism and imperialism (and for social and national liberation on the basis of a broad democratic platform), found concrete expression in the Fatherland Front movement. The leading force in this movement was the working class, in alliance with the poor and middle strata in towns and villages, headed by the Bulgarian Communist Party.

---

[1] *Georgi Dimitrov* (1882-1949): prominent leader of the Bulgarian and international communist and working class movements. Dimitrov was the outstanding leader of the Bulgarian Communist Party during decades of struggle against the Bulgarian monarcho-fascists and then the German nazi invaders which led to socialist victory in 1944. Dimitrov achieved world-wide fame for his brilliant and heroic defense of Bulgarian and international communist ideals during the infamous Reichstag Fire Trial where he placed the brutal nazi regime "on trial." He served as Secretary General of the Communist International and gave the main report on *The United Front Against War and Fascism* at the 7th World Congress of the CI, a work which has achieved the stature of a Marxist classic.

The struggle to realize the tactical slogans of the Party, as embodied in the Fatherland Front program, became nation-wide, assuming unprecedented dimensions and power. By the beginning of September 1944 it turned into a mass people's armed uprising which, under the favorable conditions created by the great victories of the Soviet Army, led to the victory of the people and opened up the way for the construction of socialism in our country.

Both central and local power *actually* passed into the hands of the working class in alliance with the working people, and into the hands of the Fatherland Front committees, in which the Bulgarian Communist Party had a leading and decisive role. Our Party, backed by the overwhelming majority of the people, became the decisive factor in the government as well.

Supported by the masses, the Party succeeded in directing the country along the road of socialist development by defeating the attempts of the internal and international reactionary forces to hinder this process. Hypocritical and hostile representatives of the bourgeoisie were gradually eliminated from both the Government and the Fatherland Front committees and the leading role of the Bulgarian Communist Party was officially recognized by all.

The distinctive feature of the development of our revolution was the fact that the working class, headed by the Communist Party, in alliance with the working peasants, did not establish and consolidate its dictatorship in the form of a people's democracy in one stroke, but in the gradual process of an acute class struggle, *without civil war*. In 1947, this process of sharp struggle climaxed in the nationalization of industry, which is a specific feature of the development of the socialist revolution and of no other kind.

It would therefore not be correct to overrate the importance of the general democratic tasks solved by our revolution nor to consider them as tasks of the bourgeois-democratic revolution.

In our country there was no "transformation," no "evolution" of the power established after the September 9th Uprising. The process of revolutionary development won new positions. It got rid of the hesitant and insincere representatives of the various parties; it gained strength and broadened its contact with the masses. *But by its class character it has always been socialist power in a popular democratic form.* Hence, the conception that two stages existed in the development of the class character and tasks of our people's power is erroneous.

Investigating an immense amount of factual material, our scientific workers and theorists in history, philosophy, economy, sociology and other fields are working out the problems of our revolution and socialist construction in order to help socialist practice.

Regarding the nature of our revolution and its specific features, I want to dwell on the character of our socialist construction and its laws of development. This is all the more necessary since the question of the fundamental laws and national traits of the transition of various countries from capitalism to socialism has of late assumed topical importance in the international communist movement. Tendencies have appeared that exaggerate the role and importance of national traits, tendencies that underrate, deny and, in the long run, revise some basic principles of proletarian revolution and socialist construction.

As far back as 1917, just prior to the October Revolution, Lenin defined the positions of the basic and of the specific characteristics in the transition of various countries from capitalism to communism in his great work, *State and Revolution:* "... Bourgeois states are most varied in form, but their essence is the same: all these states, whatever their form, in the final analysis are inevitably the *dictatorship of the bourgeoisie.* The transition from capitalism to communism is certainly bound to yield a tremendous abundance and variety of political forms, but the essence will inevitably be the same: *the dictatorship of the proletariat.*"[2]

And later on, in 1920, on the eve of the Second Congress of the Comintern, unmasking the opportunism of leaders of the Second International like Karl Kautsky, Otto Bauer and Frank Adler, Lenin speaking on the international significance of the October Revolution, elucidated the roles of the fundamental laws of development and particular traits: "In the first months after the proletariat in Russia had won political power (October 25 [November 7th], 1917), it might have seemed that the enormous difference between backward Russia and the advanced countries of Western Europe would lead to the proletarian revolution in the latter countries bearing

---

[2] *Lenin Collected Works* (English Language edition), Progress Publishers, Moscow 1964, Vol. 25, p. 413.

very little resemblance to ours. We now possess quite considerable international experience, which shows very definitely that certain fundamental features of our revolution have a significance that is not local, or peculiarly national, or Russian alone, but international."[3]

Of course, Lenin warned that it would be a very grave mistake to exaggerate this truth, and we should not dogmatically apply it to all basic features of our revolution.

Our Party has always thoroughly grasped the international importance of Marxism, and later of Leninism, and has been convinced that the basic principles of Marxism-Leninism hold good for our country, as well. It has been guided by these principles in all its revolutionary activities.

The struggle of the international communist movement and the experience of socialist construction in all socialist countries, *without exception*, confirm the truth that despite the profound changes in the world, the fundamental laws of development and the features of the October Revolution and socialist construction in the first socialist country in the world, the USSR, is of tremendous international importance.

This has been confirmed by our own experience. Although our country possesses many specific characteristics, the process of the people's democratic revolution and socialist construction in Bulgaria demonstrate the same main traits as the October Revolution and Soviet experience in socialist construction.

Just as in the October Revolution, in Bulgaria, too, the driving and leading force in the revolutionary struggle against fascism and capitalism was the working class allied with the peasant masses; in our country, too, the revolution was made under the leadership of the Communist Party; in our country, too, the dictatorship of the proletariat in alliance with the working people was established as a result of the victory of the revolution; in our country, too, big capitalist ownership over the means of production was eliminated through nationalization. And following the example of the Soviet peoples, the process of socialist industrialization, of the socialist re-organization of the rural economy, of the cultural revolution, all began along similar basic lines.

Nevertheless, the revolution in our country *is not a simple repeti-*

[3] *Lenin, Ibid*, Vol. 31, p. 21.

tion of the October Revolution; it possesses its particularities and differences from the Soviet experience as well as from the people's democratic revolutions in other countries. *These specific features are the result of differing historical, political and economic conditions existing in our country.* They are based upon the degree of skill with which our Party creatively applies the basic Marxist-Leninist laws, taking into account the concrete conditions.

The main specific feature of our socialist revolution, as Georgi Dimitrov declared at the Fifth Congress of the Bulgarian Communist Party, is the fact that it was carried out not under the slogan of Soviet power but under that of establishing a people's democratic rule. In the conditions then existing in Bulgaria, this slogan facilitated the alliance of the working class not only with the poor but also with the middle peasants in the struggle against fascism. It helped to neutralize part of the Bulgarian bourgeoisie and created conditions under which some of its representatives could take part in the struggle. As a result, after the victory of the revolution, our proletarian dictatorship was established not in the form of soviets, but in that of a people's democracy in which representatives of the petty-bourgeois and bourgeois parties participated.

Thus the active participation of the Bulgarian Agrarian National Union in the government is characteristic of our country and under the leadership of the Communist Party, this is facilitating our advance to socialism.

An important feature of our revolutionary struggle and of our social and political system is *the existence of the Fatherland Front as a specific political form* of the alliance of the working class, the working peasants and the people's intelligentsia.

As indicated, the strengthening of the dictatorship of the working class took place in an atmosphere of acute struggle against the capitalist class, *but without civil war*—a specific feature that we owe to the presence of the liberating Soviet troops in Bulgaria.

Our state, a dictatorship of the proletariat, assumed the form of a people's democratic state that successfully fulfilled its mission as the main instrument in the construction of socialism. Now that the exploiting classes have been eliminated, the economic, organizational and cultural-educational functions of our state are more and more extensive and the people are taking an ever greater part in the government and in the management of the economy.

Moreover, today when there is a world socialist system the law of socialist industrialization, of securing the predominance of the growth of heavy industry operates somewhat differently than in the USSR during the 30 years when it was the only socialist country in the world.

With this in mind, we are carrying out socialist industrialization without following in the exact footsteps of the Soviet Union and its rates of development, and without creating all branches of industry. In the development of our industries we take into account the natural resources of our country, its economic potentialities and needs, as well as those of the other countries of the socialist camp.

Co-operative farms are the form through which our agriculture has acquired a large-scale socialist character. Our co-operative farms differ from the collective farms in the Soviet Union mainly in that the land was not nationalized. The co-operative farmers have retained private ownership of the land they held when they joined the co-operative groups and they receive rent for their holdings. *It would be wrong, however, to identify this rent with absolute capitalist rent,* which is based on the monopolistic private ownership of land and on the capitalist methods of production. Actually, the rent that exists in the co-operative farms is a new economic category, since it is not an expression of relations of exploitation. It constitutes a relatively small part of the income of the co-operative farms and is distributed among the farmers on the basis of the acreage of land they brought into the co-operative rather than on the amount of labor they perform.

This specific feature—the existence of rent—does not alter the socialist charater of our co-operative farms, which are not organized in a rigid, static economic way. They are constantly developing, and along with their organizational, economic and financial stabilization, the farmers consciously and voluntarily are gradually reducing the rent or abolishing it altogether. Thus, when conditions are ripe, the land becomes public property, more socialist in character, more like collective farms.

These are the prospects for the development of all the co-operative farms in our country. The process of the abolishment of rent develops in a natural, voluntary way and this enables the mass of the co-operative farmers to understand that this is *a necessity* for the further strengthening of the co-operative farm.

There are also specific features in the development of our socialist culture that are in accord with the traditions, national characteristics and aspirations of the Bulgarian people. These are some of the main specific features of socialist construction in Bulgaria. *They are forms, methods, rates and trends in which the basic social laws are reflected.* To every Marxist-Leninist, however, *the main and decisive question is that of universal principles and laws of the revolution,* while the question of the national specific forms, and methods of application is of secondary importance. The People's Republic of Bulgaria is developing towards socialism not along a "special," "national" path, differing in principle from the Soviet people and the people of other socialist countries, but along a path that is basically the same.

At the same time, our Party fights dogmatism and doctrinairism and against the mechanical application of the general laws of development and of the experience of the Soviet Union and the other socialist countries. It fights against all attempts to ignore the specific features of our national development.

Nonetheless, the Bulgarian Communist Party relentlessly combats all attempts to minimize or underrate the international validity of the basic laws of development, to underrate and deny the international importance of Soviet experience, and to place as primary the national peculiarities for the transition from capitalist to socialist society. The downgrading and negation of the universal truths of Marxism-Leninism invariably lead to a revision of these truths, into a "theory" of "national communism" and to nationalism. The overrating of the role and importance of national characteristics and forms of development creates the danger that the communist parties and the socialist countries could drift apart, could oppose each other's "national" interests and ways of development and undermine the unity of the socialist countries and their mutual assistance. All this cannot but bring grist to the mill of international reaction.

We well know the damage the working class movement in the capitalist countries can suffer from revisionist theories on the evolutionary, parliamentarian transition from capitalism to socialism without class struggle and without the dictatorship of the proletariat. The revisionists are even trying to adapt the Leninist evaluations made in the decisions of the Twentieth Congress of the Communist Party of the Soviet Union to their pseudo-Marxist policies and theories. *It was for the purpose of dispelling parliamentarian illusions among the working class* that the Declaration of the Moscow Conference stressed that the communist and workers' parties should always bear in mind that there are two possibilities for the conquest of power and *therefore master all forms of struggle*—peaceful and nonpeaceful, parliamentarian and non-parliamentarian.[4]

Our Party unreservedly supports the declaration of the Moscow Conference, which presents a correct Leninist approach to the question of the basic laws of development and of the national peculiarities of the transition from capitalism to socialism. With redoubled energy the Party will educate its cadres and members in the spirit of loyalty to the great principles of Marxism-Leninism; it will cultivate in them the skill to apply these principles constructively and to fight relentlessly against all manifestations of revisionism; it will forward the struggle for mastering and creatively applying Soviet experience in their practical work. It will do all this because it fully realizes that the tremendous experience of the Communist Party of the Soviet Union and the Soviet peoples is a vital necessity for successfully building socialism in our country.

Another general law of our socialist development is to overcome all major contradictions in our society. The same acute irreconcilable and antagonistic contradictions inherent in the capitalist system in general were present in our own country as well. The main contradiction consisted in the contrast between the social character of production and the private character of capitalist appropriation, between the relations of production and the character of the forces of production. This basic contradiction found its expression in the uncompromising revolutionary struggle of the Bulgarian working class, in alliance with the laboring peasants, against the capitalist class, for the abolition of these contradictions and the establishment of new, socialist relations of production. The uncompromising revolutionary struggle of the working class, under the leadership of the Communist Party, against the bourgeoisie was the main motive force of our social development prior to September 9, 1944, and it was this struggle that led to the transformation of our country into a socialist state.

[4] *Declaration:* Meeting of Representatives of the Communist and Workers' Parties of the Socialist countries, held in Moscow, November 14-16, 1957.

This is not to say that the antagonistic contradictions between the people's democratic state and the overthrown capitalist class were completely eliminated. In the first years after September 9, 1944, it was still the major motive force in our socialist development, and even today antagonistic contradictions exist between the people's democratic power and the remnants of the capitalist class. There are those who have not resigned themselves to their changed position and still hope that aid will come from abroad as they continue their fight against the socialist system.

We have no reason, therefore, to think that the class struggle in our country is over and done with, that it cannot even assume acute forms. Bearing in mind the support that international imperialism gives ,to capitalist remnants, we must stress that the class struggle exists and will continue to exist for some time as the only *antagonistic* contradiction in our society. The fight of these capitalist remnants has become an integral part of the crusade by world imperialism against our country and the entire socialist camp, to the fundamental contradiction in international relations—the contradiction between the socialist and capitalist world systems. And this basic contradiction has and will have its repercussions on the ways, forms and acuteness of the class struggle inside our country.

In this context it becomes clear how false are all slogans about "freedom" in general, or about "democracy" in general, and how harmful to the cause of our working class and people are all attempts to spread pseudo-Marxist theories about the "withering away" of the state and all attempts to weaken the organs of the state, which has as one of its tasks to crush the hostile activities of the internal and international enemies of socialism.

In contrast to capitalist society, however, *non-antagonistic* contradictions are the main and typical contradictions of our socialist society. Today socialist relations of production, characterized by public ownership of the means of production, and by public distribution of its products are dominant in all spheres of our country's economy. This means that the relations of production correspond to the character of the forces of production—a conformity ensured by the planned and far-sighted policy of the Communist Party. The socialist relations of production open up boundless perspectives for the development of productive forces and of science and technology; they call to life and help advance the constant development of the forces of production.

The main force behind our progress along the road to socialism and communism remains the struggle of our society, united economically and politically. The struggle of the working class, the co-operative farmers and the intelligentsia is for the ever greater development of the forces of production and for the maximum satisfaction of the needs of the people; and against backwardness, against the forces of the past that endeavor to check our progress. All these struggles are waged under the leadership of the socialist state and of the Bulgarian Communist Party. Our people find support in their co-operation and programs of mutual assistance with the other socialist countries, and above all, in the very considerable all-round economic, technical and cultural aid rendered us by the Soviet Union.

The non-antagonistic character of contradictions under socialism makes it possible for the socialist state led by the Party to *eliminate them in a peaceful way,* without harmful conflict and in good time.

Experience has taught us that in our society contradictions between the base and the superstructure are being overcome successfully by making appropriate changes in the superstructure—in the views, the organization and the methods of work of its institutions and organs which ensures a swift development of society. The state continues, deliberately and in a planned way, to cope with the contradictions between the development of the economy on the one hand, and the forms and level of management, on the other. It continues to diminish the contradiction between the socialist character of our society and the remnants of the anti-socialist ideological influences on the minds of the people, which are obstacles in speeding-up the upsurge of the forces of production, of the economy and culture. the contradiction between production and consumption inherent in all social formations can also be solved peacefully, with deliberation and in a planned manner, under the conditions of socialism.

Thus the state is successfully overcoming the present contradictions between our progressive socialist relations of production which offer limitless opportunities for advancing the forces of production and the still insufficient development of these forces. It is also successfully coping with the contradiction between the growing needs of the members of our society and the still insufficient material and technical base to meet these needs. *Our main task–the constant development of the forces of production*–results from these contradictions.

The constant struggle to overcome the existing and constantly arising contradictions between the old and the new, between elements dying out and elements sprouting into existence, between the retrograde and the progressive factors in our movement to socialism constitute the basis of the entire state, economic and cultural policy of the Party and the government. The non-antagonistic character of these basic contradictions creates conditions in which it is possible to discover and overcome them *by means of criticism and self-criticism.*

Criticism also exists in capitalist society. But in such a society, where contradictions are antagonistic, where the interests of a small capitalist class predominate, criticisms cannot overcome these contradictions. It cannot eliminate the retrogressive phenomena in the political, economic and cultural life of society. It enters into contradiction with the social system itself and encounters the resistance of the ruling propertied classes. But criticism in capitalist society nevertheless has enormous political and propaganda importance. It helps the people to see more clearly the ulcers of the bourgeois regime and the reluctance and resistance of the capitalists to do away with these ills. It impels the working people to fight for the revolutionary transformation of the system itself.

In socialist society criticism not only exposes shortcomings, their roots and the persons responsible for them, but also helps to remove these shortcomings. Our society needs constant sharp and bold criticism of mistakes and harmful practices incompatible with our socialist system. Without criticism, mistakes cannot be corrected in good time; our cadres may be lulled into complacency; vigilance may weaken and corruption may develop in certain sectors of state, economic and ideological work. Thus our advance toward socialism will be slower and more difficult.

The Bulgarian Communist Party will continue to encourage criticism and self-criticism in every possible way, as a powerful instrument in overcoming contradictions and in eliminating shortcomings in our life and work.

What is the nature of the criticism our Party is fighting for? We resolutely oppose "criticism" whose aim is not to expose and help overcome shortcomings but to slander our socialist system, to negate our achievements, and attempt to confuse the working people and undermine their faith in socialism, in the People's Government and in the Communist Party and its leadership. We will continue to oppose the criticism that emanates from bourgeois and petty bourgeois interests and ideology. We will oppose unprincipled, destructive, biased and ill-intentioned criticism, because it is directed against the foundations of the socialist system and because it serves alien interests opposed to our own.

On the other hand, we stand for a constant deep going and rounded criticism that consolidates the socialist system, that helps it to get rid of shortcomings and accelerates its all-round development by castigating mistakes, vices and unwholesome actions, that exposes those responsible for such shortcomings, and denounces those unworthy of our society. This includes bureaucratic functionaries who have isolated themselves from the people as well as corrupt and decadent elements. In other words, we want and need constructive, honest and fair criticism showing our shortcomings in the framework of our enormous successes and the advantages of socialism; criticism that strengthens the faith of the masses in the Communist Party, that mobilizes the people and makes them more active in the struggle for the elimination of mistakes and shortcomings.

For criticism and self-criticism can operate as a powerful motive force in our society only if they become the concern of the greatest number of people. If the workers in our enterprises, offices and villages boldly oppose all harmful practices, if they struggle relentlessly and persistently for their elimination, our society will move much more rapidly and radically to rid itself of the miasmas of the old days; it will advance much more quickly.

Our Party must raise still higher the banner of bold, constructive criticism and self-criticism. The Party and the press must encourage this by every possible means. They must castigate severely those who stifle criticism; and create an atmosphere for an ever fuller and unhampered manifestation of every honest critical thought in our country.

We are faced with a two-fold task: On the one hand, it is the duty of the Party and the state, rallying the masses still closer and leaning on their consciousness and activity, to disclose and solve the contradictions and the urgent problems in good time, facilitating and speeding up the development of the production forces, technology and culture throughout the country with a view to satisfying the needs of the working people more fully. The existence of non-antagonistic contradictions in our society dictates this policy. On the other hand, it is our duty to increase the revolutionary vigilance of the masses and their preparedness and the defensive capacity of our socialist society to thwart the efforts of our capitalist remnants and of international imperialism to undermine our people's power. The existence of antagonistic contradictions between us and our internal and external enemies dictates such a policy.

2

People's Culture, Socialist Culture

Speech delivered at the concluding session
of the First Congress of Bulgarian Culture, May 20, 1967

Dear Comrades, the First Congress of Bulgarian Culture has concluded its work.

I would like to subscribe to the opinion, unanimously expressed from this rostrum, that the First Congress of Culture will be recorded in Bulgaria's cultural annals and our nation's life as a historic event.

For several days now we have encompassed in our thinking the difficult roads, the great wealth and inexhaustible treasure of the Bulgarian people's thousand-year-old culture. We again rejoiced at the fine successes achieved by our socialist cultural revolution that has made it possible for culture to penetrate every home, to become accessible to every worker and to become part and parcel of our people's lives.

The Congress itself was a splendid manifestation of the great successes of the socialist cultural revolution in Bulgaria and the advance of our national culture. At the same time it showed unequivocally that the cultural revolution and our national culture rest on the principles of internationalism and Marxist-Leninist ideology.

It demonstrated the international solidarity and the aspirations of the Bulgarian people and our cultural workers, as well as our profound respect for the progressive culture of all nations, large and small; our respect for and devotion to the liberation struggle of the working class and all working people throughout the world. We once again expressed our profound respect and love for the revolutionary culture of the great Soviet Union—daring and profoundly humane and a powerful influence upon modern civilization.

I cannot fail to note with satisfaction that the correct policy of the Bulgarian Communist Party and, more specifically, its policy in the field of culture was reaffirmed. Neither can I fail to note with gratification the unity and cohesion around the Bulgarian Communist Party and its Central Committee so vividly manifested here. It is this unity and cohesion, we may even call it comradeship, between Party and cultural workers, and between cultural workers and Party, which give promise of future successes.

The profound significance of the present Congress is also established by the fact that it confirmed cultural reform on the basis of new structure, style and methods in the leadership of our entire cultural front.

Years, scores of years, will pass and our culture will develop ever more successfully; it will grow richer and its achievements will multiply. Future congresses of culture will have to resolve new problems. Nevertheless, the First Congress of Culture in Bulgaria will go down in history as a congress of creative initiative and the fruit of the triumphant April line of the Central Committee of the Bulgarian Communist Party.

Comrades, we have all stressed our agreement with the evaluations, conclusions and undertakings for Bulgaria's further cultural development contained in the excellent report delivered by Comrade Pavel Matev.[1] It is gratifying that this was confirmed by all who spoke from this rostrum and that valuable thoughts and considerations were expressed as to the road traversed by our culture and the prospects for its future development.

To answer the question "what is important and particularly gratifying in the work of the Congress?" one might say that it is

---

[1]*Pavel Matev*, (1924 -) outstanding Bulgarian poet, Chairman of the State Committee on Art and Culture.

gratifying not only that all the comrades who took the floor attached great value to the basic factors in the development of our national culture, but also that during the Congress we took their opinions to heart and were moved by them. I cannot resist the temptation to say a few words about these factors for they are the *three inexhaustible sources* of our national socialist culture.

The first source is our rich cultural heritage—the thousand-year-old Bulgarian culture. We are proud that through the centuries the Bulgarian people with their skillful hands and their genius have created a fine material and spiritual culture. Resolutely rejecting any negative attitude towards our cultural heritage, we approach it with a sense of reverence, with love and respect for our forefathers, our talented working people and those who, under exceptionally hard conditions of bondage, ruthless exploitation and fascist dictatorship, worked tirelessly for the creation of Bulgaria's national culture. The fruit of these heroic efforts and the national genius, this culture has been and continues to be a source of inspiration.

Our revolutionary, national-democratic and proletarian cultural traditions are of particularly great importance to the development of modern Bulgarian culture. They constitute a tremendous capital for our people to draw upon. We have the obligation to continue considering these traditions attentively and carefully and to make even ampler use of them for the further progress of Bulgaria's new socialist culture.

The second source of our culture today is our present socialist life, which the people are building with enthusiasm and optimism. Creating our material and spiritual culture and establishing a new way of life in our country are processes in which the people themselves undergo a change; the socialist worker in Bulgaria is a man with a rich inner life, a new world outlook, new ideals. He is a man of bold initiative. The artistic interpretation of our life, with all its contradictions and variety, with all its many facets, along with its communist purposefulness, is a great source of inspiration for our modern culture.

The third source we draw upon is world culture—the heights scaled by human genius, thought and constructive work—mankind's progressive culture. We cherish feelings of profound respect for this culture from which we learn and will continue to learn. World socialist culture and, in the first place, the culture of the great Soviet Union, plays and will continue to play a role which is of immense and invaluable significance to us.

It is from these streams that the high flowing river of Bulgarian culture takes its nourishment today. They determine its content, its powerful current and its dynamic movement. It is from these sources that we will draw the sap of life in developing our culture, in building a new society and in educating the man of the future, the man of communist society.

The utilization of these three sources will continue to lend meaning, power and initiative to our work as it relates to the education of our people, and especially the youth, in a spirit of patriotism and internationalism. It will strengthen our national dignity, opening up new and unexpected potentialities in the enhancement of our sound and realistic optimism, increasing our confidence, self-respect and enthusiasm, protecting our working people and inspiring them to new exploits for the cause of socialism and the people's happiness.

It is our common and sacred duty to guard the swift current of our culture as it is replenished from these fresh and crystal-clear sources and to prevent anything which might muddy and foul its purity.

We have always been faced with questions that we cannot evade: what culture do we create, what are the goals of our cultural activity and policy, what values do we create and who will be, so to speak, their consumers? Modern Bulgarian culture will develop successfully in the future only if it proceeds from the interests of the working class and the people, from the positions of socialism and communism.

As we draw inspiration from the first source of our thousand-year-old culture—our cultural heritage; from the second source, which enables us to interpret artistically the life of new Bulgaria —our socialist life; and from the third source—the treasure-house of progressive world culture—we should always remember that we are serving the people, that we are working in their interest. We should always remember that there are two cultures: one that serves mankind and the progressive development of the world—social, economic, political, ideological and moral—and the other serving the exploiters and imperialists who try by hook and by crook to foist it upon us. For us, the Central Committee of the Bulgarian Communist Party, and for our whole Party, there is no criterion for checking cultural values and their utility other than whether they

have a profoundly popular character that serves the people's interests, which today are part and parcel of the interests of socialism
and communism.

We well know that the People's Republic of Bulgarian is at a
specific stage of its development. This stage has its active objective
laws as well as its own contradictions. The life of the people is
exceedingly complex, varied and contradictory and all this should
be taken into account. But if the life of the people should be por-
trayed as it is, we should never forget that our people are building a
new way of life, and it is this new way of life for which we live, work
and win fresh victories. And this is our popular, our great communist truth.

Comrades, *The greatest accomplishment of our Congress* is that it
adopted a new statute for the organization and development of culture and particularly of its leadership.

The Congress unanimously supported the considerations and
motifs for a further democratization of the cultural front and for the
reorganization of the Committee of Art and Culture into a public
and state organ. Many of the comrades who took the floor stressed
the profoundly democratic traditions of our people and the process
governed by objective law that characterizes our socialist society—a
process of steadfast development of socialist democracy in all fields
of life.

All this is perfectly valid. It is a solid, objective prerequisite to
look constantly for suitable forms, for ways and means of further
democratizing our life, including, of course, our cultural life.

In discussing this question now, in 1967, one should bear in mind
that one of the basic factors in the reorganization which is taking
place in the leadership of the cultural front is the new system of
management elaborated by the Central Committee of the Bulgarian
Communist Party. The new system introduced profound changes in
the organization and management of production and in the development of our economy. But it goes far beyond the economic
sphere: its thinking and basic principles affect all fields of public life
in the People's Republic of Bulgaria, including the complex and
varied field of culture.

This system aims at gradually raising the scientific standards of
the management of our entire social development, making full use
of the objective natural and social laws and enlisting the working

people and the men of letters and the arts more and more in the various sectors of our economy, politics, culture and the leadership of the state.

The implementation and development of the principles of the new system and their practical application in our economy have shown that under the present conditions it is possible and warranted to reorganize the leadership of the entire cultural front in the spirit of this system. What we have achieved thus far is merely a beginning. Prior to the Congress we built up a corresponding organizational structure. As you know, the chief local units for the coordination and leadership of culture were elected, there were district, town and minicipal councils on culture and art. Now the Congress has elected the central leadership: the Committee of Art and Culture.

It would not be correct, however, to think that with this reorganization and the new structure based on the new system all questions of the socialist cultural revolution will now be resolved automatically, as if by a magic wand.

It must be said that there were and probably still are people in our country who either fail to grasp the essence of this reorganization—this is natural since it concerns something new—or they do not deem that this reorganization is necessary. Some of our friends abroad have not yet had the opportunity to realize the essence of this reorganization. Indeed, what we are doing now is an experiment—but it is by no means the result of a whim.

Many comrades have said here that I am the initiator. I do not know the purpose of this suggestion. Do they want me to be held responsible in case things go wrong? I do not shirk my responsibilities, but this is not what is involved here. I would like to make it clear that the reorganization we are now carrying out is the natural result of the development and application of the principles underlying the new system of management which was collectively elaborated by the Party's Central Committee.

Comrades, one must indeed be a patriot, must know Bulgaria's history and the history of our cultural development well, in order to be able to understand fully the meaning of the experiment we are carrying out. There are specific conditions in our country, originality in the building up and development of Bulgarian culture, profoundly popular and democratic traditions in this field such as are rarely encountered in other countries.

How were the Bulgarian people able to display such maturity and such high national consciousness as to build up and develop an original culture, to set up library clubs and school boards and to form amateur theatrical companies in the dark days of five centuries of Ottoman domination?

How were our people, the progressive men of letters and the arts and our people's intelligentsia able to develop an original, progressive national culture in the face of opposition, persecution and ruthless terror under bourgeois rule and even in the period of fascist dictatorship?

Another question arises: why, in the conditions of the people's rule, of the upsurge of our people's material and spiritual resources, at a time when our men of letters and the arts are already a large army educated in the spirit of pure patriotism and the ideas of communism, should thay not take the initiative and the responsibility for the further development of Bulgarian culture?

We consider the reorganization as an expression of tremendous confidence on the part of the Party's Central Committee and our whole Party in our entire intelligentsia, both cultural and technical. It has won this confidence by its excellent work and its deeds that have shown it is indeed capable of creating cultural values, guided by the interests and needs of the great cause of communism.

We therefore need not be concerned that certain state functions in the leadership of the cultural revolution are intended to develop on a public basis, and that the role of the cultural unions, ideological institutions, etc. is enhanced in the leadership of the cultural front. This is a process governed by objective law. And if all this is being done for the first time in Bulgaria, it is because of the specific historical conditions in the development of our culture and because of the army of cultural workers—tremendous for the size of our country and vitally linked with the people and the policy of the Bulgarian Communist Party.

We are proud of our cultural workers—our writers, artists, stage and screen actors, musicians, journalists, as well as the hundreds of thousands of participants in amateur art companies, We are proud of our teachers, who tirelessly devote their effort and knowledge to educating cultured and daring young people, loyal to socialism. We are proud of our scientists, architects, engineers and inventors. We are proud of all those who spread our culture among the masses. Experienced and capable, they can assume the responsibility for the further development and advance of Bulgaria's national culture. As I have already pointed out, organization and structure cannot automatically resolve questions. In the future, we shall still have to exert ourselves to overcome contradictions in our cultural development, to combat conservatism and anything that obstructs our progressive development; we shall still have to combat ideological diversion in defense of daring creation and communist innovation.

Life moves forward. Today the stage of our development is different from what it was yesterday. Some of the laws that applied during the first stage of our socialist revolution are no longer in force—new laws of social development keep emerging.

Scientists and men of letters and the arts, therefore, are confronted with a vitally important task: to create cultural values and to develop theory. General truths cannot be applied mechanically to all facts and phenomena, to all stages of development. Theory as well as practice must also develop and improve.

Our strength is manifested by the fact that after the April Plenary Session of the Central Committee of the Bulgarian Communist Party we proceeded on a concrete basis with the constructive development of Marxist-Leninist theory and to the theoretical and practical solution of questions connected with our economy, our social, political and state development and the cultural revolution—bearing in mind the specific conditions of the construction of socialism in our country and making use of the experience of other socialist countries, especially of the Soviet Union.

In the future, too, our development, the development of the theory and practice of socialist culture, will be realized in an atmosphere of free, creative discussion. I do not think it necessary to convince you that we have in mind discussions that are based on Marxist-Leninist ideas, on popular traditions and the people's interests. We need such discussions as will unite and strengthen creative freedom and stimulate spiritual development. The development of science and socialist culture is impossible without such discussion and without a clash of opinions.

3

The October Revolution and the Historic Destiny of the Bulgarian People

Article in *Pravda*, September 29, 1967

Half a century ago, when the news of the October Revolution spread around the world, the founder of the Bulgarian Communist Party, Dimiter Blagoev[1]—our Grandpa—warmly greeted "the Russian proletarian revolution," assessing it as "one of the greatest historical events, an event of universal and paramount importance to the life of the nations."

And now, when we celebrate the 50th anniversary of the great October Revolution, the Bulgarian communists proudly recall Dimiter Blagoev's farsighted words. Today there is no man on earth,

[1]*Dimiter Blagoev* (1856-1924), first organizer of the Bulgarian socialist movement. He founded and led the Bulgarian working class party on August 2, 1891. *Blagoev*, affectionately called *Grandpa* by Bulgarians, was the outstanding proletarian revolutionary leader and Marxist theoretician in the Balkans at the end of the 19th and beginning of the 20th centuries.

friend or foe, who does not know that during those historic days the Russian workers and peasants, soldiers and sailors, led by Lenin and the Bolshevik Party, ushered in the era of socialism and communism. Today all progressive mankind welcomes the 50th anniversary as a cherished holiday of all that has been achieved during these years, as a holiday of dreams and hopes, of faith and belief in the happy communist future.

In the autumn of 1917, in the royal palace in Sofia, the dynastic clique and the leaders of the bourgeois parties frantically sought ways and means of muffling the thunder of the guns of those who had stormed the Winter Palace in Petrograd. All their machinations were doomed to failure. Bulgaria was among the first countries where the sparks emanating from Russia caused a revolutionary conflagration. And this was no accident—it was brought about by a series of profound historical reasons that made it practically inevitable.

In the first place, century-old bonds existed between the Bulgarian and the Russian peoples and between the Bulgarian national democratic liberation movement and the Russian revolutionary democrats. Russian armies had liberated the Bulgarian people from five centuries of Ottoman bondage, a fact of tremendous historical impact. There was a profound nationwide conviction that "the Russians are our brothers, our flesh and blood," as the poet wrote. Our people knew that those who fought under the banner of revolution were the sons of our liberators. Thus, our people's love for Russia was an enormous factor in the extent to which we were influenced by the October Revolution.

Second, from its very inceptions, the workers' movement in Bulgaria was inseparably linked with the struggles of the Russian proletariat. Dimiter Blagoev, the founder of one of the first Marxist groups in Russia, always had close relations with the Russian social democrats. Blagoev's followers—Bulgaria's revolutionaries—had taken an active part in the armed uprising against tsarism in 1905. Bolsheviks found a warm welcome in our country when ruthlessly persecuted by the tsarist regime. One of the safest channels for *Iskra* passed through Bulgaria. Many Russian revolutionaries, including Lenin, lived as emigrés with Bulgarian passports provided by Blagoev's Party. And many Bulgarians took an active part in the

October Revolution. In the thick of the revolution Lenin sent his personal courier to Blagoev.

The Bulgarian Left-wing Socialists knew the state of affairs in the Russian social democratic movement, which enabled them to assess correctly the actions of Lenin and the Bolsheviks and to give the October Revolution their unreserved approval and support at a time when social democratic leaders in other countries were reacting with hostility.

Third, at the turn of the century the Party of the Bulgarian Marxists emerged as one of the most consistent revolutionary currents in international social democracy. Its stand on the questions of peace and war was correct and steadfast, and its representatives supported the Bolshevik faction at the Zimmerwald Conference.[2] The heroic, anti-military propaganda of tte Bulgarian Workers' Social Democratic Party (Left-wing Socialists) helped to enlarge its ranks and enhance its authority among the masses, to step up revolutionary unrest at the front and in the rear, and to properly organize it.

All of these conditions explain the powerful political impact of the October Socialist Revolution on Bulgaria. October set an infectious example; it gave the signal for immediate revolutiionary action as the only way out of the unbearable situation that had been created in our country. Insurrection broke out in various military units in quick succession and armed clashes occurred in different parts of the country. In the autumn of 1918, under the slogan of "Let Us Follow the Example of Our Russian Brothers!" the great Vladaya Soldiers' Insurrection broke out.[3] This is what Lenin wrote about it: "At the price of *national* sacrifices we have preserved such *international* revolutionary influence that now Bulgaria is directly following our example!"[4] We, the sons and daughters of the Vladaya

---

[2] *The International Socialist Conference*, held in Zimmerwald, Switzerland, September 5-8, 1915, was the first such gathering during World War I. It was attended by 38 delegates from 11 European countries. Lenin formed a Left group, against the Kautskyite majority, in which the Bolsheviks alone adhered to the correct and consistently internationalist stand against the war.

[3] *Vladaya Soldiers Insurrection*, 1918: the first armed attempt to overthrow the bourgeois monarchist power in Bulgaria and establish a people's democratic republic.

[4] *Lenin Collected Works* (English Language edition), Progress Publishers, Moscow 1965, Vol. 28, p. 112.

heroes, are proud of our country, which succeeded in "following directly" the example of the nation that was the first to raise the banner of the socialist revolution!

The defeat of the Vladaya Insurrection failed to stop the revolutionary process in Bulgaria. When international reaction tried to thwart the revolution, the Bulgarian Communist Party, fulfilling its sacred international duty, took the lead of the popular movement against attempts to use Bulgarian soil as a springboard for an invasion of Soviet Russia. Meetings, demonstrations, strikes and peasant unrest rocked the country. Although there was a shortage of bread at that time, ships loaded with wheat left the Black Sea and Danubian ports for the free shores of the first workers' and peasants' state.

The intensified struggle in support of Soviet Russia strengthened the influence of the Bulgarian Communist Party among the broad masses—a proof that genuine internationalism contributes to the development of the national revolutionary movement. The history of the Bulgarian communist movement from October 1917 until September 1944 confirms this conclusion, bearing out the truth that the greater the authority and influence of the Soviet Union in a country, the more developed and consolidated its revolutionary movement becomes, along with the power and influence of its communist party.

Under the powerful ideological impact of the October Revolution, our Party reassessed the long road it had traversed in a Leninist direction. It assumed the name Communist Party, became co-founder of the Communist International, adopted the ideological, political and organizational principles of Bolshevism and, gradually overcoming its social-democratic errors and shortcomings, turned into a party of the new Leninist type. The Septerner 1923 Uprising[5] it had led—the first anti-fascist uprising in the world-—played an exceptionally significant role in the Bolshevization of our Party. The Uprising had been crushed with unprecedented ruthlessness. But the impassioned and proud appeal "Let Us Follow the Example of Our Russian Brothers!" born in the stormy October

---

[5] *September 1923 Uprising:* a mass uprising of the Bulgarian people, led by the Bulgarian Communist Party, which aimed to overthrow the monarcho-fascist power and establish a government of workers and peasants. It was the first anti-fascist uprising in world history.

days, survived our bloody defeat. Glorified by the heroism and the self-sacrifice of the Septembrists, this appeal was never forgotten by our people.

We drew a profound lesson from the defeat of the September 1923 Uprising and the Party began to reorganize those forces which had remained intact. It offered firm resistance to Left and Right deviations from the Leninist Party line, steeled its ranks, consolidated and expanded its ties with the masses and prepared for the final decisive battle.

During these years of fierce class struggle, the moral influence of the October Revolution and of socialist construction in the USSR was of great importance to the members of the Party, of the Young Communist League and to the broadest strata of the population. The deeds and example of the heroes of the Revolution—the St. Petersburg workers and Red Army men, the shockworkers, the champions of the Stakhanov movement, Pamfilovists and the young guards—all inspired our working people. In the face of the danger of execution by firing squads or on the gallows, the sons and daughters of our people raised revolutionary slogans and greeted the great land of the Soviets. What many of them said before they died in the struggle constitutes a magnificent anthology of boundless love and gratitude for the communist exploits of the Soviet people and Lenin's party. The treasure house of Bulgarian and world proletarian literature has been enriched by verses inspired by October, verses about the swift Red squadrons of the Revolution and about Moscow—the lodestar of the new era—and about the Russian Prometheus who lighted the torch of the future. There were verses about the new man, the citizen of socialist society, and the supreme principle of our own life—friendship with the Soviet Union— —written by Bulgaria's most outstanding poets, from Hristo Smyrnenski to Nikola Vaptsarov.[6]

Under the leadership of the tremendous and many-sided activity of the Bulgarian Communist Party, our people met the nazi attack against the Soviet Union as if it were an attack against their own

---

[6] *Hristo Smyrnenski* (1898-1923), outstanding Bulgarian proletarian poet and author.
Nicola Vaptsarov (1909-1942) famous Bulgarian revolutionary poet.

country, against their lives and destinies, their dreams and ideals.
Our Party organized a mass struggle against the capitalist military-royalist dictatorship and against German fascism and its stooges in our country. Because of their correct approach the communists also won supporters in the army, including General Vladimir Zaimov, an honest patriot and great friend of the Soviet Union, who was executed by the fascists. The powerful popular resistance movement in Bulgaria prevented the German occupiers and the bourgeois rulers from sending a single Bulgarian soldier to the Eastern Front. The partisans, political prisoners, outlaws, partisan supporters, communists and their sympathizers lived, fought and died with the proud consciousness that they were soldiers of the great army which, headed by the Soviet communists, was routing the nazi aggressors.

Lenin's idea of a worker-peasant alliance, so brilliantly realized in October, found its expression in our Fatherland Front, set up on the initiative of the Communist Party. This program proved to be salutary for Bulgaria, mobilizing the masses who, in September 1944, with the decisive assistance of the Soviet Army of Liberation, took power into their own hands. Our people are right when they say that the September 1944 Uprising would have been inconceivable without that of the great October Revolution. The socialist revolution in Bulgaria was a natural continuation of the October Revolution.

*   *   *

Socialist construction in Bulgaria has fully confirmed Lenin's assessment of the significance of Soviet experience, and continues to do so. In 1918, Lenin said, "The experience which the workers now united in trade unions and local organizations are acquiring in the practical work of organizing the whole of production on a national scale cannot be taken away, no matter how difficult the vicissitudes the Russian revolution and the international socialist revolution may pass through. It has gone down in history as socialism's gain, and on it the future world revolution will erect its socialist edifice."[7]

Not so long ago the Bulgarian people solemnly celebrated the 23rd anniversary of the socialist revolution in Bulgaria. From the

[7] Lenin, *Ibid*, Vol. 27, p. 413.

viewpoint of our own experience during these 23 years, we examined the road traversed by our people under the leadership of the Bulgarian Communist Party. It is a brilliant confirmation of the tremendous role of the all-round fraternal assistance and support rendered by the Soviets to a young socialist state. There were historic successes and victories, there were work and struggle, there was a road of inevitable difficulties to overcome in our advance along the path of adapting Soviet experience to our own conditions.

Today the People's Republic of Bulgaria is developing into a modern socialist state. Compared with 1939, a mere 23 years shows that the gross social product has increased seven times and the national income has quintupled; industrial production has increased 27 times and the production of the means of production 59 times, while agricultural production increased more than 2.5 times. During the period of the Fourth Five-Year Plan alone, as much fixed capital was created as during the whole existence of the Bulgarian state up to 1961.

The political line of our party, mapped out by its Fifth Congress (1948), the April 1955 Plenary Session of the Central Committee of the Bulgarian Communist Party, and further developed by the Seventh, Eighth and Ninth Congresses, is a creative application of Marxist-Leninist teachings and of Soviet experience in Bulgaria.

We look upon a number of formulations and decisions of our party, typical of socialist construction in our country, as an original and creative approach in accordance with our national and other specific objective conditions. They are a further development and modification of the experience of the October Revolution and its results by a later revolution, a transforming social activity based on the experience and support of the first socialist revolution in the world. We will point out a few of these formulations and decisions.

The main unit in the creative search on the front of socialist construction at the present stage is the new system of management and its consistent application and development. This new system is based on the full application and development of Lenin's principles on management. It consists in adapting the system of management to the objectively acting mechanism of the economic laws of a developed socialist society, and thus securing the country's still more rapid development toward socialism and communism.

In the past few years, our Party has made an important advance in expanding the sphere of action and the utilization of the law of concentration, specialization and co-operation of socialist production. To accomplish this end, some undertakings have already been carried out that are exceptionally large for the scale of our country's economy.

First, we have the merger of the co-operative farms. Our Party found that under our conditions co-operative farms were the most suitable form for the socialist reconstruction of agriculture. We were the second in the world after the Soviet Union to achieve the triumph of socialism in the countryside. This co-operative farm merger is actually a further development of Lenin's co-operative plan under the conditions of victorious socialism. The process of increasing the degree of socialization of the means of production in agriculture has provided ample opportunity for applying the economic laws of socialism in all spheres of expanded reproduction and creating real prerequisites for the development of agriculture on a modern industrial basis. This enables us to gradually resolve another complex task of historic significance: the elimination of the age-old socio-economic differences between town and country.

The formation of the Union of the Co-operative Farms and the impending merger of the Union of the Co-operative Farms with the Central Co-operative Union are of great importance in the further development of the co-operative system in the countryside. What it means is that a qualitatively new socio-economic organization will actually be created—a form of the economic integration of co-operative producers and co-operative trade organizations that will facilitate the linking of kindred and mutually related economic spheres in the reproductive process of agriculture.

Second, the setting up of state trusts. It has been confirmed by our experience that these are an efficient form of the further concentration of socialist production—a qualitatively new, higher form of economic management under socialism which fully corresponds to the present state of the development of the productive forces and production relations and to socio-economic life as a whole. In establishing the state trusts, we were guided by Lenin's idea about the socialist trusts in seeking forms of concentration of production under the conditions of the modern scientific and technical revolution.

Third, the reorganization of the Committee of Art and Culture into a social and state organ. The first Congress of Bulgarian Culture (May 1967), which took into account certain specific historical conditions, as the originality and profound democratic traditions in the formation and development of our culture, found that the necessary prerequisites were at hand in Bulgaria to further democratize leadership on the cultural front on the basis of Lenin's teaching about the cultural revolution and on the basis of our new system. A social and political body was established that will coordinate the rights and possibilities of state power with the increased role and autonomy of the cultural unions and ideological institutions with the competence and interests of the workers in this field, which is vitally important for the triumph of socialism.

Life has taught us that after the complete victory of socialist production relation, the creation and consolidation of the people's moral and political unity, the joint work of the Communist Party with its allies, the Bulgarian Agrarian Union, is an exceptionally important task. Indeed it is a necessity for successful socialist construction, especially in the countryside. The Fatherland Front, the largest socio-political organization of Bulgarian patriots, also uses new forms in enlisting almost all politically active citizens in our social life.

The People's Republic of Bulgaria is confidently advancing along the road of socialism. The Bulgarian communists and the Bulgarian working people see the surest guarantee of the prosperity of their country in the indissoluble friendship between their Party and the Communist Party of the Soviet Union, between the Bulgarian and the Soviet peoples, and in the establishment of ever closer contacts between our two countries.

The slogan of the heroes of our revolutionary battles "Let Us Follow the Example of our Russian Brothers!" is still valid for us, acquiring new meaning that makes it an ever greater moral and material force yielding abundant fruit every day.

Because it has been built up naturally in the course of long and stubborn struggles, drawing its vital strength from deep roots, the alliance between the People's Republic of Bulgaria and the Union of Soviet Socialist Republics is the most significant fact in the centuries-old history of our state. The alliance, reaffirmed by the new treaty of friendship, co-operation and mutual assistance between our two fraternal countries, has enhanced and consolidated the international prestige of the People's Republic of Bulgaria in the Balkans, in Europe, and throughout the world. We are happy and proud that between the BCP and the CPSU and between our countries, relations are a model of contemporary proletarian internationalism and of socialist internationalism in action.

The great October Socialist Revolution gave a gigantic impetus to the world revolutionary process. It showed the world revolutionary forces most convincingly that a triumphant socialist revolution was possible, and it opened up before them immense prospects for victory in their own countries. Under its influence the international communist movement expanded, turning into a powerful organized political force which has no equal and to which the future belongs.

The decisive impact of the great October Revolution on the world revolutionary process resulted in the world revolutionary system which is the greatest gain of mankind's struggles, next to the October Revolution itself and the establishment of the Soviet State. The contribution of the Soviet Union and of the CPSU to the establishment of the world socialist system and of a new socialist type of international relations is invaluable, based as it is on the principles of equality, respect for national sovereignty and fraternal mutual assistance in building a new society and in fighting unitedly against imperialism. The economic, political and military might of the Soviet Union has become the bedrock of a rapid and successful development of socialist construction in the fraternal socialist countries and a guarantor of their prosperity and might. It ensures the transformation of the world socialist system into the chief revolutionary force of the present period and an indestructible foundation for the development of the world along the road to communism.

The example of the October Revolution and the scope and power of the world communist movement also gave a strong impetus to the struggle against the age-old colonial system and led to its collapse. The vast colonial territories and peoples have been transformed, as Lenin predicted, from a reserve of capitalism and imperialism into a reserve of socialism, into allies in the struggle against imperialism.

As a result of the joint efforts of millions of fighters and, in the first place, of the communists of the Soviet Union for over half a century, communist ideology has become the pre-dominant ideological force in the world. Anti-communism is not only losing influence, but it is more and more frequently turning against its authors and disseminators. Nevertheless, the failure of anti-communism does not mean that communist ideas have now become easily accessible to all the people in the world. Imperialism is not ready or resigned to perish. This can be seen from the history of the 50-year period following the October Revolution and from the latest world developments. In spite of the protests of millions of progressive people, the unbridled escalation of US aggression against the Vietnamese people is expanding. Israel's aggression against the Arab nations has led to a serious aggravation of the climate in another part of the world. There are also many other signs that show that world reaction, steered by the United States, is trying to turn back the gains people have made in the last half-century.

Our Party is quite confident of the power of the world communist and revolutionary movement, of the power and might of the world socialist system, and the inevitable triumph of communism. But communist optimism must include revolutionary vigilance. Communists are not idle dreamers but fighters of a Leninist character. Our Party harbors no illusions with regard to developments, whether near or distant. We are taking all necessary measures to defend, if the need arises, side by side with the Warsaw Pact member-states, the gains and peaceful prosperity of our country and of the entire socialist community.

The Bulgarian Communist Party is well aware of the fact that the principal condition for bridling the imperialists and frustrating their plans is the unity and cohesion of the countries of the world socialist system, of the international communist movement and of the progressive forces all over the world. That is why the Bulgarian communists and the entire Bulgarian people are profoundly indignant at the actions of Mao Tse-Tung and his adventurous group. We find no justification for any action directed against the Soviet Union, against the CPSU, the international communist movement and against our unity and cohesion in the face of our sworn enemy. We cannot assume a postion of "neutrality" as if it were a matter of ordinary difference between two parties and not of frenzied slanderous attacks by the Chinese leaders against the Soviet Union and the entire world communist movement, attacks which betray the interests of communism everywhere, including China.

The international creed of the Bulgarian Communist Party was expressed by the great son of our people, that outstanding militant of the international communist movement, Georgi Dimitrov. On the 20th anniversary of the October Revolution, Dimitrov wrote in Pravda:

"There is no and there cannot be any surer criterion for determining who is a friend and who is an enemy of the cause of the working class and socialism, who is a supporter and who an opponent of democracy and peace, except one's attitude toward the Soviet Union. The touchstone for checking the sincerity and honesty of every militant of the workers' movement, of every workers' party and organization of the working people, of every democrat in the capitalist countries is their attitude towards the great land of socialism."

We have been educated by Georgi Dimitrov and his words are deeply impressed on our hearts and minds. We, Bulgarian communists, see that there is something suspiciously similar in the slogan of the counter-revolutionaries "for Soviets without the communists" and the suggestions for unity of the international communist movement without and against the CPSU and the Soviet Union. No, he who is against the CPSU and the Soviet Union is not and cannot be a friend. He is not and cannot be a fighter for communist unity and for the communist cause.

A year ago the Ninth Party Congress found that conditions were ripening for convening an international conference of communist and workers' parties. Today, the necessity of holding such a conference is even more obvious. The unity and cohesion of our forces are more necessary than ever, and no consideration can prevent us from accepting the historic responsibility that rests on our shoulders.

4

Party Work with the Youth and The Dimitrov Young Communist League (Komsomol)

BCP Thesis on the Youth and the Komsomol,
October 12, 1967 (Excerpts)

The education of the youth in a spirit of patriotism is of paramount importance, but here, as in other activities, a radical change, a new approach is called for in order to meet the present conditions.

We have in mind the intensification of this education, the proper combination of internationalism with patriotism, and the avoidance of any imbalance between internationalist and patriotic education.

We believe that special attention should be devoted to the following formulations:

First: Our Party has always followed a consistent line in educating the people, the youth, in a spirit of internationalism.

Dimiter Blagoev, Georgi Dimitrov and their collaboraters, the Party itself, have for many decades educated our members and the Komsomol in the spirit of proletarian internationalism; in the profound love of, and indestructible friendship with, the Soviet people; in the spirit of solidarity with the working people of the world and with peoples who are fighting for freedom, independence and social progress. The attitude of deep affection and gratitude to the Soviet peoples, to the great Party of Lenin, is accompanied by a readiness to safeguard, consolidate and develop Bulgarian-Soviet friendship as our most valuable possession, as the source of great creative power. It must continue to be an inseparable part of the patriotic and international education of our youth and people, a law of our new development along the road to socialism and communism.

In this spirit, the Party and its present leadership continued after September 9, 1944, to promote internationalism and friendship with the Soviet people, the peoples of the socialist countries and the working people all over the world. It is in this spirit that the Party and its leadership today educate Bulgarian communists, Komsomol members, the Bulgarian people in general. We believe that those who succeed us will carry on this glorious tradition, since it is determined not only by our communist views but also by the vital interests of the Bulgarian people, of our state and of socialist and communist construction in Bulgaria.

In the years of struggle against capitalism and fascism, the communists and the Komsomol members manifested their *consistent internationalism and profound patriotism,* their boundless love of the people and the homeland.

The activities of the Party and the Komsomol in the years of the people's government are examples of *patriotic tasks in the interest of Bulgaria* and, at the same time, of an honest and worthy *fulfillment of our international duty.*

Second: Nevertheless we should state that, *considering the line of development of our international traditions, we have tended in our general work to underestimate the importance of the patriotic education of the people and the youth in particular.*

It is true that much has been done in recent years for the education of the younger generation in the spirit of patriotism, but what has been done so far is still inadequate. For our youth in not just an abstraction. It was not born and is not living in a no man's land; it has its own genealogy, its own motherland, whose history is full of dramatic events and heroic feats.

Do we make proper use of this past in educating our youth? I submit that we do not, and that, even worse, there is hardly any other nation that permits such underestimation and even defamation of its own historical past.

We need to assess Bulgarian history from a Marxist-Leninist point of view. The popular masses are the creators of history, and the historical figures who were leaders of the people and the country in various periods were the spokesmen of the people's social aspirations and tendencies.

A Marxist assessment of the objective role of Bulgaria's eminent figures is therefore essential. Our predecessors wto lived in this countryside, at these crossroads, fought selflessly over centuries under extremely difficult conditions to preserve the Bulgarian state, to save the Slavs from assimilation. This was a mighty struggle involving prodigious efforts, great sacrifices to save Bulgaria from the threats of the modern Byzantine Empire, of the Franks and the other barbarians who made frequent incursions into our lands. Yet we do not emphasize this.

We do not speak of Khan Asparouh, the founder of the Bulgarian state; we do not speak of Kroum the Terrible, who saved the Slav peoples from assimilation. The Slavs should all erect monuments to him. We do not speak of Tsar Simeon and the Golden Age of Bulgarian literature; we rarely speak of Tsar Samuil, Tsar Kaloyan and Tsar Ivan Assen II, nor of the Bogomils, of Ivaillo and of the peasant uprisings.[1]

Before Slav tribes settled here, our region was inhabited by Thracian tribes, creators of one of the great European civilizations of antiquity. Thracian blood runs in our veins; Thracian monuments dot our lands; we are Thracian civilization's legitimate heirs. But we do not speak about all this; our history and archaeology do not point to our inheritance from Thracian culture.

Many additional facts, many examples from history and present-day life, can be adduced that bear our our tendency to underestimate our folk art.

---

[1] *Khan Asparouh* (644-701) first ruler (Khan) of the Slavonic Bulgarian state. *Khan Krown the Terrible, Tsars Simeon, Samuil, Kaloyan, Ivan Assen II:* Bulgarian rulers from the 11th through the middle of the 13th centuries.

Naturally our history should not be studied as an end in itself, but in closest connection with the present and with due consideration of its relevance to the proper education of our people and our youth. The isolation of the present from the past, like other deviations from the Marxist-Leninist approach to elucidating and interpreting historical facts, runs the danger of leading to nationalism.

Education of the youth in a spirit of patriotism, in the love and respect for the *history of the people*, for its struggles against *foreign oppressors*, for the struggles of the working class and of the people against *capitalism and fascism*, for *the construction of socialism*, should without doubt be intensified and based on a new approach.

Our youth should be educated in the spirit of:

—love of the *Bulgarian state*, which, for 13 long centuries has withstood all the vicissitudes of its history, through all its trials and tribulations;

—love of the *native land*, of all its scenic beauty, of its native villages and towns;

—love of the Bulgarian way of life, the folklore, round dances, songs, folk costumes and customs, etc;

There should be an end to the *nihilist approach to our history*, to the underestimation of our heroes in the educational work among the youth. We should be proud of our history, of our past, of our glorious revolutionary traditions.

A feeling of profound respect for *our flag* should also be inculcated in the younger generation; the flag of the Proto-Bulgarians-—the *horse mane*—should become something sacred; the *green flag of the haiduks,*[2] under which the Bulgarian people fought for five centuries for their liberation; the tricolor, under which our people, in the new historical conditions after the Liberation, fought for their reunification; the *red flag,* under which our working class and the working people fought against capitalist exploitation and which today embodies past struggles and the new society under construction in Bulgaria—a socialist and communist society.

It is necessary to review and interpret our historical past from a Marxist-Leninist point of view and to clarify the role of eminent historical figures.

[2] *the green flag of the haiduks:* Bulgarian peasant guerrilla fighters against the Turkish Ottoman Empire oppressors.

Concerning history textbooks and studies, the emphasis has been placed primarily on the wars our people waged, the poverty in which they lived and their lack of democratic rights. All this is true—the khans and the tsars of the First and Second Bulgarian Kingdoms certainly did not strive for the triumph of socialism in Bulgaria. But in those days, other tasks of a socio-historical nature, quite progressive in character, were accomplished. Without these accomplishments, the Bulgarian state and the people would not have existed; Bulgaria would not be what it is today—no communist nation can be formed without a history.

Our history textbooks should therefore get rid of all that defames our people and their eminent historical figures; they should emphasize the emotional and ideological influences that existed, and the past should not be isolated but skillfully linked with the present.

As to our *archaeology:* This can play a significant role in the patriotic education of children, adolescents and youths. Many excavations are now taking place in our country; many Thracian tombs, monuments of Thracian culture and other archaeological treasures are being found. But they are under ninefold lock and key.

Archaeological museums are kept closed—they are neither well-kept nor popular enough. Let us unlock the museums; their doors should be thrown wide open to the people and especially to students and the entire youth. It may be well advised to establish in Plovdiv a large *museum of original Thracian civilization,* showing the influence it exerted on both the Roman and the Byzantine civilizations—a museum that should be known to every Bulgarian and demonstrates that we, Bulgarians and Slavs, are the heirs of Thracian culture.

Youth rallies, marches, excursions to familiarize the young with the scenic beauty, the historical past of native regions, of the villages and towns, would be of particular value in the education of youth in a spirit of patriotism. Initiatives of this character should be increased in number and further extended.

Third: On the military education of the youth, and on youth training before consscription as an integral part of communist education:

The Komsomol should fulfill its obligations in the training of youth men before conscription. In this respect, the education of the youth in a spirit of patriotism is the most important factor in their training before going into the armed forces.

The *armed forces* should also sponsor the training of the conscripts before they enter military service. The best army officers should be selected and sent to the Komsomol in other to train the young men, so as to ensure that they have good training in the period preceding their military service. Close relations of confidence and cordiality should be established between the Komsomol and the armed forces; the youth men should be psychologically, to a large extent militarily, and technically prepared to fulfill their duty.

Fourth: Youth should participate in socialist construction more actively, and its labor education should be improved.

Komsomol members and other young people are making a great contribution to the building of our socialist economy. Our greatest socialist constructions bear witness to the work of the Komsomol and youth. In the future as well, they should devote all their efforts, knowledge and energy to the development of production forces and the economic and cultural advance of our country. The most important projects of our five-year plans should be accomplished by the work of the Komsomol and youth.

We should also consider *the problem of the voluntary youth brigades.* In the new conditions, they should acquire a new content, A new approach to the youth brigades and some of the other forms of work should be established; new ways and means should be sought.

The participation of young men and women in the construction of socialism and their labor education should be the active basis, an important aspect, of their education in the spirit of communism.

Fifth: Today the education of the youth in a spirit of patriotism is a major task on the ideological front:

All our forces should face up to this task. *The unions of writers, artists, the press, the radio and TV, the publishing houses, the cinema, theater, opera and vaudeville–all the links in the formation of public opinion that exert an influence on the shaping of the human personality should reappraise their work.*

The state and public organs that work among the youth, should take a decisive part in the activities of all these institutions in order to ensure that their programs include all that is essential for the communist education of youth and for living up to their needs.

We need *mass songs* that will be sung by our youth; *show business* should not go in for triviality and imitation but should strive to develop loftier feelings and thoughts. Obviously, we cannot expect our youth to sing only folk songs, to sing them the way they have been sung for centuries, or to go about dressed in national costumes. But in music as well as in fashion there should be no room for triviality, imitation, decadence—we should remain Bulgarians, with our differences from other nations. We should therefore make use of the wealth and variety of our national costumes in tailoring modern clothing; we should use them not mechanically but creatively. Our clothing should be well-fitting and beautiful, achieving and satisfying esthetic requirements.

We need *melodious modern songs,* based on the musical traditions of the Bulgarian people. They must be songs that will capture the hearts of youth. We have poets to write the lyrics of these songs; composers to create good music. All that is necessary is to organize and properly assist their efforts.

We need *books of fiction reviving our heroic historical past,* powerfully and movingly depicting crucial moments in the history of our people and our state, books that will imbue the younger generation with lofty feelings of national pride.

We need books, films and performances which reflect our turbulent present, which tackle the major problems of our development, fighting for the real truths of our life and vividly depicting our present life and the greatness of our cause. It is not only our past but our heroic present as well that is a powerful source for patriotic feelings of pride and spiritual élan.

We must make sure that all this is reflected in radio and TV programs, in the films we produce, in our books, theaters, exhibitions and concert halls, in the arts and in our spiritual life.

It is high time for *the leading workers on the ideological front, the front of art and culture* to take concrete measures for the creation of works of this nature, to see to it that they find their place in life by making use of all forms and means of influencing and encouraging writers, artists, etc.

The entire ideological front and all its branches should elaborate a *specific program for the education of the youth in the spirit of patriotism and internationalism.*

Sixth: The underrating of the patriotic education of the youth, the acceptance of any national nihilism are not *only harmful and dangerous* from the point of view of our national interests, but also *run counter to internationalism,* to education in a spirit of internationalism.

No proper education in a spirit of internationalism is possible without cultivating the love of one's own people and its socialist homeland. And, on the other hand, there is not, nor can there be, genuine patriotism without the love of and solidarity with the working people of the world.

Dialectical unity exists between socialist patriotism and internationalism. This unity should permeate our educational activities.

The education of the youth in a spirit of patriotism necessitates that we do not in the future neglect its *education in the spirit of internationalism.* Patriotism and internationalism are two elements of the alloy called communist education. For Bulgarian communists this is a fundamental truth.

Placing the emphasis on patriotism today, we want to overcome the existing lag, the temporary disparity, not in order to produce chauvinists but patriot-internationalists, harmoniously developed communist personalities.

This is what counts most for us; this is the task before us!

5

On the Further Development of Our System of Government

Excerpts from the Report to the Plenum of the Central Committee of the Bulgarian Communist Party, July 24, 1968

The construction and development of a socialist society is a law-governed historical process. After having done away with private ownership and having established socialist ownership of the means of production, the socialist revolution created the objective prerequisites for a planned, proportionate development of society and for the scientific leadership of all social processes. The policy of our Party is based on Marxist-Leninist theory and on scientific principles and achievements.

We are guided by the principle that the construction of a socialist society is a process of forming a qualitatively new social system, characterized by a specific structure and its own laws of functioning and development. These determine the theoretical and practical considerations as to the development of society, the growth of the productive forces, the perfecting of production relations as well as questions as to the "structure" of this society, its anatomy. *The more thoroughly the laws governing the development of socialist society are mastered, the more correctly relations between the various fields of social life are regulated and coordinated, the more harmoniously society functions and develops as a whole social organism—the more effective party Party and state leadership becomes.* This leadership is in a position to direct socialist construction correctly and successfully only when it does not lag in taking into account changes that have taken place in the functioning of society, the contemporary needs of its development and perfection which will overcome the disharmonies and disproportions arising among the different spheres of social reality.

A socialist society is a dynamic, rapidly developing society. In unprecedentally short historical periods socialism radically changes the economy, the mode of life and the culture of the people, indeed the whole system of social relations. The present scientific and technical revolution makes this difficult process still more complicated. If it is not directed properly, in conformity with objective laws and needs, serious contradictions and violations of the normal functioning of the entire social organism may arise.

After the historic April 1956 Plenary Session of the Central Committee of the Bulgarian Communist Party, a salient development was our Party's endeavor to guide socialist construction by seeing that its own activity in public administration was kept in conformity with objective laws. This constructive implementation enabled us to achieve outstanding successes in the country,s industrialization during the past decade. Similar successes were achieved in the socialist reconstruction and development of agriculture, in the improvement of social relations and in the development of socialist democracy in all spheres of life.

Guided by scientific principles, the Party has always taken into account the fact that progressive changes in this system cannot take place automatically, that they must not take place spontaneously. On the contrary, *a decisive role is and should be played by public administration that is based on Marxist-Leninist science.*

The immediate task that the Ninth Congress of the Party established was that *scientific and technical progress should be stepped up, that we should pass over to intensive economic development and that the scientific leadership of social life as a whole should be improved in all its phases.* Our society has reached such a high stage of development that without fulfilling this task it could no longer secure its normal functioning as an integral social organism nor the possibility of planned improvement. *The questions of raising the level of scientific management of technical progress, of intensifying economic, political, social and cultural life, of developing society as a whole, of improving the system of public administration, are now becoming the alpha and omega in Party and state work.*

Why is it Necessary to Perfect the System of Public Administration?

Comrades, The perfecting of the system of government, of society as a whole, is mainly determined by the stage we have achieved in our country, the stage of the construction of a mature socialist society, by the nation's general economic, social, political and cultural development and by the scientific and technical revolution in motion throughout the world.

After the April 1956 Plenary Session of the Central Committee of the Bulgarian Communist Party, substantial quantitative and qualitative changes occurred in the development of the country's productive forces. Fixed capital funds in the period of 1957-66 nearly trebled the sum that existed in 1956. Industry and particularly those progressive branches that are characterized by high growth rates, now hold a leading place in the whole reproduction process. This accounts for the sharp upswing of the country's whole economy. Bulgaria now holds a foremost place with regard to the growth rate of its national income. The growth rate of social labor productivity is also high: while in 1961-65 it was 7.5 per cent, in 1966-67 it rose to 8.6 per cent, and in 1968 the increase is expected to be about 10 per cent.

The rapid growth of the productive forces will also be characteristic of our future development. From preliminary projections of the Sixth Five-Year Plan, it can be seen that the average annual growth rate of the national income will be more than 8 per cent and will grow to 15-16 billion leva in 1975, i.e., about 10 times more than in 1948.

A substantial expansion in the scale of social production is envisaged as well as further changes in the structure of the country's economy. According to preliminary estimates, by 1975 the relative share of the chemical and machine-building industries, electric power production and metallurgy will account for more than 50 per cent of the total industrial output as against the present 38 per cent.

This intensive development of social production now surpasses the hitherto established forms and methods of leadership. On the other hand, substantial qualitative and quantitative changes have also taken place in other fields of social life, in harmony with the powerful economic upswing. Inevitably, all this calls for perfecting the entire social organization of production and for perfecting a system of public administration that corresponds to the new tasks that we shall have to resolve in the near future.

The modern scientific and technical revolution also makes new demands on the system of public administration. As science and technology develops more and more rapidly and the process of social production becomes increasingly complex, we need better forms of organization and government, and greater flexibility and coordination in leadership. The scientific and technical revolution puts at the disposal of the public administrative system hitherto unknown means, of which we must make maximum use.

This revolution embraces all phases of social life, exercising a powerful influence on production and manpower, on the people's mode of life and culture and on social relations and ideology. The link between science and production becomes ever closer and more dynamic; science becomes ever more deeply integrated into production, becoming its heart and soul, and opening up the roads and prospects for further advances. It is becoming the main factor in the rapid growth of labor production; and this is, in Lenin's words "the most important, the main thing for the triumph of the new social system."

Only Socialism can achieve conditions for the widest development and most thorough utilization of the achievements of the scientific and technical revolution in the interest of the working people and of society as a whole—rather than in the interest of monopolies and imperialistic aggressions, as is the case under capitalism. The world socialist system also intensifies the objective prerequisites for uniting the efforts of all the socialist countries towards the acceleration of scientific and technical progress. *This progress is the main factor in creating the necessary conditions for accelerating the construction of an advanced socialist society, and for the fuller satisfaction of the steadily growing material and spiritual needs of the people.*

This should not be considered as merely a technical or economic question—*it is also an important political and socio-economic task in the struggle for the definitive construction of an advanced socialist society in Bulgaria* and for creating the conditions for a gradual transition to a higher future stage—the construction of communism.

As a country and people we are vitally interested in the development of scientific and technical progress both inside the country and in the world socialist system. Achievement of this objective depends directly on the mechanism used in implementing our economic policy, on the planning system, on the capital investments policy, on the system of material incentives, on the working people's active participation in production and public life as well as their socialist consciousness, and on the effectiveness of public administration.

Our society's present stage of development and the acceleration of technical progress, therefore, dictate that an effective economic organization should be created and the whole system of government perfected.

Consistently pursuing the line of raising the scientific level of leadership, the Central Committee of the Party has in the last decade implemented a number of measures aimed at improving the mechanisms and functioning of our socialist society along with establishing a better structure for our system of government. The most substantial and radical initiative along these lines is the new system of economic management, which is a natural result of the profound changes in the economy, the growth in numbers and quality of cadres and the country's entire social life. *The consistent application of the new system of economic management is now the key for creating strong economic incentives and pressures, for developing the scientific and technical revolution in all fields of life and intensifying the country's economy.*

In improving the system of government, we have taken into account the fact that the various social phenomena are interrelated, that a reconstruction in one sphere of social development presupposes and requires changes in other spheres, as well as in the Party and state leadership, At the same time, however, we know that in deciding these questions the stages, conditions and possibilities of development must be taken into account and that all problems cannot be solved with one sweep of the hand. The Central Committee of the Party has correctly focused its attention, above all, on the elaboration of the new system.

Insofar as the economy is the foundation of social life, the objective need for the new system has become the main factor in looking for forms of management and in perfecting the structure of the social organism. It is with its assistance that, first of all, high and stable rates of economic and social progress, then an accelerated transition to intensive development, technical progress and a steady increase in the people's living standards must be secured.

At the present stage, the further improvement of the structure and mechanism of public administration is a general necessity for our entire social system. In brief, *from the reconstruction and improvement of individual fields, we now have to pass over to perfecting the whole mechanism of the functioning of the entire system of public administration.* In other words, we have to complete the reconstruction started with the new system for a given stage by establishing a better and more stable structure of public administration, one that will more fully correspond to the tasks of building an advanced socialist society and will give wider scope to the laws of our society.

In establishing the new system, we have reached: "a." The logic of development now expects us also to say "b." At its Plenary Sessions and at its Ninth Congress the Party elaborated and reaffirmed the principles of the new system. What we have to do now is to bring the whole mechanism of public administration into conformity with the principles of this system. We must secure the most favorable "medium" for its consistent application and resolve all additional problems that may arise. *This is now of decisive significance for the normal functioning of all the cells of the complex social organism as an integral whole in the accelerated development of our society.*

The necessity of improving public administration puts four main groups of questions on the agenda:

First of all, are questions connected with the improvement of the mechanism of the new system of leadership and with the creation of the economic conditions needed for its consistent application and normal functioning.

Second, there are the questions connected with improving the organizational structure of government and securing all the necessary conditions for its optimum functioning. At the present stage, substantial changes will have to be made in the content and functions of a number of forms presently established in Party, state, economic and social government. We shall have to go on establishing new forms in the system of public administration, and we shall have to put aside other forms which have already had their day. *In making these complex decisions, we are guided by the Leninist principle of democratic centralism, by the requirements of the objective laws of socialism* and by the achievements of science, particularly cybernetics.

The third group of questions is connected with perfecting the system of information as an essential element of modern government and with strengthening the role of science in the government of society. And finally, the task of perfecting public administration calls for measures *aimed at decisively raising the level of the work in all links of the ideological front and improving the communist education of the working people, so that the current problems of our educational system will be consistently resolved, as well as those of the system of selecting, training and promoting cadres, of labor and state discipline.*

All this will create more favorable conditions for the attainment of a fresh upswing in our economy and culture, for the acceleration of scientific and technical progress, for the elaboration and implementation of a far-flung program for the further improvement of the people's living standards, for a fuller utilization of the advantages offered by the socialist system. The possibilities of the country for a more active participation in the international division of labor, the development of fraternal co-operation and mutual assistance with the socialist nations, and for enhancing still further the prestige of the People's Republic of Bulgaria will be increased.

Perfecting the system of social administration, solving the current problems of our social development, will lead to bringing still closer together the economy of the People's Republic of Bulgaria and the economy of the Soviet Union and to expanding our all-round cooperation – thus deepening and enriching the Bulgarian-Soviet friendship which is so dear to all of us. We have always considered this friendship as one of our greatest achievements. The creative use made of the historical experience of the Soviet Union—which is of such world significance—are and will continue to be a decisive factor for the successful construction of socialism and communism in Bulgaria and for defending the freedom and national independence of our country and ensuring its all-round socialist progress.

Changes in the Structure and Functions of State Organs

After the April 1956 Plenary Session of the Central Committee, side by side with the establishment of a fresh approach to economic problems, the Party devoted great attention to the political superstructure in our society and undertook a number of measures to improve the system of public administration.

The present conditions make it necessary for us to proceed to a further improvement of the government. A leading principle in the process must be the consistent application of the Leninist principles of the organization and activity of the socialist state. These principles and especially the all-round development of socialist democracy—the active participation of the public—will continue to be the unshakeable foundations of our government. The improvement of state government should be effected along the following lines:

—through a consistent application and constructive development of the Leninist principle of democratic centralism—the fundamental principle in the construction of the socialist state and government—by establishing the most effective combination of centralized leadership and socialist democracy;

—the Marxist-Leninist principle of the unity of legislative and

executive-administrative power should be applied unreservedly in the structure and functioning of the system from top to bottom;

—this structure and functioning should be brought into line with the *principles and requirements of the new system of management and the full introduction of the achievements of governmental science;*

—*the system of self-government should be developed in the various spheres of life,* and in the participation of the working class, and their socio-political organizations in the leadership of society, and their contribution to the leadership of society as a whole should be extended and enriched;

—*the activity of the state power's organs from top to bottom will continue to be implemented under the leadership of the Bulgarian Communist Party;* their leading principle will be the policy of the Party, its general line and the fight for its implementation.

Only under a consistent and correct implementation of the leading role of the Party on the basis of the Leninist principle of democratic centralism can the system of state government operate entirely in the interests of the working people and the development of genuine self-government.

In a socialist society there is no room for either a factual or formal division of power; legislative power should never be opposed to the executive activity of the state. This conclusion is confirmed by historical experience and the experience of today's socialist countries. One of the salient features of the Paris Commune was that it merged legislative and executive power, which Marx described as a "working corporation," which at the same time both issued and executed the laws. Lenin also called attention to the necessity of uniting the legislative and the executive work of the state, and he came to the conclusion that the merger of legislative and executive labor "brings the state apparatus closer to the working people."[1]

Unity in state power, unity in making decisions and fulfilling them are of decisive significance for the consistent development of the content and functions of the representative organs. They must have their say on all the fundamental questions that arise in life, the state and society, The work of the representative institutions is now

[1] Lenin, *Ibid*, Vol. 27, p. 154

usually connected with general leadership and control, and the decisions on concrete questions, often of great importance, are left entirely to executive bodies.

It would be expedient, in connection with the preparation of the new Constitution of the People's Republic of Bulgaria that the special committee elected by the National Assembly should discuss and introduce into the Draft Constitution the necessary amendments to the system, structure and functions of the organs of state power and government.

The Central State Organs

National Assembly. Although measures have several times been taken to enhance the role of the National Assembly as the supreme body of state power, to a large extent it continues to fulfill its functions only formally. The main reason for this is the fact that for many years the executive organs usurped the functions of the National Assembly, replacing it in many respects.

This situation must be changed radically. First of all, the National Assembly must have a larger role in the preparation, discussion and adoption of laws. The National Assembly must discuss and decide the main questions of our state, economic and cultural policy; the development and distribution of the productive forces of the country, foreign policies and economic questions, financial policy in the field of prices and wages, the raising of the people's living standards and of their cultural, educational, public health and other activities.

From now on the National Assembly must also be an organizer of the planned leadership of society. In this regard it must determine the trends in the solution of current socio-economic problems and instruct the executive bodies on the elaboration of the state plan, organizing its preliminary discussion and approve it. The National Assembly must approve the long-range plans—the five-year plans and those for longer periods. It must hear reports by the government and other state organs on the fulfillment of the plan and present recommendations and conclusions.

The enhanced role and competence of the National Assembly in the government call for an improvement in the electoral system in the methods of submitting candidacies and recalling national representatives.

A State Council of the People's Republic of Bulgaria. The National Assembly, which does not function permanently but from session to session, is not always in a timely position to settle all questions, nor to organize the fulfillment of such decisions as it has already taken. *It is therefore necessary to establish new organs that will facilitate these functions.* To a certain extent such committees are already in operation, but they are not and cannot be authorized to issue regular state acts and to decide definitively important questions of state. As to the Presidium of the National Assembly, it functions, above all, as a supreme organ of state power that represents the state in the country and beyond its boundaries.

Under these circumstances, a correspondingly active organ of the National Assembly is obviously needed which will be able in the future to decide those questions that the National Assembly is not in a position to decide at given periods of time. Such an organ might be the State Council of the People's Republic of Bulgaria.

This is not merely a question of replacing or renaming the existing Presidium but of setting up a new organ of the National Assembly in principle. It should be elected by the National Assembly itself, and combine the making of decisions and their implementation.

As a permanently functioning organ of the National Assembly, the State Council should be vested with executive and administrative power in connection with the principal questions of the Government, enabling it between sessions to fulfill all important tasks arising from the laws passed and decisions made by the supreme organ of state power. For its entire activity, the State Council will be responsible to the National Assembly.

The State Council should have the power to make decisions, issue decrees and other juridical acts on all fundamental questions arising in connection with the laws and decisions of the National Assembly, as well as on questions of principle affecting the government. They should require of the government, and other state organs, the study and settlement of the individual questions as well as reports on the fulfillment of the National Assembly's decisions. They should discuss and make decisions on the reports of various committees; coordinate the activity of all state organs; exercise control over the central organs of state government and over the local bodies of state power and government. It would also be expedient to vest the President of the State Council with the duty to implement a number of functions and, in the first place, with the right to represent our state in international relations.

The State Council should also direct and coordinate the work of the local bodies of state power. This makes it necessary to set up a *single organ for the People's Councils* instead of the present People's Councils Department of the Presidium of the National Assembly and the People's Councils Administration at the Council of Ministers. This would direct and help in the work of the People's Councils and coordinate their relations with the central state organs.

With a view to applying a scientific approach to the organization of the government and to the functioning of the central state organs and their subdivisions, it would be expedient to set up an *Institute of Government Organization* under the State Council of the Republic.

In connection with the enhanced role of the National Assembly in the preparation of the laws, it would be advisable for *the Legislative Council* at the Ministry of Justice to be placed under the subordination and guidance of the State Council of the Republic.

It is also necessary to enhance the role of the *Chief Public Prosecutor's Office* and of *the Supreme Court* as supreme organs that function to ensure the correct application of the country's laws. The competence of the Chief Public Prosecutor's Office and of the Supreme Court should be re-examined in order to free them of functions that do not properly belong to them. The Supreme Court should strengthen its activity in the supervision of the work done by the courts and the observance of the laws and their correct application. The Supreme Court and the Chief Public Prosecutor's Office should be vested with legislative initiative, substantially widening their scope. It is necessary, however, to improve and perfect relations between the Public Prosecutor's Office and the Supreme Court, on the one hand, and the Ministry of Justice, on the other.

Council of Ministers. In connection with the consistent implementation of the principle of unity between legislative and administrative executive state activity, the government should become a real executive organ of state power, working under the guidance and immediate control of the National Assembly and the State Council.

In order to enhance its efficiency, the government should be freed of functions that do not belong to it, so that it can get a fuller grasp of the questions of the operative administration and functioning of the state, the coordination and control over the work in various fields of life. One of its important duties is to make manifestations of bureaucracy impossible in the activity of state organs; another is to become more exacting and improve its control over their work, and to bring about conditions for the development of initiative in the organs of government and in the economic organizations.

It is also necessary to specify in greater detail the *tasks of the Government in the field of planning*, whose functions should be: to organize the elaboration of long-range forecasts for the development of science and technology, and programs for the development of the main branches of production. In accordance with the economic and social policy of the Party, it must organize the elaboration and discussion of the variants of the five-year national economic plan, together with its annual sub-elaborations, and to present the most effective variant for approval by the National Assembly. In addition, the necessary changes in the annual five-year plan must be approved along with concrete criteria of economic efficiency in production, trade, capital investments, etc.; long-range norms must be set up, as well as limits and quotas and other means of economic regulation. The activity of the various branches of the national economy must be directed, as well as the trusts and enterprises, in accordance with the mapped-out policy and the fundamental tasks envisaged in the state plans.

The development of social production and the steadily increasing complexity of relations in the country's economy call ever more urgently for coordination to be implemented, especially in the field of economic activity. This calls for day-to-day operative intervention by the Government in the settlement of one or another problem.

Under the present scientific and technical revolution, the present far-reaching economic relations and high dynamism, it is impossible to decide the problems of concentration, specialization, co-operation in production, etc., in the old way. What comes forward, in all its seriousness, is the question of securing in the whole system of society such a competence and interaction between the different sub-systems, that it will enable us to guarantee the coordination of activities in all units of leadership.

Concerning Negative Phenomena in Our Life

In the process of shaping the new man, the actual social conditions in which he works, creates and lives should be taken into consideration. Man's social consciousness and conduct in a socialist society are fundamentally conditioned by his life in society and by his social environment.

Our socialist reality is increasingly acquiring the characteristics of an advanced socialist society. At the same time, however, we encounter quite a number of negative phenomena, survivals and manifestations of bourgeois influence. We are in the presence of *two truths in our lives* that actually interact and clash with each other.

The first, which characterizes the positive side of reality, is the construction and steady progress of our socialist society, expressing the progressive social relations, the conscientious attitude towards work, public interests and the socialist system. Its protagonist is the builder of socialism who becomes ever more emancipated from the selfishness and individualism of the past and begins to feel that he is an integral part of society. Highly conscientious, idealistic and with a broad intellectual background, the builder of socialism with these typical traits is steadily being strengthened and steadily gaining more ground.

At the same time, we must not close our eyes to yet another phase of our reality. It is a question here of selfishness, indifference, careerism, bureaucracy, kowtowing, haughtiness and similar phenomena. There are such negative manifestations as unprincipled friendships at the expense of social goals, unjustified intercession and so forth. Although they do not determine the true character of our society, we should not lose sight of their existence and should try to circumscribe and eliminate them.

The process of perfecting social relations and the shaping of a builder of socialism is beset with many difficulties. We, as a Party and state, are looking for ways and means to overcome them and to increase the solicitude for the common man, the common citizen of the People's Republic of Bulgaria. It is true that the care of the common man in socialist Bulgaria is placed on a height conceivable only under a socialist system. The general problems of the present and future of the common citizen are decided in accordance with his radical interests as well as with socialist principles. We should not, however, overlook the fact that there are still many unsolved problems which, though not of prime importance, infringe on man's personal rights and his position as absolute master in his own country. There are still cases when citizens are not sufficiently defended, when their interests are unjustly affected. They are at times subjected to undeserved humiliation and insults by individual bureaucrats and arrogant officials.

The time has obviously arrived when we must still further extend the material guarantees of defense of people's rights, honor and dignity. To this end, our legislation must be strengthened. We should create all the conditions necessary for increasing and safeguarding the rights of the common man in all spheres of social life, including the administration of society.

In this respect, we still do not make full use of the possibilities of the new system of management, which permits the worker not only to produce but also to take an active part in the management of production; to have a stake not only in the fulfillment of his personal work quota but also in the work of his neighbor, of other teams and shops, in the organization of labor, and in supplies and sales of finished goods. All these are sources of stimulation to the worker, encouraging him to express himself, to come forward with his own ideas, opinions and initiatives in all phases of production.

These possibilities of the new system, however, are not yet accompanied by sufficient material guarantees, Why don't we, for instance, consider the problem of broadening the rights of workers in assessing the work of their managers, superiors, heads of shifts and shops, directors, and so forth? This should be done in an organized way and not spontaneously but guided by the Party, trade union, Komsomol, and higher state organs on a legal basis. For this purpose, obviously, we must have the respective legal and normative acts.

It is essential to deal again with the question of *grievances of the working people*, not only as an important channel for obtaining information but also as one of the forms for defending the rights and interests of the citizens, of criticism and control and as a manifestation of our socialist democracy. On many occasions we have come up against incorrect and illegal acts of the organs of the government that encroach upon the rights and legal interests of the individual. These acts are in flagrant contradiction with the policy of our Party and the essence of our system—the process of extending democracy in our country. Moreover, impermissible sluggishness is often permitted, along with lack of competence and efficiency and indifference, in examining the grievances of citizens.

It is without any doubt necessary to draft a law on the order in which the organs of state government will issue their individual administrative acts affecting the rights of citizens or organizations. This law will have to offer solid guarantees for the implementation of the rights of citizens, preventing their infringement.

It will also be expedient to introduce changes in the procedure thus far followed in our work on the grievances of the working people, with a view to establishing prompt response, higher competence and efficiency. It may be advisable to set up special groups of experienced and duly empowered officials of the respective state bodies. These groups will promptly, if possible on the very same day, give their decisions on proposals in connection with the complaints and, in cases when the questions are complicated, study and resolve them within a short time. The prompt settlement of legal and just complaints will produce a positive effect at least along two lines. It will help consolidate the citizens' faith in socialist legality and in the state organs and, on the other hand, will play the role of a warning of coercion with respect to the violators of the law.

We must no longer suffer the anomaly that an application of complaint submitted by a citizen to a certain institute or department may be returned for solution to the same organ as that against which the citizen has complained. Of course, complaints that are slanderous must be attributed to those who are responsible.

Or let us take a few other spheres of our social life: trade, transport, communal services, and so forth. Here again in our everyday practice the citizen as an individual is often disregarded and his interests are trampled underfoot.

When a citizen, in fulfillment of his patriotic and civic duty, signalizes or fights against the rude behavior of an official and proves that the law and the rules of socialist society have been violated, why is it that there are no sufficient guarantees for his defense? Why don't we take advantage of the great possibilities that socialism offers for publicity about these manifestations? Why don't we demand the co-operation of society as a whole and of public opinion in the fight against these negative phenomena? Again, more material guarantees are needed in defense of the common man and for the implementation of his constitutional right to take part in the management of state and social affairs.

Or let us take communal services, where some things happen that we must no longer tolerate. In a minor transaction the common citizen is not only sometimes robbed economically but is also subjected to humiliation and insults to his dignity. This obviously can no longer be endured, and strict rules should be introduced in the services rendered to the population. A man is sometimes compelled to beg, to wait a long time, to listen to rude remarks and sermons and to pay illegal tips in order to obtain the service to which he is entitled.

Strict order must finally be introduced also in *the fight against squandering and theft of public property, profiteering and the robbing of citizens.* Our society sustains serious losses through the activities of unscrupulous and greedy people eager to lead an easy life at the expense of others. The organs of state government wage a steadfast struggle against those people, yet despite this the squandering and theft continue and many thieves find ways of escaping the law.

It is necessary to substantially raise the role of society, of the industrial work forces, of state, social and economic organs and organizations in the fight against thieves and against the squandering of public property. To this end, all organs and forms of control must be activated and a complex system of resolute economic, administrative and ideological measures be elaborated to make it really hot for such shameful phenomena in our socialist system.

Obviously, the organization of the fight against squandering and thieving must be decisively improved and *a special law should be drafted and adopted for this purpose.* The respective organs should be vested with the right of checking on the origin of suspicious property, as has been the case in the past with regard to those who had accumulated wealth illegally. Such checking will not only make possible the discovery of hidden crimes and their material and legal retribution, but will also play a serious preventive and educational role.

In discussing this problem, we should not forget that squandering and thieving inflict not only material losses and damages on society. More important are the moral losses, the corrupting influence of criminal actions, absolutely incompatible with socialist norms and rules of conduct, hostile to them and the tasks set for the education of the new man.

The genesis of anti-social phenomena undoubtedly goes deep into the pre-socialist stages of social development. But it would be wrong to think that they do not find favorable soil even in the objective conditions of our present life. We must attribute these conditions not only to the survivals of the past in our economy and way of life, but also to certain aspects of socialist relations still insufficiently high in respect to the development of socialist production, as well as insufficient maturity in our social relations. The negative phenomena in our life may also be nurtured by certain difficulties and disproportions in the nation's economy that lead to a temporary revival and a multiplication of negative phenomena.

Along with the objective conditions that may delay either overcoming or reviving the negative phenomena, there are also a number of reasons of a subjective nature. To these we must, first of all, refer to the flaws in the application of the socialist principles of management and distribution, the insufficiently consistent application of check-ups in the quantity and quality of expended labor and the amount of consumption. There are shortcomings in the organization of work and production, etc., and experience has shown that every violation of socialist principles brings material and moral losses to society.

As can be understood, the negative phenomena in our life arise from both real, objective causes and from subjective ones. Overcoming these phenomena is possible only by eliminating their sources and the preconditions that nurture them or lead to their revival and multiplication. This is a complex process. Can it be achieved at once or automatically? Our development has hitherto shown that this is impossible. We would be utopians, unacquainted with life, to imagine that by empty promises or in a brief period we would be able to stamp out these negative aspects of our reality. But if we cannot eradicate them with a sweep of the hand, we still must have a clear line of action and must wage a stubborn fight against them.

The fight against the negative phenomena in our life must be waged with every possible means and in various directions.

–*The material and technical foundations of the socialist system, the entire socialist economy, should be developed and consolidated; social relations should be perfected;* the conditions of life of the working people should be improved; the principles of socialism should be systematically applied.

–*Social democracy should be broadened, the role of public opinion enhanced* and the potentialities for society to detect, condemn and stamp out manifestations of an anti-socialist character should be increased.

–*The role of the personal examples set by communists should be reinforced.* In this connection we should require of communists that they abide strictly to the statutory stipulations: to serve as examples in their work, to guard and increase the value of socialist property, to serve as examples in their personal life, to be intransigent towards philistinism, moral laxness and other surviving flaws of the past, and to strictly observe Party and state discipline and socialist legality.

–*Legal measures should be taken against violators and criminals by further consolidating social legality and issuing new laws* that correspond to the changes which have taken place, and to the present stage of our development. The new laws must secure wider possibilities for mobilizing the working people and their conscious participation in the fight against negative manifestations and those who exhibit them, and for the observance of the legal norms by all, regardless of rank and position in society.

–*Socialist legality* should rest on its natural foundations—the people and their conscious observance of the laws, their endeavor to live and work in a new way. Here the most serious sector is the younger generation. All efforts to secure legality will be futile without *legal consciousness*, a proper attitude towards state order, a readiness to react against injustice and lawlessness, and unless these attitudes are cultivated from a very early age. Education and teaching also have to contain a socialist legal consciousness.

Of particular importance is *the consistent and full application of the principle of equality before the law*. The greatest enemy to equality before the law is the *"habit of putting in a kind word"* in behalf of the contending parties. This gives rise to violations of the laws; raises to important positions incompetent men and condemns brilliant minds and talents to dealing with petty matters. The custom of such favoritism is and should be alien to our socialist reality. We must give this matter legal expression in our future laws.

Effective struggle can be led against negative manifestations only if society as a whole participates and if Party and popular control is developed and perfected. The uncompromising edge of the mass means of communication must be turned against them, and if every citizen who is fully responsible morally and before the law for his conduct is at the same time given the guarantee that his rights will be defended, he will be protecting his own interests as a builder of socialist society before any organ in the state.

The construction of an advanced socialist society is a process of changing and developing not only the productive forces, the foundation and superstructure, but also a process of shaping and perfecting the new man. Moreover, the successful development and perfecting of socialist society is impossible without a constant development and perfecting of the new man, the builder and main figure in this society. Socialist consciousness is a job for the millions who, under the leadership of the Party, in changing the nature of the country also change themselves and in doing so change society.

That is why the struggle for a higher socialist consciousness, for the shaping of the new man, must be waged without respite and on a broad front, in all sectors of life, among all strata of the people, with all the means and methods at the disposal of the Party, the state and our socialist society.

Raise the Role of Science in Public Administration
and in the Nation's Socio-economic Development

Science and revolutionary theory have always been guides to action for the Bulgarian Communist Party, both in the struggle against capitalism and in the period of building a socialist system. With a number of its theses and decisions, our Party has made its modest contribution to the collective development and enrichment of the Marxist-Leninist theory and of socialist practice.

The profound meaning of the measures aimed at perfecting the whole system of public administration and the mechanism of its operation now being proposed consists in the endeavor to decisively raise the scientific level of administration. But however perfect that structure and mechanism of public administration may be, however fully they may correspond to the stage of social development, the system of public administration cannot function in an optimum manner unless it is based on science and especially on the social sciences.

To raise the role of science in the elaboration and implementation of Party policy has today become a vital necessity and a typical feature of present-day development This is so because of the very character of our society, a scientifically governed society.

The link between public administration and science is two-sided. The correct understanding of this question is not only of theoretical but also of great practical significance.

In building the advanced socialist society, as practice has shown, along with the role of the organs of public administration, the subjective factor is steadily increasing in importance, This, however, dows not mean a strengthening of subjectivism in economic management and the other social processes, As we know, freedom of will is only a consciously perceived necessity, a taking into account of the requirements of the objective laws. It is only on the basis of the action of these laws that society can be properly governed and that social development can be accelerated. *This calls for an ever deeper knowledge, mastery and utilization of the laws governing the operation and development of socialist society.* Every underestimation of science and the results of scientific investigations, every neglect of non-compliance with the laws of social development may inflict serious damage on socialist development. The scientific governing of society, and of the nation's economy in particular, is incompatible with all manifestations of subjectivism and must be eliminated.

The decisive role of science in securing the scientific character of public administration and in creating the best possible conditions for its functioning and development make up one side of the question. But an equally important problem now is to improve the management of science itself by securing optimum conditions for its development. In nature and content this question is complex and many-sided. Here we shall touch upon only a few of its aspects.

First: It is necessary, above all, to elaborate a *scientific strategy and tactics in the field of scientific policy* that takes into full account the present and future requirements, the specific conditions and possibilities for our country. This task is now paramount and we must solve it in a short time.

In this connection we should specifically do the following:

—Determine the correct correlation in the development of the various kinds of natural and social sciences and in the various kinds of scientific research (fundamental, practical elaboration).

—Elucidate more fully the questions of in what fields of science, on what problems, on what scales, in what periods of time should we concentrate the country's scientific and financial resources for independent scientific and research work—and what will be the main results of all this. There can be no doubt that we shall develop scientific and research work, especially in the fields in which Bulgaria is specializing, along CMEA lines, and in which, therefore, we are mainly responsible for the development and introduction of scientific and technical progress.

—Co-operation and coordination with the Soviet Union and the other socialist nations in the field of science should always be broadened and deepened. It is necessary to understand in what forms we can implement our participation in the research institutions of the USSR and the other socialist nations. We must also decide in what fields we shall seek knowledge principally or exclusively from the other socialist nations.

—It is also necessary to revise the practice and forms of studying the achievements of science and technology in the capitalist nations, with a view to making better use of them.

—A effective organization should be set up for the rapid introduction into production of the new achievements which are on and above the world level. Measures should be taken for the mass production of special articles based on these achievements for the whole socialist camp, for an excellent organization of advertising and for maximum sales of these articles in the nonsocialist countries (in the developing nations and, eventually, also in certain capitalist markets).

—The problem of incentives for the introduction of scientific and technical elaboration in production has not been solved. But technical progress cannot be accelerated without it. It is necessary to increase the material incentive to enterprises connected with the introduction of scientific and technical achievements—without allowing this to become a source of trouble for them and to produce an adverse effect on their economic indicators.

To secure a scientific strategy and tactics in the field of science, and proper leadership in the organs entrusted with the management of science, we should subject science itself to research, increasing our contribution to the theory and general method of Marxist-Leninist philosophy, and to the elaboration of the problems of sociology and political economy in our studies, as well as to theories of government organization and information, etc.

Second: We are very seriously faced with the task of *elaborating a far-reaching program for the development of the social sciences.* In our country, as well as in the other socialist countries, Marxism-Leninism and the other social sciences have been going through a real upsurge in the last few years. For the most part, the simplistic view that the social sciences are characterized by only or mainly propaganda functions may be considered to have been overcome.

This does not give us any ground to believe that the social sciences in our country are marching in step with our ever growing needs. In view of the requirements of public administration in particular, we need to have their increased help in perfecting the management of the various production processes, in the people's way of life, culture, education, all social life, and in the entire superstructure—so that they may make use of all the advantages offered by the socialist system. This calls for the establishment of still closer ties among our philosophers, sociologists, economists, jurists, etc., for practical socialist construction and for a profound study of the phenomena of social life.

In achieving these ends, we should place emphasis on the following activities:

—the social sciences should be so developed that in the final count they will be able to secure the necessary and sufficient information as to all modern social structures and processes. They should give timely warning to the leading organs as to the need of replacing outdated forms, methods and means with others which are abreast of the requirements of the new conditions, proposing changes supported by scientific arguments.

—concrete sociological, economic and other social investigations should be organized, with a view to elucidating in the nature, structure and trends of the new phenomena in our society and the new forms and manifestations of social laws. The results of these investigations of social laws. The results of these investigations should be so adapted as to make possible their optimum use by the respective governing Party and state organs.

—the social sciences should be so elaborated as to offer possibilities to map out scientifically our development over a certain period of time. Of decisive significance are systems of mapping out social developments such as the planning and forecasting of social processes.

Third: The structure and functions of our organs charged with the direction of science should be perfected in accordance with the need to make it possible for science to develop under the best possible conditions and in a manner that will intensify scientific research. In the various units charged with the direction of science, from top to bottom, the principle of a correct distribution of labor, of full consonance and coordination, and the elimination of all parallelism should be applied. It is only through a thorough coordination and consonance in the work of the State Committee of Science and Technical Progress, the Bulgarian Academy of Sciences, the Academy of Agricultural Sciences, the higher educational establishments and the departmental research institutes that a maximum and most effective utilization of scientific research can be achieved. This question should be deeply investigated and analyzed, so that an adequate organization of science for the present needs of our social development may be established.

The authority and significance of the Bulgarian Academy of Sciences, its initiative and responsibility for the development of the country's sciences, should be further enhanced. At the same time, the initiative of the research institutes should be encouraged and their functions broadened so that they may indeed become basic units in the system of the Academy.

Through its role and significance, the Bulgarian Academy of Sciences must be a powerful scientific mainstay of the Party in its all-sided activity.

Fourth: The planning and financing of scientific research and the stimulation of scientific activities should be further perfected. In our country these problems have, on the whole, been correctly solved. Stages in planning have been established, including the forecasing of scientific and technical research, the elaboration of basic trends, the drawing up of long-range plans, of current plans for scientific and technical investigation and of concrete programs for the development of the individual branches. The work in connection with the selection of subjects has been improved so as to correspond to the needs of the nation's economic, cultural and social development. The branch scientific organizations have been established on the principle of financial autonomy—a process which has brought good results.

Special attention should be paid to the question of *scientific coordination.* That is most closely related to the problem of a more thorough and consistent application of the principle of systematic planning of scientific research so that it may embrace the whole cycle of investigation: from the long-range scientific and technical forecasts and fundamental investigations to their transformation into corresponding technologies and constructions capable of being introduced into the national economy.

For a small country like ours, with limited financial, natural and human resources, the problems of planning, financing and coordinating scientific investigations acquire exceedingly great significance. Not only the effectiveness of scientific research but also the destiny of our strategy in the field of science depend upon their correct solution.

We are faced with the acute problem of the proper organization of scientific research (scientific auxiliary technical bases, administrative staff) and the training and preparation of scientific cadres.

The training of young scientific cadres and their proper utilization are of very great importance in raising the role and effectiveness of research work.

In a number of scientific institutions the Party principles of selecting cadres are often violated. Good scientific leadership and an atmosphere of solicitude and strict standards towards aspirants, assistants and young research associates are not always attained. Measures should be adopted that will place on a sound foundation the selection, growth and distribution of the new scientific cadres. This is all the more necessary because our research institutions are either new or they have widened the front of their investigations in the last few years. Flaws in the qualifications and education of cadres can produce a lasting negative effect on their work and development.

Fifth: We have established a good *national system of scientific and technical information* which "delivers" the necessary information straight to scientific workers and technical cadres. This established network and its methods and operations in the field of scientific and technical information, must now be expanded and improved.

Our enterprises, trusts, ministries, research institutes, technical development centres, higher educational establishments, scientific societies, etc., must be able to quickly receive and make fuller use of the latest achievements in science and technology as well as in the organization of production all over the world, on every general and special problem that may be of interest to them.

Concluding Speech

Comrades, the present Plenary Session of the Central Committee of the Bulgarian Communist Party, which discussed questions of paramount importance to our social, economic, political and cultural development, achieved an exceedingly high level. Unanimity, great activity and a constructive attitude were evidenced, and the collective mind of the Party leadership was demonstrated.

It could not have been otherwise. Our Central Committee comprises in its ranks worthy representatives of the communists and the working people from all sectors of life of all Party generations. As the militant general staff of the Party, the Central Committee represents the country's heart and mind and is closely connected to the Party, the people, to socialist construction and to the aspirations of the working people. And this constitutes its great strength.

The creative work of the Plenary Session is one more proof of the fact that only the collective mind is capable of determining the fundamental trends and mapping out ways and means for our successful advance. The most important conclusion we can draw is that in the future, too, the collective thought of the Central Committee should be developed to a maximum in summarizing and lending meaning to socialist practice in the correct solution of the current problems of the Party's home and foreign policy, and to avert any manifestations of subjectivism.

In the statements made here, some personal contributions on my part in elaborating the problems under discussion were pointed out. I see my contribution as part of the joint comradely work of our collective. No one could by himself shoulder a task of such vital significance to our whole social development; such a task can only be an undertaking of the entire collective, the Politbureau, the Central Committee, the Party.

In the discussions of the Plenary Session, a number of problems were further elaborated, new questions were posed, additional proposals were made, The lively discussion and the constructive attitude displayed will obviously be of great significance to the final formulation of the decisions of the present Plenary Session of the Central Committee, to their implementation, and to our future work.

It was pointed out quite correctly that far-reaching explanatory and organizational work is needed among the cadres, the work forces and working people, in order to bring about a turning point in their consciousness and a new attitude towards the fulfillment of their set tasks. This is absolutely necessary in order that the Central Committee, all Party organs and the entire Party should be up to the high level demanded by the problems discussed here and that they may become tasks of all communists and of all the people.

We listened and gave general approval to Comrade Georgi Traikov's statement of the assessment made by the Standing Board of the Bulgarian Agrarian Union in connection with present and future joint work of the Bulgarian Communist Party and the Agrarian Union. The assessment of the latter's leadership and its positive attitude has been discussed at our Plenary Session. I wish to express our thanks for this assessment and to re-emphasize that we, communists and agrarians, have marched and will in future continue to march together for the implementation of our common cause—the construction of a socialist society.

In conclusion, I wish to join in the optimism that was expressed here as to the fact that the Central Committee and our Party will continue to mobilize the efforts, talents and enthusiasm of the working people in the same constructive and purposeful manner, and that, on the basis of the decisions of the Ninth Party Congress and the present Plenary Session of the Central Committee, they will continue to inspire and lead the whole people to work and fight for the socialist advancement of our dear country—the People's Republic of Bulgaria.

6

On Questions of Education

Memorandum to the Political Bureau of the Central Committee of the Bulgarian Communist Party, July 30, 1969

Recently, and more particularly since the session of the Politburo which approved the materials to be submitted to the Plenary Session of the Central Committee of the Party on the reform of our educational system, I have been considering certain basic principles of education under socialism. Today's discussions at the Plenary Session made me reconsider them once again and induced me to share with you some of my considerations.

We have set ourselves a big task, the perspective of introducing compulsory secondary education for all our young people. Naturally, we members of the Politburo have agreed that for many reasons the solution of this problem should not be implemented too hastily. But the task itself has been properly set. Universal secondary education is the chief means through which the aims of our educational reform can be attained, and that aim is to prepare the younger generation to cope with life. It is also the main method of linking our education with all other aspects of our socialist development.

Now all this is true — the problem of education in a highly developed socialist society has been properly formulated. The question, however, is what kind of secondary education is to be aimed at?

Is it right to identify universal secondary education with the three types of secondary schools now existing—the secondary professional and technical schools, the technical colleges, and the secondary polytechnical schools, and to establish these three types of educational institutions as final forms of our secondary education?

In doing so, it seems to me, we would be laboring under certain conceptions that have been established under our people's rule, conceptions which we already consider a traditionel system for the education and training of our youth. The correct thesis on the future type of school, I believe, is that given by Marx and Lenin for a comprehensive polytechnical institution that will link teaching with work and work with teaching. I am wondering why we should retreat from that thesis?

The polytechnical schools in our country have not altogether been a success and other socialist countries have had the same experience. This has led to a certain confusion, to a tendency to try to find other ways of solving the problem, chiefly by splitting up the comprehensive type of school. Both in our country and in other socialist countries this has been discussed and various types of specialized schools have been created—secondary polytechnical schools, technical colleges, secondary vocational schools and so on. What is more, the so-called polytechnical secondary school is "polytechnical" in name only, not in its actual character.

Is this correct? Is it proper that we should give up the idea of a comprehensive polytechnical school, as our party used to call it in its program, and look for different types and establish them as the only expedient forms of education?

It is my opinion that this would not be right. For our failures with the comprehensive system of education based on polytechnical principles are not due to a fault in those principles but to other factors. Chief among these is the lack of theoretical clarity, insufficient study of a number of problems concerning methods and methodology, lack of experience and proper organization, conservatism and formalism in educational work, insufficient training of teachers and leading educational workers, certain difficulties connected with the technical facilities in schools and the poor organization of the enterprises, factories and co-operative and state farms responsible for supplying them.

As you see, these are not reasons that would justify deviating from the thesis of Marx and Lenin on the education and training of our young generations for socially useful work. On the contrary, the reform of our educational system can be implemented most fully and advantageously only on the basis of a comprehensive polytechnical school. For only this type of school, properly organized, is able to offer the most favorable conditions for all young people to independently advance their training, to forge closer links between themselves and the working class and agricultural workers through productive labor and social development while promoting their ideological training.

Marx has also explicitly stated that from the age of 16 or 17 all young people would engage in socially useful work. Our educational system must create the necessary conditions for implementing this principle by giving young people the training needed for participation in production and other socially useful work. And since this does not concern a few strata of our young people only, but all youth in general, it is obvious that the problem will not be solved by setting up various specialized schools for a greater or smaller section of our youth but by a general reform of our educational system, notably of the secondary schools, which must be attended by the entire young generation. This is another important argument in favor of the comprehensive polytechnical school.

Under such a system of education, the question of the so-called primary school training, which has been the subject of many discussions, ceases to exist, since with the introduction of compulsory universal secondary polytechnical schooling there will be no need for an independent school unit of that kind.

We should also bear in mind that at present the course of higher training for specialists is far too long. It continues up to the age of 23 or 24 and, if we add the years of military training for men, to 25 or 26. This is a considerable loss to society since, as we know, the most productive and creative age for research work, especially in mathematics and physics, is between twenty and thirty-five. By keeping our young people away from the field of independent creative work, we are retarding their development by five or six years—the years of the greatest creative daring.

Obviously this further bolsters the argument that a comprehensive secondary polytechnical school would create the conditions for shortening the course of higher training.

If secondary polytechnical education takes, say, ten years, young people will finish school at 16 and enter life ready to work in various spheres of material production and social development. At 17 or 18 they will be ready to take up leading positions in production; at 19 or 20 they will be fully qualified university or college-trained specialists.

I am also deeply convinced that with the broad and many-sided human knowledge that exists it is impossible to acquire a rounded education exclusively at school. We should also bear in mind that modern science develops at a breakneck pace and even if we assume that some unusually gifted and studious young people may, on finishing their university training, have familiarized themselves with the most recent achievements of science and technology in their particular fields, they will within a few years lag behind if they remain at the same level of knowledge. This is even more true of the majority of present-day experts. That is why they must constantly refresh and enrich their knowledge and experience and keep in step with the latest achievements of the scientific and technical revolution. Therefore a more efficient system of further training must be created and socially useful work must be closely linked with education and self-education.

If we are to find the right solution to these problems, we should shelve our present conceptions of schooling and set ourselves the task of building up a streamlined system that will link together secondary and higher school training with the various forms of further study, with material production and its development, with research institutes, with ideological training and so on, What is needed is a system that will guarantee the smooth evolution of the two mutually linked processes—on the one hand, the merging of the higher educational establishments with the various research institutes and, on the other, the merging of the latter with the practical work done in the respective fields which will constantly produce a fresh stream of new challenges. Only such a system can produce highly qualified experts and scientists trained in a communist spirit, keeping them abreast of the level of scientific and technical progress.

It is evident than that one of our main tasks at present is to build up a pattern for the future comprehensive polytechnical school. In constructing this pattern, we must be led by the idea of bringing nearer to each other and merging the two types of training of young people that have been established so far, general education and vocational training. We are constantly advancing towards a merger of physical and intellectual work; we are steadfastly marching on the road to becoming a technically-minded people. Radical changes are taking place in our society and these are bound to lead to an abolition of class divisions and to the building up of a classless communist society. To create an all-round human personality is the ideal we pursue for the citizen of tomorrow. The road to that ideal passes through the comprehensive polytechnical school, which must give every boy and girl the opportunity not only to acquire a knowledge of nature and society and the general necessary cultural and polytechnical outlook, but also to enable them, even while in school, to participate in socially useful work. Indeed, all young students after a certain age should combine their schooling with practical work in material production.

We should also stress that such an approach, apart from its contribution to preparation for life, is also invaluable as a political, moral and educational factor. It will be helpful in eradicating petty bourgeois prejudices and will inspire all young people with respect for physical, socially useful work and with a sense of belonging to the working class, to all workers for socialism, no matter what field of human endeavor or human knowledge they engage in after finishing secondary and higher training.

We should like to add that the comprehensive polytechnical school places all young men and women under equal conditions and solves in a most equitable way the problem of compulsory education and the choice of a profession—a problem of great personal, social and political importance.

It would be of interest to inquire how the adherents of the three different types of schools would proceed in their choice of school for children before they have shown their special bent and abilities. Seemingly, they would have to be subjected to a choice based on caste. But ours is not a caste state. The Constitution of the People's Republic of Bulgaria grants every citizen the right to education, primary education being free of charge and compulsory. In our new Constitution a clause will read that secondary education is to be compulsory and free of charge as well! Only a secondary polytechnical school can provide an education equal to secondary.

Naturally, we cannot at present give up our established structure and system of education and we cannot, therefore, proceed to a sudden radical solution. We do not yet have the necessary basis, the experience, the trained experts and the funds. It would also be a mistake if we were to solve the question in advance at the present Plenary Session. For we cannot afford to fail to reckon with our present needs, which call for speedy training of experts in certain new branches and which compel us to postpone the introduction of comprehensive education such as I have proposed. It is essential, however, to remember that educational reforms are not carried out during every five-year plan and that the reform we are advancing now will extend over the next 20 years or so.

Therefore, without committing ourselves to any categorical formula, we ought to include in the decisions of this Plenary Session certain carefully considered statements that will delineate the general trend in sufficient clarity and indicate the final aims.

The second question I wish to dwell upon concerns our higher educational institutions and the scientific field in general.

The essentially new element that the reform introduces into our higher education is the linking together of teaching with research work. It is disquieting that research work in our higher educational establishments is still only a side activity. It is no less disquieting that our research institutes occupy themselves with peripheral problems, while the main problems connected with the advance of the scientific and technical revolution remain as a whole outside the pale of their attention.

The basic concepts and principles of reform suggested for our higher education and for the concentration and integration in the field of research work are correct.

It is indisputably necessary that research work in our institutes and higher educational establishments should be centered round certain leading and progressive branches of our national economy, in conformity with the forecasts for its development over a considerable period of time. It is also beyond dispute that research work is more fruitful and effective when it is closely linked with practical activity, when it is accomplished by teams consisting of scientists, instructors, students, experts and innovators from the enterprises, Such teams will also guarantee the swiftest implementation of new scientific achievements in practice. This will put an end to the often observed lack of continuity between research work and the practical implementation of its results in production.

All this will be of major importance in eliminating the existing subjective attitudes in the choice of workers in research institutes, in the two academies and their sections. It will guarantee a constant fresh stream of talented specialists; it will rejuvenate those institutes, some of which have gone rather stale, owing to the strange principle according to which, once a research worker takes "holy orders", he cannot be discharged even though he may not be accomplishing anything for the advancement of science, and may even have forgotten his "Old Testament"!

Hence, it is necessary to organize research work in all fields in such a way as to direct them towards the main problems of our technical, economic and social development, and to make science a genuine productive force.

We have at present two academies of sciences, numerous higher educational establishments and over a hundred research institutes and technical development centers. Besides these, there are a number of institutes of higher education and of research institutes that either have none of the necessary facilities or are still in the process of receiving them. Obviously, this is not only a luxury for a country the size of ours, but also a grave handicap in carrying out efficient teaching or research work and directing them towards the solution of basic problems. It will therefore be necessary to concentrate and integrate research work with the higher training of experts, which will lead to considerable changes in the structure and organization of the entire field of research and teaching. On these points, too, it seems to me we ought not to commit ourselves to categorical statements. We ought to be quite precise in formulating our decision so as to be able in future, after due deliberation and inquiry, to reach the best solution of these problems.

These, comrades, are my arguments and my suggestions. If the Politburo agrees with them, I request that it ask the Plenary Session to introduce certain amendments and specifications in the decision concerning a reform of the educational system.

7

Master Science and Technology

Excerpts from a speech to the 8th Plenum of the Central Committee of the Dimitrov Young Communist League (Komsomol), October 29, 1969

I should like to begin by expressing my profound gratification at being able to participate in the work of the current plenary session of the Central Committee of the Dimitrov Young Communist League.

Personally course, I have always enjoyed being among young communists and particulary among those to whom the Party has confided the direct leadership and responsibility for work among young people, for their communist education and participation in socialist construction.

My satisfaction is due not merely to my being among you again but also to the circumstance that I am attending a session of the Komsomol Central Committee which has placed on its agenda problems that are of crucial importance for the scientific and technical revolution, for the construction of the infrastructure of socialism, for speeding up the rates of building an advanced socialist society in the People's Republic of Bulgaria.

The Party and its Central Committee, have stressed time and again that *the Dimitrov Young Communist League is the foremost assistant and reserve of the Party.* These are not just words but a historical fact; they recognize the real status won by young communists, by youth in general, in decades of devoted work and struggle under the banner of Marxism-Leninism, under the leadership of our Party.

The Central Committee of the Dimitrov Young Communist League, the entire Komsomol, have always responded readily to the decisions taken by the Party Central Committee in implementing its policy. The Komsomol and its leadership have always adopted as their own the tasks set by the Party and Government. It is gratifying to note here that the Komsomol Central Committee is worthily performing its role by mobilizing the forces of the Komsomol, the forces and the enthusiasm of the whole youth for the implementation of Party policy.

This occasion marks yet another demonstration of the responsible place and role of the Komsomol in our society. Only a month has elapsed since the September Plenary Session of the Party Central Committee, and here you are, ready to discuss the problems before you arising out of the decisions of the Plenary Session, to map out measures for the most active participation of Komsomol members and all young people in putting these decisions into effect. This is magnificent proof that the Komsomol continues to be the Party's foremost assistant and reserve, that it jealously guards and develops its rich revolutionary traditions, that the Party and the Bulgarian people can fully rely on it.

Foresight and Daring, a Class Approach to Pressing Tasks

I am sure you are quite familiar with the issues discussed at the Plenary Session of the Party Central Committee and the decisions taken there. I shall not, therefore, repeat to you the contents of these documents. I would merely like to note that the problems discussed by the September Plenary Session of the Central Committee are extremely important and urgent ones that have a direct bearing on Party policies at the present stage. They have been formulated in the spirit of the decisions of the Party's Ninth Congress and are, in substance, a further, more detailed elaboration of the ideas and decisions of the July 1968 Plenary Session of the Central Committee, principally in the economic field.

What is the significance of the fact that the Plenary Session of the Party Central Committee discussed not only in general theoretical terms but in more specific terms such cardinal problems as the scientific and technical revolution in Bulgaria, the concentration and automation of production, the concentration of research and integration of science and production, the introduction of automation in management and the refinement of the new system of economic management?

It shows; first, the high standards that Bulgaria has attained and its increased potential. And second, the foresight and daring of our Party and nation which, in close unity with the Soviet Union and the other socialist countries, puts forward for solution not only the pressing tasks of the present day but also tasks that will provide a bridge to the future, to the further accelerated development of the socialist system.

If we were to make a political and class appraisal of the work undertaken by the Party and the people who will speed up scientific and technical progress in order to effectively develop the productive forces and to improve the administrative system of our socialist society, we should say that it is a continuation, under the new conditions, of the class struggle, which has been steadfastly waged by our working class, in alliance with the other working sections of the people, and under the leadership of the Party for several decades. This work is of major importance for the implementation of the policy that the Party and its Central Committee have undeviatingly pursued ever since September 9, 1944. It is a policy aimed at lifting the country out of its centuries-old backwardness and at eliminating vestiges of the capitalist past. It is a policy of developing Bulgaria as an advanced socialist state, creating wider and better conditions for raising the material and cultural standards of the people and for the free, all-round development of the human personality.

After the victory of the proletarian revolution, the Communist Party, the universally recognized leader and inspirer of the working people, begins to solve new historic tasks connected with the final elimination of the capitalist system and the building of a new socialist society. In the course of this struggle the economy is gradually reformed along socialist lines, exploiter classes are done away with, the proletariat becomes a free and rapidly growing working class, the principal class force of society; the class of co-operative farmers takes new shape and evolves as a unified socialist class; socialist relations of production prevail and develop in town and countryside, and a cultural revolution gets under way. All this creates conditions for profound changes in the material, spiritual and cultural life of the working people and for a steady improvement in the general standard of life.

From the point of view of the policy which the Communist Party pursues after the victory of the socialist revolution, from the point of view of the particular country's domestic situation and its international position, all these are class tasks which, in their totality, constitute a further development of the class struggle of the victorious proletariat. The class struggle goes on in the field of the economy as well as in the political and ideological spheres. This is class struggle in the deepest sense, for it expresses the class interests of the working class and at the same time affects the vital interests of all classes and social groups. What is more, it affects the very existence of classes, having a direct relationship on their class nature.

This struggle then is a profound class battle, because it is waged from an internal and an international point of view, in the face of the stiff resistance of the class enemy, and in the conditions of overcoming the vacillations of petty bourgeois classes and strata and sometimes, their active resistance.

In Bulgaria, socialism has finally and irreversibly triumphed. Socialist social relations prevail in the whole of society, in all spheres of our life. But, even in such conditions, every step forward, every one of our achievements in the construction and development of socialism has a profound class character.

Why is this so?

Because they consolidate the positions of the working class, a class that is the most revolutionary, the leading class of our society.

Because they promote the class homogeneity of society and

gradually create conditions for attaining a classless communist society.

Because every one of our victories is a modest contribution to the battle of the international working class against capitalism and imperialism and for socialism.

For that reason the drive to outstrip the capitalist countries in raising labor productivity, the drive for technological progress in the socialist countries and for a wider, speedier application of the achievements of the modern scientific and technical revolution in production, is at the same time a class struggle since it is one of the fronts, and a decisive one at that, of the victorious proletariat.

Science and technology are now developing at a breakneck pace, so rapidly, in fact, that if the present rate is maintained, according to the estimates of certain scientists, by the middle of the 21st century all the people on our planet will have to work in the field of science. This is, of course, carrying it to an absurdity. But I have cited it merely to show how dynamically the class struggle must be waged on that front and how important the active participation of the socialist countries in the scientific and technical revolution has become.

To lead in the scientific and technical revolution has now become the priority issue in the strategy and tactics of the proletariat, of the world socialist system, of the struggle and the triumph of the communist ideal in the world.

Only on the basis of the most recent advances of modern science and technology is it possible to build the infrastructure of socialism and subsequently of communism.

Only on the basis of the most recent advances of modern science and technology can the new system achieve the abundance of material and spiritual wealth necessary to the working man under socialism and communism.

Cybernetics, electronics, automation, nuclear power, laser and missile technology, microbiology and the other modern products of human genius form the natural material foundation on which the socialist and communist system can develop, flourish and yield abundant fruit. On that foundation the material prerequisites are created for socialism to outstrip capitalism in all spheres, including the decisive one of social life: material production.

Spearheading the modern scientific and technical revolution has produced and will continue to produce a strong revolutionizing impact on the minds of the broad masses of our planet. It helps us to reinforce the magnetic attraction of communist ideas.

We all remember quite well the tremendous impact on people's minds, especially in the capitalist countries, of the first sputnik and the catapulting of the first man into space. That scientific and technical exploit of the Soviet Union smashed to smithereens the imperialist propaganda that was trying to ram into the minds of the working people in the capitalist countries that under socialism science and technology could not properly develop.

There is no doubt that in the future, too, under the unceasing care of the fraternal Parties, our nations will continue to develop the scientific and technical revolution, to conquer its summits. It is not capitalism, a system rent by class contradictions; not capitalism, where everything including the progress of science and technology is subordinated to business, profit and super profit—but socialism, under which all classes and social groups have a stake in the progress of science and technology, socialism, where everything is put in the service of man, and provides the natural social climate that can offer unlimited scope to the scientific and technical revolution.

This is how we Marxist-Leninists see the role of modern science and technology in the development of the national economy, in the economic and political balance of power on the world scene, in the competition between the two systems and in the development of the world revolutionary process.

The task facing our Party, the Komsomol, our people, our youth today is to step up scientific and technical progress, to master and apply the modern scientific and technological advances, and to build up and strengthen the socialist society. This is at the same time our Peter's pence to the general contribution of the Soviet Union and the other fraternal countries, to the consolidation of the world socialist system, and to the triumph of socialism.

The tasks we are now tackling are not fortuitous nor the product of somebody's whim. They are prompted by the stage of development we have reached, by the new requirements of the nation's further improvement. The Party and the people will be able to solve these tasks successfully, if Party policy continues to be based on science, if its is constantly being developed, enriched and reassessed in the light of the experience of the millions of people in Bulgaria.

What is the primary need?

The primary need is to avoid looking at these tasks solely from the positions of technology and economy, from purely departmental positions. The decisions of the September Plenary Session of the Central Committee are not only of major importance for science, technology and the economy, but they also have tremendous political and ideological significance.

Their implementation should be regarded as a component of the class struggle for the development and consolidation of the positions of socialism inside the country and on the international arena.

The main thing is to step up scientific and technical progress in all spheres of socialist construction, to create ever improved prerequisites for the communist education of the people and of youth, for raising the general standard of life. This is the principal yardstick for measuring the correctness and effectiveness of our activity. For we cannot consider the Party to be doing a good job if our society's material basis is not being broadened and consolidated, if living and cultural standards in town and village are not rising steadily, if the working people are not being educated in a communist spirit. Once the working class has taken power, it has to do more than do away with the old social system; its duty is to build a new society, to show in practice its superiority over the old system.

A Militant Program of Party, Youth and Nation

Comrades, I should like to swell quite briefly on *some of the problems of the scientific and technical revolution.*

Why are we paying so much attention to this issue? Why are we dealing with its general and more specific problems at Party congresses, at plenary sessions of the Party Central Committee, at sessions of the National Assembly and the Government, plenary sessions of the Komsomol Central Committee and so on?

What does the modern scientific and technical revolution comprise? What is the principle thing in this discussion?

As we have pointed out more than once, we are living in a time when the scientific and technical revolution is assuming ever greater proportions and making ever stronger claims in the whole world, in the socialist as well as in the capitalist countries. It has an impact on production, politics, ways of life, spheres of social life; and it has become an essential object of state policy.

More than once mankind has gone through periods of radical scientific and technological change. They have led to man's physical force being replaced by natural forces. They have led to a hundred and thousandfold increase of the strength, speed and skill of human hands and feet and of the receptivity of man's senses, which, at the same time, are being displace, in part or in toto, by machines.

Accomplishing revolutionary changes on that basis, the bourgeoisie created, in Marx's words, a base that was adequate for itself and finally settled the victory of capitalism over feudalism. In so doing, however, it created the prerequisites for its own destruction, and its gravedigger, the proletariat.

The contemporary scientific and technical revolution has brought about a giant leap forward in the development of the productive forces, in the domination of natural forces and an active influence over them. The introduction of automation, of electronics, of cybernetics in social production and administration, of mathematics in scientific knowledge, the discovery of new, practically inexhaustible sources of energy, of new materials and substances with properties hitherto unknown, etc.—these are some of the principal achievements and characteristics of the modern scientific and technical revolution. This revolution is removing, gradually but surely, not only the barrier of limited sources of energy, of the limited possibilities of substances and materials found in nature, but even the so-called "barrier of information flows," the barrier of the limited human memory.

Unlike previous technological revolutions, therefore, under the modern scientific and technical revolution, the machine begins to take over part of the mental work of man, and a gradual separation of man and machine begins, whereby he ceases to be its appendage. Self-instructed and self-controlled systems of machinery will begin to operate even more extensively in production.

The scientific and technical revolution is having great economic and social repercussions both on the capitalist and on the socialist systems. The economic and social consequences of the scientific and technical revolution will have a significant impact on the people's way of life, and especially on the younger generation in Bulgaria, on their working and living patterns.

One of the foremost social implications of the scientific and technical revolution is the sudden acceleration and vast increase in the redistribution of manpower among the spheres of social production: hundreds of thousands, even millions, of people have to start working in a different field of production. You can see how in our agriculture, for instance, the number of those employed in production has been appreciably decreasing. This is bound to happen in industry as well, i.e., in the whole sphere of material production. Many are those who will have to change their professions and their jobs. For people unprepared for such changes, and in a society where the necessary conditions are not created, such shifts can be a source of great human tragedy.

The growth of the productive forces, the introduction of mechanization, automation and cybernetics into social production under our system will speed up the process of bridging the gap between mental and physical work as well as advancing the process of raising rural to urban standards. Important changes will occur in the correlation between, and the content of, working and nonworking time and especially in the working people's leisure. There will consequently be greater opportunities to enrich the general knowledge of the working people. Their way of life, their ways of thinking and behavior will gradually incorporate features and virtues that are characteristic of the communist personality. The increase of leisure time implies some very important tasks for our Komsomol, as has been pointed out here. The development of science today is a collective undertaking. Joint creative quests, the new conditions of production, the improvement of the system of social administration, will strengthen the collective spirit, comradeship, mutual aid and respect.

On the other hand, the interpenetration of science and industry and the ensuing intellectualization of society, if I may put it that way, considerably raise the demands on workers' skill, on the general and special education of those employed in production and, in general, in socially useful work.

It is impossible to step up scientific and technological progress and to improve social administration, without tightening and strictly observing labor, technological and state discipline. The September Plenary Session of the Party's Central Committee quite correctly brought up this matter in a very urgent fashion. This current Plenary Session has also given it a special attention. These are only some of the problems that we are now encountering in the course of the scientific and technical revolution and that have particular importance for young people. Naturally, under socialism there are all the objective and subjective conditions and prerequisites for solving these problems correctly, in the interest of the working people. This, however, does not mean that they will be solved automatically.

Scientific and technical progress, the accomplishment of a scientific and technical revolution is now a key problem for us in the further construction of a socialist society.

It is true that up to now we have devoted considerable time to this problem and that we have achieved quite a few successes. In spite of this, however, we cannot say that we are satisfied with the present state of affairs.

What do I have in mind?

Automation on the basis of electronics and the application of cybernetics in social production and administration—this is the main thing in the modern scientific and technical revolution. But we were very slow in properly assessing these matters.

We have also failed to face up to the fact that the scientific and technical revolution presents, in a new way, the problems of concentration and specialization, of complex automation, of the technology of production and management.

What are the main problems in that field which present-day reality raises for us? They can be described as follows:

—building up systems of computers and automation equipment as a material base for the new processes;

—training scores of thousands of experts to man these machines and, particularly important, training cadres—economists, engineers and mathematicians of a new type, to work out control systems and computer programs;

—the introduction of technologies, basically new in principle, into management and production, and the use of a number of materials of an entirely new structure and quality;

—changing people's way of thinking and overcoming the conservatism in their approach to things and phenomena so that they can understand the problems of the scientific and technical revolution and their practical resolution. This is the principal and perhaps the most difficult question.

We are now faced with a major task: to provide the best possible conditions for the development of the scientific and technical revolution in our country. What we have to do is to create a better climate in which scientific and technical progress will thrive at all levels from top to bottom.

For all leaders and rank-and-file workers, for our scientists, engineers, construction men, designers, technicians and technologists, for all specialists and for the entire work force, resolving the problems of scientific and technical progress must become as necessary, as vital as daily bread, We are inspired by the noble ambition to advance the nation's production potential at such rates and to such a level, to master the achievements of modern science and technology to such a degree, as to make sure that the People's Republic of Bulgaria will within a short time catch up with the industrial countries that are advanced in the spheres of science and technology, and become a technically-minded nation, a communist nation.

You are already familiar with the two programs submitted at the September Plenary Session, on the setting up of automated systems of management on a nation-wide scale and on the setting up of systems of management in the key enterprises and corporations. You are aware of the scope and of the main tasks and objectives we have to achieve in this sphere in the period up to 1975. We are, indeed, embarking on a bold and daring undertaking, but our work is based on scientific principles and rests on solid practical foundations.

These programs, naturally, will be implemented stage by stage, in conformity with our resources, the level of the nation's economic infrastructure and the stage reached in the development of our country.

Obviously, we are not yet in a position to introduce automatic lines, complex mechanization, computer techniques and the like everywhere. What we can and must do is to pursue unswervingly the policy of consistent modernization in all the existing plants and production processes. In the implementation of scientific and technical progress in our country we shall draw not only on our own experience and achievements but also on the experience of other countries, socialist as well as capitalist. But we shall, above all, continue to rely on Soviet experience and achievements.

The problems of the scientific and technical revolution in Bulgaria cannot be formulated or resolved successfully without specialization and co-operation within the framework of the Council for Mutual Economic Assistance (CMEA), and bringing our economy ever closer to that of the Soviet Union. I shall not deal with this question in detail here; I would only like once more to underline, that for us socialist integration is a matter of vital importance, since it permits us to overcome the limitations imposed by our small territory and population. It is an integration that will open up before Bulgaria broad vistas for the development of the scientific and technical revolution.

The execution of this tremendous work and the fulfillment of Party directives on scientific and technical progress will depend on the people, on their tireless work, on the working class, co-operative farmers and the intelligentsia, experts, scientists and the millions of builders of socialism.

It may be said categorically that the fate of scientific and technical progress is in your hands, dear Komsomol members. It is in the hands of Bulgarian youth.

Youth has always been the fiery agent, the dynamic force in revolutionary drives and today, too, it is an energetic, ardent force in the promotion of the scientific and technical revolution in Bulgaria.

We are certain *the Party's program of broad advance all along the front of scientific and technical progress will in the time to come also become the practical program for our glorious Komsomol and for our entire patriotic, industrious Bulgarian youth.*

8

The New Party Program

Excerpts from the Report of the Central Committee of the Bulgarian Communist Party to the 10th Congress of the BCP, April 20, 1971

One of the most important specific features imparting a historical character to our Congress is the fact that it will discuss and adopt a new Program of the Bulgarian Communist Party.

The text of the Draft Program was published and submitted to wide discussion in the Party as well as in our social, political and mass organizations and our entire society. I do not think that it is necessary to make a detailed analysis of the contents of the draft here but I shall dwell only on some key problems.

More than one hundred and twenty years have elapsed since the day when the founders of our great revolutionary science, Marx and Engels, armed the working class with the communist program, the first in human history —*The Manifesto of the Communist Party.* Appearing at the dawn of the international communist movement, *The Communist Manifesto* today continues to call, mobilize and inspire the struggle for freedom and happiness and for a bright communist future.

Our Party has always estimated the Party Program to be an exceptionally important *theoretical, ideological and political document* that expresses the principles, goals and tasks of the Party and defines the ways and means of achieving them. The Program is a *guide to action* for our entire Party and for all working people. It arms us with a clear perspective and points to the right road for securing our historical goals.

The need for a Program is dictated by the objective logic of social development and by the historical task of the Communist Party to direct and lead it. It is meant to reveal the "line" linking the separate parts and stages of the revolutionary process, our past, present and future activity, "so that we do not get lost," as Lenin pointed out, "in the zigzags, in the turnings of history but bear in mind the general perspective . . . so that we can see the beginning, the continuation and the end."[1]

The Program of the Party is a comparatively long-lasting document which acts as a guide to action during a whole historical period of the revolutionary struggle. The Party introduces some changes and amendments to its program or adopts a new program only when the social and historical development and its own development face the Party with qualitatively new tasks. Marx compared the programs of the Marxist parties to "milestones, by which people judge the level of the Party movement"[2] They are milestones marking the key moments, the basic stages of development of the revolutionary movement of society.

Since its very beginning, our Party has had an established tradition in this respect. It adopted its *First Program* as early as its *Constituent Congress* on Mount Bouzloudja in 1891. This was the first program document of the Bulgarian socialist movement.

The *Program Declaration* was adopted at our first Congress after World War I in 1919, when the Party was renamed "Communist Party." The Program Declaration of the Bulgarian Communist Party

[1] Lenin, *Ibid*, Vol. 27, p. 130

[2] Karl Marx, *Critique of the Gotha Programme*, New York: International Publishers, 1973 edition, p. 35.

included substantial additions and amendments to the old Party Program, called for by the new historical period, by the victory of the Great October Socialist Revolution, by the development of the Party, the initial stage of adoption of the ideas of Leninism and by the founding of the Comintern, one of whose founding members was our Party.

In October 1922 the Party Council approved the draft for a new Party Program submitted by the Bulgarian delegation to the Fourth Congress of the International in November, 1922. The events of 1923, however, prevented the discussion and adoption of the draft by a Party Congress.

Later the Bulgarian Communist Party worked out other program documents, among which were the decisions of the *Fifth Congress of the Party in 1948* and the decisions of the *April Plenum of the Central Committee of the Bulgarian Communist in 1956*. But no matter how significant, these documents were not, nor did anyone claim they were, a Party program.

The problem of working out a new program of the Party was raised as long ago as the *Fifth Congress,* the first Congress of the Party after the victory of the socialist revolution in Bulgaria. But no program was worked out, owning to Georgi Dimitrov's death and the events which followed.

Only after the Seventh Congress of the Party was the problem raised again, and the July Plenum of the Central Committee in 1968 decided that a program of the Party should be worked out and submitted for discussion and adoption to the present *Tenth Party Congress.*

What has made it imperative for our Party to adopt a new program?

We have already stated the general principles that determined the necessity for Party programs. We were guided by these principles when we decided to work out and adopt a new program for our Party.

We rely and are led by the basic principles of Marxist-Leninist theory in all our activities. Marxist-Leninist science on the development of society is the scientific basis of the activities of every communist party. Historical experience, however, has shown *that our theory must be applied in a creative way by making it concrete and by developing it.* In *the first* place, the concrete conditions in each country at a given stage must be taken into consideration; and, in *the second,* the changes in the international situation, in the development of the world revolutionary process and in the interrelation of all world forces.

In this connection, it is not difficult to see that the need has long been ripe to work out and adopt a program. Since the adoption of the *Program Declaration* of the Bulgarian Communist Party in 1919, more than half a century has elapsed, and during this time deep, fundamental changes have taken place in the world and in the development of our Party and in our country. I do not consider it necessary here to give a detailed picture of these changes.

I shall merely point out that all program documents of our Party have long since been carried out. It is more than a quarter of a century now since our country has been developing along the road to socialism, passing through various stages of formation and development. Today our people are building an advanced socialist society in the People's Republic of Bulgaria, under the leadership of our Communist Party.

All this requires that the Party should adopt a new program that will theoretically sum up and give meaning to the historical experience of the past and the present and also discern future trends of development of our country. We should apply Marxism-Leninism creatively and develop it further in accordance with the requirements of the new stage of development. We must scientifically define and substantiate the present historical task of the Party, the main trends, and ways and means for its realization.

It is true that the congresses of the Party also dwell on the problems of socialist construction and the basic tasks of the Party for a given period. Neither the resolutions of the congresses, however, nor the reports of the Central Committee to the congresses, nor the social and economic plans can be substituted for the program.

We know that the stages of historical development of society as a complete system last much longer than the periods between congresses. We cannot exactly foretell when the building of the advanced socialist society will be completed but obviously it will cover an extended historical period. We also know that the dynamics of development increase together with the ascending development of our socialist society and of the world socialist system. At the same time, the construction of an advanced socialist society is taking place under the conditions of the speedily developing scientific and technological revolution today. It is connected with the development, practical application and utilization of the achievements of this revolution in all spheres of social life that further accelerate the rate of development of society.

Since this is so, and because of its leading role, today more than ever the Party needs to have a clear view of the future development of the social processes, and this can only be provided by the Party Progrm.

No less important is the fact that in accordance with the Leninist teaching on the Party, *one of the conditions for membership in the Communist Party, inscribed in the Statute of our Party is the acceptance of the Party Program.*

What are the characteristic features of the Draft Program?

The principal feature is that it is a program for the construction of an advanced socialist society in Bulgaria.

Bulgaria has entered the stage of building advanced socialism as a result of the socialist revolution, of the successful ending of the transition period from capitalism to socialism and the complete victory of socialist production relations, as well as of the results of the qualitative and quantitative changes in the whole system of social life. During this period, the construction of the material and technical basis of socialism must be completed, socialist production relations must be improved, culture must be enriched, the well-being of the people must be improved and irregularities in the development of the social system must be overcome.

Consequently, the major immediate historical task of the Party is the construction of an advanced socialist society in our country.

Hence the task of the Program is as follows:

—to analyze the domestic and international conditions under which we are constructing the advanced socialist society;

—to formulate the basic characteristic features of this stage of the development of socialist society in Bulgaria;

—to trace the basic laws and tendencies of development during this period;

—to map out the major tasks of the Party in the different sectors of life and to define the basic methods and means for solving them. In working out these problems we have relied on the principles of Marxist-Leninist theory and, more specifically, on Marxist-Leninist science in connection with the two phases of communist social and economic formation. We have relied on the experience of our Party and country in their historical development till now, and on the historical experience of the Communist Party of the Soviet Union in building socialism and communism in its country and its contributions to the creative development of Marxist-Leninist theory. We have also relied on the historical experiences and creative contributions of the Communist Parties of the other socialist countries as well as on the documents of the international communist movement—the result of collective efforts. In working out our Program we were greatly aided by the *Program of the Communist Party of the Soviet Union,* by its wealth of theoretical content and by the discovery of the laws and perspectives of the further development of society towards communism.

This is only natural, first, because we are a Marxist-Leninist Party, an internationalist Party. And, second, because the process of the construction and development of socialism in Bulgaria is part of the unified world revolutionary process that follows objective laws valid for all countries throughout the world. *The construction of an advanced socialist society is not a specific Bulgarian task.* Other countries and other peoples who have taken the road to communism are passing, or will pass, through this stage. That is why *the laws functioning at this stage are common laws of development.*

At the same time, however, *these common objective laws function in a specific way in every individual country.* Every Party works out and solves concrete problems in accordance with the conditions in its own country, its national traditions and its historical past. That is why, in mapping out the ways of development during the stage to come we have tried *to link in one organic unity the international tasks with the national tasks of the Party, the general with the specific. We have tried to lend a Bulgarian character to the content and form of our Program so that it will not only reflect what holds good for all countries and peoples, but also the specific, concrete conditions and tasks of our Party and of our people.*

For this purpose, while working out the Program, we have relied,

above all, on the historical experience of the 25 years of development of socialism in our country, on the achievements of Marxist-
Leninist theoretical thought in Bulgaria and, more specifically, on
the historical experience and achievements of Marxist-Leninist
theoretical thought in our country during the period after the historic April Plenum of the Central Committee of the Bulgarian
Communist Party in 1956.

It should be stressed that it would have been extremely difficult
to work out our Draft Program if, in recent years and especially
during the period after the Ninth Party Congress, we had not solved
at different plenums of the Central Committee, and *more precisely
at the July Plenum,* important theoretical problems connected with
our economic, social and political life.

In developing the Draft Program we were guided by the
Marxist-Leninist requirement for *the Program to be scientific and
realistic to the maximum:* to be thoroughly in accordance with the
concrete conditions and the degree of development of our country,
not overlooking certain stages while mapping out our tasks and
avoiding subjectivism and illusions. "The program," Lenin wrote,
"must be built on a scientific basis."[3] . . . . "It must take into consideration facts which are absolutely and precisely ascertained."[4]
The Program must be founded on a strictly objective, scholarly
Marxist-Leninist analysis of the socio-historical processes and their
laws; it must solve new theoretical problems and at the same time
put forward only such historical goals and tasks that can be realized.
"This and only this," wrote Lenin, "is the attractive power of our
program. And if we put forward the slightest claims which we ourselves cannot fulfill, then this will weaken the force of our program,
because the masses will become suspicious and decide that our
program is only fantasy."[5]

That is why the Draft Program outlines only the most general
tasks and trends of development. Now, under the conditions of the
scientific and technical revolution, it is especially difficult to define
the concrete indices and rates of development over such a long
period of time.

---

[3] Lenin, *Ibid,* Vol. 29, p. 190
[4] Lenin, *Ibid,* Vol. 27, p. 131
[5] Lenin, *Ibid,* Vol. 27, p. 148

In working out the Program we were guided by the premise that the entire activity of the Party *to construct an advanced socialist society must be subjected to the task of ensuring the constant rise of the material and cultural level of the people and the all-sided development of man.* That is why there are good reasons to say that the Program is the living embodiment of the Party's slogan, "*Everything in the name of man, everything for the well-being of man!*"

We were also guided by the desire that the Program should be *in form, as it is in content, close to the thoughts and feelings of the working people so as to be understood by them.* The requirement that the Program be scientific and theoretically substantiated does not mean that it should be an abstract theoretical treatise comprehensible to only a narrow circle of specialists. The Program is a document for the instruction of the entire Party and the millions of working people in the ideas of Marxism-Leninism, of socialist patriotism and consistent proletarian internationalism, for the purpose of involving the working people in the actual struggle for the victory of socialism and communism. As Lenin put it, every paragraph of the Program must contain "material for agitators to use in hundreds of thousands of speeches and articles. Every clause of our program is something that every working man and woman must know, assimilate and understand."[6] That is why there is an attempt to express the most difficult theoretical problems in the Program in simple and comprehensible language. In the Program there is also a degree of emotional content that contributes to a stronger impact.

The elaboration of the Program is a great collective effort in which, under the guidance of the Central Committee, members and collaborators of the Central Committee participated, as did a considerable number of representatives of our Marxist-Leninist scientific thought. Its discussion became a nation-wide effort, in the real sense of the word. In all the towns and villages throughout the country, in plants and on construction sites, in cooperative farms and offices, in educational institutions and scientific institutes, everywhere, communists, Komsomol members, members of the Agrarian Union and of the Fatherland Front participated with great interest in the discussions of the Draft Program. It can be said that

[6] Lenin, *Ibid*, Vol. 29, p. 190

this was one of the widest mass polls of the communists and the people carried out by the Central Committee. It was one of the most outstanding examples of the unbreakable link between the Party and the people.

What did the nation-wide discussion of the Draft Program show?

Above all, the poll showed the *universal approval* of this document by all the working people in our country. The assessments of our work so far and the formulations of our forthcoming tasks have been unanimously approved. The Draft Program has been estimated as a historical document. Its creation is an outstanding event in our life. The discussion has convincingly shown that by creatively applying the principles of Marxism-Leninism, the Central Committee of the Party has been able to cover the most important problems of our development and to find the proper solution for them.

The discussion has again proved *how much the political and ideological maturity of our people has grown*. This is shown by the high level of activity, by the numerous opinions and suggestions sent to the Central Committee of the Party directly, or through the district Party committees, the leadership of the public organizations and through the editorial boards of newspapers, magazines, radio and television. The careful study of these suggestions has shown that the overwhelming majority of them have a constructive character, that they are permeated with a high consciousness of unity with and devotion to the ideas of our Party and the cause of socialism and communism.

The discussion of the draft Program has eloquently demonstrated the unity and cohesion of the Party ranks; the unity and cohesion of our entire nation with the Party's general policy; and the unity of all the generations in our country—the generation of the Party veterans, the middle generation and the youngest—all of whom have readily assumed the historic responsibility of building the advanced socialist society in Bulgaria.

The nation-wide discussion of the Draft Program of the Party was *a remarkable theoretical, ideological and political* schooling for our people. It is also a clear indication that the ideas and perspectives mapped out by the Party, once they have taken hold of the masses, will become a great material force. This is a guarantee that the Program will be put into effect.

Some Theoretical Problems Concerning the Construction
of the Advanced Socialist Society in Bulgaria

Comrades, the new Draft Program of the Party reflects a great number of *new* theoretical problems of extremely great importance. I would like to touch upon some of those, and which are of great practical significance as well.

The most important refers to the *place and character of the advanced socialist society* as a stage in the development of the first phase of the communist formation.

As we know, Marx and Engels scientifically established the inevitable doom of capitalism and the creation of a new communist social system. Developing the theory of the communist socioeconomic formation, they proved that in its development this formation would inevitably undergo two phases—a lower and a higher one. Marx, Engels and Lenin discovered the basic laws governing social development during the period of transition from the capitalist to the communist formation and during the first phase of the latter, which is socialism.

Summing up the experience of the socialist revolution, Lenin extended and enriched the characterization of socialism and communism. In a number of his works, he was the first to speak of socialism in formation, advanced socialism and fully developed socialism.

Naturally, it was not the task of Marx, Engels and Lenin to make a detailed analysis of the communist socio-economic formation and its phases and stages. That was neither possible nor necessary at the time. But they have left us a great theoretical heritage that we must further develop and enrich in new conditions.

I must stress the fact that the Soviet Union has accumulated considerable theoretical and practical experience in the course of building communism. Much experience has also been gained by the other fraternal countries and by the international communist and working class movement. All this helps us a great deal in throwing light on our further development.

Now that the construction of an advanced socialist society in the People's Republic of Bulgaria is our immediate historical objective, and the task of our everyday practice, we are confronted by the question: What is an advanced socialist society and what are the characteristic features and basic laws of development in force at this stage? What is its place in the development of the first phase of communism and of the communist formation as a whole? *This is the key question of our present-day Marxist-Leninist theory and practice.* The correct working out of the remaining theoretical problems relating to our social development depends to the highest degree on the correct theoretical elucidation of this key question.

In addition, in the final analysis this question predetermines the concrete strategy and tactics of the Party at the present historical stage. Whether we advance forward, or slow down the rates of social development, will largely depend on how we answer this question. Shall we resort to rash steps and subjectivism in our movement forward or will our policy be scientific and correspond to the objective requirements of social development? It is precisely these considerations that required us to analyze and define the characteristic aspects of this stage of the advanced socialist society.

We do not claim that our treatment of this question in the Program is exhaustive. We have not tried to offer a complete, an all-out characterization of this stage. This was neither possible nor necessary for such a Program. On the basis of the achievements of the theory of Marxism-Leninism and on the basis of our practical experience accumulated in building socialism, we have tried to give the main outlines of the advanced socialist society in Bulgaria.

In addition, I would like to stress that our Program has not set itself the task of giving the advanced socialist society the kind of characterization that could be applied by all fraternal parties. We have no such claims, nor have we set ourselves such a task. What we really tried to do was to use not only our own experience but also that of other countries so that the characterization of the advanced socialist society would be as full as possible and scientifically grounded. I would like to emphasize, however, once again that it applies chiefly to the advanced socialist society in the People's Republic of Bulgaria.

The theoretical basis upon which we place the examination and clarification of the advanced socialist society is Marxist-Leninist science for the *emergence, formation and development of the communist socio-economic formation.*

The development of society is a complex and contradictory process, in the course of which society passes through different

*socio-economic formations, while in its turn each formation passes
through different phases, stages and degrees of development.*
Let us take capitalism, for example. This social formation today
does not have the same appearance or shape as it did at the beginning of its development. We think of manufacturing capitalism, of
industrial capitalism and of imperialism as the highest and last stage
in its development. But life has shown that this last stage, so brilliantly analyzed by Lenin, also undergoes various phases. We are
now witnessing a new phase, in which the most characteristic feature of imperialism is state-monopoly capitalism.

We know that Lenin also spoke of different stages during the
period of transition from capitalism to socialism.

As the first phase of communism, socialism also passes from lower
to higher forms of social organization, from lower to higher stages of
development. The classics of Marxism-Leninism expressly emphasized the necessity of considering the communist formation and
its phases, including socialism, *in their dialectical development* and
not as static or frozen.

One should not forget that capitalism began to develop its production relations deep within feudalism. But we know that socialist
production relations arise and begin to develop only after political
power has been won. Apart from this, as shown by historical experience, during the period of transition from capitalism to socialism it
is not possible to build up completely the material and technological
basis typical of the socialist system. Socialist production relations
are gradually built up during the period of transition but afterwards
they must continue to develop and be perfected. The period of
transition is not a long enough period to complete the socialist
cultural revolution and fully establish socialist ideology in the consciousness of the people's masses. The period of transition is not
sufficient to form the new type of man, capable of building the
second phase of the communist formation. The period of transition
is not sufficient to ensure a harmonious development of the entire
social system.

Therefore, after the period of transition from capitalism to
socialism, society does not have either the objective or the subjective prerequisites for the transition to the highest stage of the communist society. *A more or less continuous period is needed during
which socialism develops to the point where it reaches its highest*

stage, which Lenin described as the advanced socialist society, when it reveals and realizes all its potentialities for growth in its productive forces and in its production relations and culture and the living standards of the masses, as well as in man's personality—the stage when it most completely discloses its indisputable superiority over capitalism in the main spheres of the life of society.

The analysis of social development and of the present-day material and cultural conditions in which our society is developing shows us that Bulgaria has reached the stage of building the advanced socialist society, the stage when we shall complete the construction of the material and technological basis of socialism, when we shall perfect socialist relations of production, when we shall further develop and extend all elements of the superstructure typical of the mature form of socialism.

Therefore, in our country the construction of the advanced socialist society *is an objective and historically necessary process governed by objective laws of development*, brought about by the stage reached in the development of the productive forces and production relations as well as by the objective laws governing the transition of socialism to communism.

In working out the question of the advanced socialist society, we have come to a new theoretical formulation, on which I would like to dwell briefly.

As we know, Marx wrote as follows in *Critique of the Gotha Programme* in describing the first phase of the communist socio-economic formation, i.e., socialism: "What we have to deal with here is a Communist society, not as it has *developed* on its own foundations, but, on the contrary, as it *emerges* from capitalist society; which is thus in every respect, economically, morally and intellectually, still stamped with the birthmarks of the old society from whose womb it emerges."[7] On the other hand, communism, which is the higher phase of the communist formation, arises from and develops on its own basis.

The Draft Program, however, says that "the advanced form of socialism is built and developed on its own socialist basis."

We believe there is no contradiction here but a further specification and development of one and the same concept on the basis of

[7] Karl Marx, *Ibid*, p. 8

rich and new historical experience. Marx speaks of a socialist society *just* arising out of capitalist society. It is perfectly clear that such a society inevitably bears and will bear the distinctive birthmarks of the old society in all respects—economic, moral and mental. Can one describe our socialist society, which has already undergone a long period of intensive development and which is confidently approaching its maturity, as a society that has just arisen out of capitalist society? Can we say that the construction of an advanced socialist society proceeds also on the basis left us by capitalism in political, moral and mental respects and not on its own basis? I think that the answer is in the negative and this more than ever clear today.

What are the main prerequisites created in our country for the construction of an advanced socialist society?

The first prerequisite is *the absolute domination of socialist relations of production in town and countryside, as well as unified socialist relations of production for the development of the whole society.*

The second prerequisite is the degree reached in the development of the productive forces. We have succeeded in creating a *comparatively high material and technological basis* as well as a higher level of qualification of the labor force. This has now enabled us to solve qualitatively new tasks in the promotion of industry, the rural economy and in the other sectors of our socialist economy.

The third prerequisite is the new social and class structure, which is radically different from that of capitalism, as well as the ideological, political and moral unity of our society.

The fourth prerequisite is the *complete domination of the socialist political and ideological superstructure.* The people's democratic state plays an enormous role in the country's socialist construction. Marxist-Leninist ideology is the unshakeable foundation of our country's entire cultural life.

The fifth prerequisite is the strengthened world socialist system, the *new type of mutual relations* among the countries of the socialist community and the growth of *international socialist integration.*

All this constitutes our own new socialist basis, created during its formation and upon which the advanced socialist society is to be built and developed further.

We now know from the experience accumulated in our social

development that the phase of socialism will cover an entire, lengthy historical period. The socialist society in Bulgaria and in the other socialist countries, not to mention the Soviet Union, already has a long and extremely rich history. True, it is much shorter than the history of capitalism, but, on the other hand, it is immeasurabley richer in creative work in the economic, social, political, moral and cultural fields.

It is precisely on the basis of this perfectly new, rich and all-sided creative work that we are building and we shall be building the advanced socialist society. In this sense we say that mature socialism is built and developed on its own socialist basis. Unlike the kind of socialism that appeared and developed directly from the heritage left us by capitalism, with respect to development of productive forces, living and cultural conditions, education, and so forth, *advanced socialism is being built and developed on the basis of firmly established socialist production relations; on the basis of the material and technological foundation under construction; on the basis of a highly developed political and moral life; on the basis of the socialist state system and democracy; on the basis of an advanced socialist culture and ideology and the education of the overwhelming majority of its population. In a word, we are building the advanced socialist society on a social and economic basis that is radically different from that on which capitalism was grounded.*

As for the birthmarks of capitalism of which Marx speaks, they will indeed be historically overcome and outlived, finally disappearing only when our society enters the highest phase of the communist system.

As experience has shown, however, these birth marks are also subject to substantial changes in the different stages of development of the socialist system. When Marx spoke of socialism as a society that still bears the birthmarks of capitalism, he had in mind the vast historical heritage of certain negative aspects from the point of view of ultimate communism. This heritage includes such phenomena as the differences between town and village, between mental and manual labor; social classes, with all their differences and contradictions; the state; the church, etc.—all of which socialism inherits directly from capitalism. It also includes the vestiges of the past in life style, mentality, ideology, consciousness and education, which continue to manifest themselves in one sphere or another of man's public and personal life in socialist society. Marx saw vestiges of the bourgeois law even in the socialist principle of distribution of goods according to one's work. This historical heritage can neither be skipped over nor abrogated by decree. It can be done away with and cleared away only with the tremendous and tireless efforts of the working people and, in the first place, of the working class and the Communist Party, in the process of socialist and communinst construction.

This historical heritage is not mechanically transferred on to socialism, however, and does not remain unchanged, It is refracted through socialist reality and assumes a qualitatively new context, manifests itself in new forms and fulfills qualitatively new functions. Here we do not have in mind such vestiges of the bourgeois society as the moral, religious, political and other ideas which are hostile to socialism and against which we must wage an unabating struggle. We have in mind something else.

Under socialism, too, there are *classes* and *class distinctions*, but *these are classes of a new type with new inter-relations.* Under socialism, there are no exploiter classes but *friendly classes* where the working class plays the leading role.

The socialist state is also *a state* but a state of a *new type*—the first in the entire history of mankind governed by a non-exploiter class, whose historical mission consists in building up a society in which there will be no classes nor a state.

Under socialsim, too, there are *differences between mental and manual labor, between town and village,* but these differences do not constitute essentially anatagonistic contradictions.

Therefore, in speaking of the birthmarks of capitalism, we must also bear in mind the new context, the new forms and manifestations and the new functions of the heritage from the past.

Thus, the view as to the advanced socialist society's own foundations does not at all deny Marx's conception about the birthmarks of capitalism that socialism carries within it, but rests on the further specifying and development of this concept on the basis of modern historical experience.

Another theoretical problem, which has a highly important bearing on the activities of our Party, is the problem of *the character and trends of the development of socialist ownership* during the period of building the advanced socialist society. As we know, socialist ownership is the economic basis on which the socialist society is established, developed and perfected. That is why the Draft Program pays special attention to this problem.

What will be the basic tendencies in the development of socialist ownership in this country during the next few years?

First and foremost, *the continued expansion and enrichment of the two forms of socialist ownership–the forms of public (state) and cooperative ownership.* The expansion of socialist ownership does not mean quantitative growth alone; it also means a process of qualitative changes.

The further development of state ownership can, at the present stage, be ensured above all through *perfecting the forms of this ownership.* In this respect, the role played by *the concentration of production,* and on this basis, the merger of economic units is of great importance. There have been set up in the past few years state economic trusts that are powerful economic units. These collectives are in a position to solve the basic problems of their branches.

The cooperative socialist form of ownership is developing chiefly along the lines of further socialization of the means of production. The establishment of large-scale co-operative farms, and particularly of the agro-industrial complexes, indicate the main lines along which this tendency is developing. The socialization of the means of production in the cooperative sector will continue to expand in the coming years, and this will be an important aspect of perfecting the cooperative form of ownership.

Hence, the conclusion that during the construction of the advanced socialist society the Party must concentrate its efforts towards preserving, expanding and perfecting both forms of ownership, and on helping to intensify the public character of socialist ownership as a whole. Every underestimation of the form of co-operative ownership and of its importance for the development of our economy is harmful and contrary to the objective trends and needs of socialist development. The cooperative form of ownership has not exhausted its economic potentialities by far. It has its historical place and its role to play in the further construction of socialism in our country. The fact that in the process of the general and constant growth of social production the production concentrated in the hands of the state will grow at a higher rate is quite a different matter. In this way the scope of public ownership, which is the basic form of socialist ownership, will expand; its leading role in the development of the economy and in the promotion of the socialization of the needs of production in the cooperative sector will grow; the positive effect of the scope of public ownership on the major processes in the development of society will become greater.

Alongside the development and enrichment of socialist ownership, another important tendency, typical of this stage, will be given wider scope to expand. What we have in mind is *the gradual convergence of the cooperative and state forms of ownership that will result in their future fusion into a unified form of public ownership.*

This trend is developing on the basis of the rapid growth of the productive forces of both sectors in our national economy, and on the basis of the *steady dialectical process of interpenetration and enrichment of the two forms of ownership,* while both state and cooperative forms of ownership are gaining greater maturity.

This process of interpenetration and enrichment and gradual fusion is developing *along several main lines:*

—Along the line of standardizing the methods of production in both sectors of our economy. Of particular importance, in this respect, are the industrial methods of production in agriculture. This is now being undertaken in the countryside on an ever growing scale.

—Along the line of standardizing the forms of economic organization of social production in the state and cooperative sectors, and of setting up joint state and cooperative enterprises, agro-industrial complexes and enterprises in the fields of industry, transportation, building and communal services. At the present stage of development the agro-industrial complex emerges as the basic form of economic organization in agriculture—a form that will promote, to the highest possible degree, the increase of production, the perfecting of the cooperative form of ownership, and the gradual fusion of the state and cooperative forms of ownership. As we know, in the formation of the agro-industrial complexes two forms have been combined in different ways: in some case, the complexes were set up on the basis of one form of ownership, and in others, on mixed forms of ownership. The mixed type of agro-industrial complexes now accounts for about 40 per cent of the total. With the further development of horizontal as well as vertical integration, the pro-

cess of interpenetration and the perfecting of the forms of cooperative and state ownership will tend to increase.

What form of ownership the new means of production will assume
as a result of the activities of the agro-industrial complex, in which
cooperative and state ownership are inseparably linked in the
cooperative and state farms, is now a highly topical problem.
It is evident that the newly formed funds will be neither solely
state nor solely cooperative property. Obviously, *something new is
being born*, which in its further development will gradually lead to
the formation of an over-all national ownership.

The interpenetration of the two forms of ownership will also proceed along the lines of unifying the methods of management of state
and cooperative production units along the lines of leveling the
incomes received by the working people employed in state and
cooperative production and so. on.

In other words, *in the course of building the advanced socialist
society the state and cooperative forms of ownership will continue to
develop still further;* the process of their interpenetration and enrichment will gain momentum and, on this basis, they will gradually
converge and will in the future fuse into a unified public form of
ownership.

The strengthening of international socialist economic integration
will greatly affect the nature of the socialist forms of ownership. In
this process of integration the cooperation of production between
the fraternal countries will expand, the international division of
labor will grow, and there will appear an ever greater number of
joint interstate economic organizations. *In this way the socialist
forms of ownership will gradually be carried out within the entire
world socialist system. This will create the basis on which the elements of the international form of socialist ownership will develop as
a new phenomenon in the common development of the fraternal
countries along the road to socialism and communism.*

Comrades, the question raised in the Program of *the development
of the social structure* at the present stage of the advanced socialist
society in our country is of also special theoretical significance. The
Program substantiates the Marxist concept that *the differences between the social classes and groups cannot be completely overcome
at the present stage. Those differences, however, are reduced to*

such a degree that the socialist society finds itself at the threshold of social homogeneity.

What reasons are there for drawing such a conclusion?

Radical, revolutionary changes have been carried out in the social and class structure of our society in the years of the people's rule. The classes of exploiters have been eliminated; the sharp contradictions between town and countryside, between intellectual and physical labor has also been eliminated. The essential differences between them are gradually being overcome. The nature of our society is determined by the life and interrelation of workers, cooperative farmers and people's intelligentsia, who have all been freed from exploitation.

The relationships between the classes and the other social groups are not only friendly, they are also relationships of the people who are, generally speaking, equally related to the means of production, who take an active part in the social organization of labor, who are coming closer together in respect to the size of their income, their way of life, their cultural and social status.

All this provides the prerequisites for the promotion of the process of bringing the social groups closer together and of strengthening the characteristic social features which the working people in this country have in common. Relying on the achievements scored so far, the Party is in a position to direct, in a consistent and planned way for the coming decades, the law-governed process of the gradual formation of social homogeneity in the People's Republic of Bulgaria. The attainment of *complete* social homogeneity is the task of the second phase of communism.

The Program defines one of the important aspects of the process of overcoming social and class differences, and this aspect is a matter of *principle* for our Party. But what we are indicating here is that *the process of bringing the social groups closer together will be carried out on the basis of the historical mission of the working class, that the growth of the social, ideological, moral and political unity of society depends on the degree to which the interests of the different social groups come close to and fuse with the basic interests of the working class.* It is this law that explains why the Communsit Party does not lose its class character in the process of becoming the Party of the entire nation. It also makes clear why, in spite of the fact that

the rates of its quantitative growth diminish, the working class preserves its leading role as a class in the building of the advanced
socialist society. In the light of this theoretical view, it becomes
clearer that revisionist "theories" are anti-scientific and anti-Marxist
when they assert that under the conditions of the scientific and
technological revolution the working class ceases to be the leading
force in the socialist revolution and in the development of the
socialist society.

In the advance socialist society the social activity of the individual
will become greater as will his awareness that work constitutes the
main meaning of life. His ambition to assimilate the best achievements of science and the arts will also become stronger. Man will be
the bearer of high moral virtues. There is no doubt that in the
gradual convergence of the various social groups and in the shaping
of their common social and spiritual features, *the most important
will be the historical virtues of the working class as the most progressive of the classes.* There is no doubt that the working class will have
made the greatest contribution to the process of the gradual convergence of the various social groups and of strengthening their
common social and cultural features.

The strengthening of these features does not at all mean that
individuality will be leveled, that originality will be stifled and that
people will be reduced to a common denominator. *Communism
means a rejection of bourgeois individualism but not of individuality.* Many-sided individual development is a necessary condition for
social progress. *The advanced socialist society offers a wide scope
for the expression of creative talent and the possibilities of man. It
provides still better conditions for the development of his individual
abilities and qualities, and for the development of man's natural
talents, which Marx considers to be the basic feature of every higher
social system.*

The process of shaping the new individual and of establishing
social homogeneity does not take place automatically or as a matter
of course. The scientific guidance of the process requires that the
social aspects and effects of the scientific and technological revolution be studied and taken into consideration; that a rational territorial deployment of the forces of production be carried put; that the
educational system be reorganized; that the working force be qual-

ified to accord with the new requirements and tasks; that work in the sphere of ideology be intensified, and that every individual cultivate and develop an awareness of the social, political and ideological unity of society.

We expect thorough investigation from our philosophers, sociologists, economists and other workers in the field of the social sciences as well as their theoretical conclusions as to the dynamics of the social and class structure, the processes of inner- and inter-class changes, the strengthening of social unity and the development of the individual.

The problems of the development of *the state and socialist democracy* in our country elaborated in the Program will be of great importance during the coming period. The experience of the Soviet Union, the analysis of the character of the socialist system and its laws and of the nature of the socialist state and the perspectives of its development, confirm the conclusions of the Program that at this stage *"the state of the dictatorship of the proletariat will grow into the state of the entire nation,* which, under the leadership of the working class, voices the will and interests of the entire nation," and that at this stage *"the democracy of socialism reaches the highest and fullest form of expression."*

We accept the principle that both the state and the democracy of socialist society are not established once and for all. Together with the development of the socialist system as a whole, the state and democracy also develop and change, passing through various stages with their individual peculiarities—but retaining their socialist character.

As we know, the socialist state goes through two stages of development, determined by changes in the social structure. The state of the dictatorship of the proletariat, which in this country assumed the form of a people's democracy, corresponds to the transition from capitalism to socialism.

The state of the dictatorship of the proletariat undergoes the process of constant perfecting, gradually changing into a state of the entire nation in the process of building the advanced socialist society.

In this connection, two tendencies become apparent. As a result of increased unity between the classes of the working people, the social basis of the state expands in a gradual transition into a state of the entire nation. On the other hand, a process of combining the state and non-state forms of social government sets in. This will be a step in the transition towards communist self-government. *which means that the state of the entire nation is a final stage in the development of the socialist state that introduces the general transition toward communist social self-government.*

Important changes will take place in the state system and in socialist democracy in the course of this process.

Democratic centralism will be preserved as the basic principle of the organization and functioning of the state. But within the state of the entire nation this principle will become richer in content and form. The gradual tranisition toward the state of the entire nation cannot be made without changes in the functions of the state. The principle of the unity of power will receive fuller development. The representative organs will make decisions and implement them to a greater degree.

One of the most characteristic features of the transition of the state of the dictatorship of the proletariat into a state of the entire nation will be the growing participation by the working people in the government of society directly or through their representative bodies. More and more frequently we shall resort to the practice of submitting major problems to the entire population for discussion and approval through referendums and similar forms. In this way the working people will participate directly in the government.

On the other hand, representative democracy will continue to develop and improve. The competencies and control functions of the representative bodies over the executive apparatus, in particular, and over the whole state organization, in in general, will be further extended. This will inevitably lead to certain changes in the electoral system as well.

The state bodies will not be in a position to express the will and interests of the working people fully and completely if they do not more effectively enlist the Bulgarian Agrarian Union and the public political and mass organizations in their manifold activities. In the future these organizations will also exert greater influence on all spheres of state activities—legislative, executive, administrative, juridical and control. The joint activities of the state bodies and the public organizations will be continuously enlarged and enriched. This enhancement of the role of the public organizations in the system of public administration will of necessity require a considerable increase in the scope of their legislative initiative and direct participation in making important State decisions.

The gradual transition of our state into a state of the entire nation and the extension of socialist democracy *are unthinkable without the further consolidation of the hegemonic role of the working class, and without the enhancement of the leading role of the Communist Party in the entire system of public life.* The leading role of the working class is a key factor in the development of the socialist state and of socialist democracy because the working class, owing to its place in society and its historical mission, is the natural leader of all the working people—until such time as the classless society of communim is built. The socialist state is in a position to enlarge its social base continuously and to express the interests of the entire people more fully only because the social unity of our society is built and grows on the basis of the historical mission of the working class, under the leadership and the guiding activities of the Communist Party.

Comrades, *The Communist Party, as it continues functioning as the Party of the working class, is gradually becoming the vanguard of the people, the Party of the entire nation.* This is one of the most salient laws in the construction of an advanced socialist society. It is an expression of the new changes taking place in the economy, the political system, the social and class structure and the intellectual life of this country.

The Party is a living organism that is continuously developing. Eight decades ago our Party was founded as the Party of the working class, its headquarters, its leader and organizer in the struggle for the communist idea. Traversing a difficult path the Bulgarian Communist Party has been fulfilling its historical tasks with honor and has now become the universally recognized leader of the working masses in this country. Under the new conditions, it is continuing to develop and gradually change into a Party of the entire people. This is a reflection of the real changes taking place in the working class, the class of cooperative farms and the people's intelligentsia, of growing socialist consciousness and the strengthening of the socio-political and ideological unity of our society.

The fact that we take into consideration these changes does not mean that we are belittling the leading role of the working class nor that we are substituting petty bourgeois ideas for Marxist-Leninist science and confusing the ideology of populism or abstract humanism with the communist idea. We firmly denounce the thesis of the dogmatists and the extremists who believe that the role of the working class can be carried out by the intelligentsia or the peasants or the youth. We also reject the thesis of right-wing opportunists as to the merging or dissolution of the working class into the other social strata. *In the period of building a mature socialist society the Communist Party continues to be the Party of the working class and at the same time it gradually turns into the Party of the entire people.*

Obviously, one of the main features of this process will be the changes taking place in the social composition of the Party, and in the relationship between working class, cooperative farmers and intelligentsia. The main tendency in these sectors will be to reflect the changes within the social structure of our society more fully.

In the future as well, the Party will continue to regulate its social composition, but this tendency to bring the classes closer together and strengthen the social and political unity leads *to placing in the foreground more than ever the personal qualities of the candidate, when applying for membership,* without minimizing social background. The shaping of the new type of socialist worker, the conscientious bearer of the Marxist outlook, the fighter for the communist idea, will create conditions for a continuous extension of the social basis of the Party. All strata of the people will ever more actively and conscientiously support the Party policy and render it effective assistance. The Party policy, in turn, will ever more fully express the interests of the entire nation.

We are fully aware of the fact that the process through which the Party will gradually change into a Party of the entire people is continuous and complex. It depends on the objective processes of the development of the socialist society as well as on the purposeful organizing, ideological and educational work of the Party among its members and all the working people.

The Bulgarian Communist Party is the blood and flesh of the people. In its long history it has never had any other interests but those of the **working class, the working people, socialism and** communism. It will continue to hold aloft the red banner of the revolution, high and pure, guiding the struggle of the people for happiness, for the still greater advance of our country, and for the complete victory of the communist idea.

On the Significance of the Program

Comrades, *the new Program will play an extremely important role in enhancing and improving Party leadership in its entirety. It synthesizes and formulates the general Party line,* which will be the guiding principle of all the future congresses and plenums of the Central Committee and in the work of the whole Party and the state.

We are making great efforts to raise *the scientific level of Party and State leadership.* The existence of a scientific program, of a scientifically elaborated general Party line, and of scientifically determined basic trends, ways and means of attaining the goals we have set for ourselves, creates conditions for raising the scientific level of social management in our society. *The Program will help us in our efforts to meet the requirements of the objective laws of social development.* This is the *first* aspect of the historical significance of the Program of the Bulgarian Communist Party.

The second important aspect of the Program lies in the fact that it will serve as the basis of a further elaboration of the theoretical problems of our social development.

The Program does not claim to be absolute truth in the highest degree. In giving theoretical answers to a number of problems, it predetermines the future development of theory but it does not set limits to further creative quests. We might say, paraphrasing Engels' words, that the Program of the Bulgarian Communist Party is not a dogma but a guide to action.

The third aspect of the significance of our Program is that it is addressed not only to the Party but to the entire people as well. And this is quite natural, when one takes into account the fact that the cause of socialism in this country has been the cause of all the working people, led by the Communist Party, for a long time now. The Program is, *literally,* not only that of the Party but of the entire people.

As a basic theoretical and political document, the Program is of great improtance to the entire ideological work of the Party, the Komsomol, the trade unions, the Fatherland Front and the other mass organizations. It is of great importance to the correct education of the working people and of the youth, in particular, in a spirit of communism. The Program makes the ideas of Marxism-Leninism much easier to understand, brings those ideas closer to the masses and mobilizes them. Linking the past, the present and the future of the country together, linking the immediate task with the final goal, the Program exerts strong ideological and political influence on the masses, bringing meaning and light into their practical activities.

Along with this, the Program provides the ideological workers and our entire ideological front with new weapons for a more active and effective struggle against present-day bourgeois ideoloogy and anti-communism, against revisionism and dogmatism. this is *the fourth* aspect of the significance of the Program.

And, lastly, we should mention its international significance. The Program we are now going to adopt is our own—the Program of the Bulgarian Communist Party for the construction of the advanced socialist society in Bulgaria. Summing up the historical experience, revealing the achievements of the people and the Party and the wide vistas opening up before them, the Program demonstrates the basic advantages of the socialist social system over capitalism. By building up the advanced socialist society, we fulfill our international duty to world socialism and the world revolutionary movement.

Now, when we are asked about the achievements of the people and the goals of our Party, we can answer with pride: *Read the Program of the Bulgarian Communist Party!*

After discussing the draft submitted here in all its aspects and with all due consideration, the Tenth Congress will, undoubtedly, adopt the Program of the Bulgarian Communist Party. Inspired by its objectives, by its Marxist-Leninist ideas, the Party will lead our people to new victories.

Comrade Delegates, the Central Committee has reported to you on the main results achieved in our work during the period under review and on the tasks of the Party and the country in the next few years. You have been acquainted with the Draft Directives for the Sixth Five-Year Plan and with the Draft Program of our Party concerning the construction of the advanced socialist society in Bulgaria.

Now, the Congress, the supreme body of the Party, will proceed to a discussion of the report and the draft documents. There can be no doubt that, just as during the preliminary nation-wide discussions, the deliberations at this Congress will be business-like and will display the vital concern and high Party principles typical of Bulgarian communists. There can be no doubt that the Tenth Congress of our glorious Bulgarian Communist Party will be on the same level as the documents under consideration, because these are the fruit of the collective thought of our Party and are based on the magnificent achievements that our country has won under the Party's guidance.

We are all deeply convinced that the decisions to be made by the Tenth Congress will be transformed into reality by the working class, the cooperative farmers and the people's intelligentsia. The guarantee for this is our Party, its unity and its unshakeable loyalty to the great revolutionary science of Marxism-Leninism! The guarantee for this is the fact that we have the solidarity and support of the international communist movement and all the progressive forces in the world! The guarantee for this is the fact that we are a part of the world socialist community, that we have unbreakable friendship and cooperation with the fraternal socialist countries and with the great and invincible Union of the Soviet Socialist Republics, which is confidently marching towards communism!

Long live the Bulgarian Communist Party!

Long live the world communist and workers' movement!

Long live communism!

9

The New Constitution of the People's Republic of Bulgaria

Report to the 16th Session of the Fifth National Assembly, May 7, 1971

Comrade Members of Parliament, 1971 will go down in the history of the Bulgarian nation and of the Bulgarian Communist Party as a memorable year. It will be remembered, above all, by the Tenth Congress of the Party and its decisions, and by the adoption of the Program of the Bulgarian Communist Party—a program for the building of an advanced socialist society. It will also remain memorable because of another important event: the adoption of a new Constitution of the People's Republic of Bulgaria.

The Fifth National Assembly has been entrusted with the historcal responsibilty of working out the new Constitution and of proposing to our people for adoption in a nation-wide referendum.

As Chairman of the Commission on the drafting of the new Constitution and upon its instructions, I take particular pleasure in informing you that the task with which the National Assembly entrusted us March 15, 1968, has been fulfilled. The Draft of the new Constitution is ready.

The work of the Draft was a difficult and responsible job. The Draft was prepared with the active participation of scores of Bulgarian politicians and statesmen, MPs, scholars and experts. Its fundamental principles were disclosed at a plenum of the Central Committee of the Bulgarian Communist Party as well as at the Tenth Party Congress. In our work we were invariably guided by the Marxist-Leninist teaching on the socialist state, and on the role and significance of the Constitution in the administration and development of socialist society. We relied on the achievements of the social sciences, on our own experience in state building and on the rich epochal experience of the Soviet Union, as well as on the experience of the other socialist countries.

The nation-wide discussion of the Draft of the new Constitution was a brilliant expression of the democracy of the socialist system. The active participation of the working people in the discussion clearly showed that *our working class, the peasants and the intelligentsia are vitally interested in ensuring that the fundamental law of our state correspond fully and in every possible respect to their will as citizens and builders of socialist Bulgaria.* The Draft was discussed at more than 30,000 meetings, in which over three million people took part. Nearly 14,000 proposals for amendments and additions to the draft were made at these meetings. in this way *the new Constitution really became a product of the efforts of the whole nation, a genuine people's Constitution.*

This is the third Constitution that Bulgaria has adopted since its liberation from the five-centuries-long foreign bondage. The first, the Turnovo Constitution[1], which in certain respects reflected the aspirations of the people and the ideals of the national liberation struggle, was a bourgeois Constitution. It consolidated the power of the bourgeoisie, the exploitation of the working people and the institution of the monarchy, which was hated by the people.

The socialist revolution of September 9, 1944, relying on the assistance of the Soviet liberating army, overthrew the rule of capital. This victory had to be consolidated constitutionally as well, so we could turn once and for all from the monarcho-fascist past and give full scope to the liberated forces of the people.

On December 4, 1947, the Grand National Assembly, under the

[1] *Turnovo Constitution,* a bourgeois democratic constitution adopted on April 16, 1879 in the town of Turnovo.

leadership of Georgi Dimitrov and with his direct participation, adopted the first Bulgarian socialist constitution. Georgi Dimitrov spoke the truth when he said that it had been written with the blood that our heroic and freedom-loving people had shed in the long struggle against the monarcho-fascist and bourgeois tyranny.

The first socialist Constitution of the People's Republic of Bulgaria legally consolidated the achievements of the people, attained under the leadership of the working class. It was on the basis of that Constitution that people's rule asserted itself, private capitalist property was expropriated, agriculture was made cooperative, a socialist state apparatus replaced the destroyed bourgeois state machine and the socialist cultural revolution was carried out.

For more than 20 years this Constitution has well served our people, and now that we are adopting the draft of our new Constitution, we would like to declare onec again: the 1947 Constitution will remain in Bulgaria's history as a document of which our nation is and will always be proud.

Every Constitution, including our new one, reflects the relations existing in society. These can be reduced to the following basic groups:

first—the character and form of the state and of the political structure of society;

second—the forms of ownership and the socio-economic structures;

third—man as a citizen and his rights and obligations to the state and to society;

fourth—the state organs through which state power is exercised and the relationship between them.

The social function of the Constitution consists in the legal consolidation of these basic social relations.

Bourgeois constitutions are demagogical in character. It was no accident that Lenin called them fictitious. Bourgeois constitutions consolidate the rule of the capitalist class and the exploitation of man by man. They grant certain rights to the people but these rights, far from being guaranteed, are also restricted and they are constantly violated by the bourgeoisie in the interest of the ruling class. In our history, too, there are examples to this effect. The Turnovo Constitution granted certain rights to the people, but the bourgeois ruling circles quite unceremoniously violated them by suspending the Constitution, issuing laws at variance with it and systematically pursuing a policy of alienation and suppression of fundamental personal freedoms.

The social function of the constitution manifests itself fully and consistently under socialsim. Socialist constitutions consolidate the political power of the working people that has been established as a result of their long struggle, under the leadership of the working class.

Reflecting the relations existing in society, the constitutions change whenever major changes occur in these relations.

The substantial changes in our country's socio-political and economic situation after 1947, as well as the qualitatively different tasks, conditioned by the new stage in the development of socialist society and of the socialist state, have made it necessary to proceed to the elaboration of a new Constitution of the People's Republic of Bulgaria.

What are these changes and the new tasks?

1) *The social and class structure of our society has undergone radical revolutionary changes.* If, at the time of the adoption of the first socialist Constitution, industrial and office workers accounted for 25 per cent of the country's population, on the eve of the adoption of the new Constitution they account for 69 per cent. Or take the number of peasants: in 1947 they constituted nearly three quarters of the population and at present they account for less than one third. Moreover, while only four per cent of our peasants were cooperative farmers at that time, today the class of cooperative farmers, builders of Socialism, works throughout the entire countryside. The exploiting classes have been done away with; the relations between the working class, the class of cooperative farmers and the intelligentsia now reflect the unity of interests typical of a socialist society, They are relations of cooperation and alliance under the leadership of the working class, relations reflecting the moral and political unity of our people. This alliance has a single common purpose: the building of a classless communist society.

2) *The evolution of our state into an all-embracing political organization of the working people.* The socialist state is the main instrument in the building of an advanced socialist society. The state of the dictatorship of the proletariat gradually grows into a state of all the people. On the basis of the revolutionary changes in society

as a whole and in its individual spheres, as well as on the basis of the political evolution of society, socialist democracy continuously extends and improves. The working people take an ever broader part in the activity of the state organs; the state and social forms of administration become increasingly interrelated.

3) *The necessity of consolidating the socialist relations of production.* While at the time of the adoption of the 1947 Constitution the means of production were almost exclusively private capitalist property, today this type of ownership belongs to the past. Socialist ownership of the means of production prevails completely in our country as our society develops in a planned manner.

4) *The profound changes in the consciousness of the working people* brought about by socialist property and the continuous strengthening of the moral and political unity of society, the vast ideological and educational work done by the Party, the socialist state and the mass organizations. The main features of the consciousness of the working people and of the nation are now characterized by socialism, and they are constantly increasing to the point where they eclipse all vestiges of private ownership.

5) *The objective material and cultural prerequisites created during the process of socialist construction for a further extension of the rights of the citizens,* for their growing involvement in the administration of society and the state and for the all-round development of the individual.

6) *The fact that Bulgaria is now entering upon the stage of the construction of an advanced socialist society.* The abolition of the capitalist social system and the complete triumph of socialist social relations in all spheres of life are decisive changes that have come about as a result of the socialist revolution. The period of transition from capitalism to socialism has been completed; socialism has become a living reality, and society has gradually entered upon a new stage of development—the stage of building a mature socialist society. The specific laws of the capitalist socio-economic system have vanished from the stage of history.

The objective laws of socialism now operate in our society. All this makes it necessary for us to build a better structure of state organs by consistently applying the principles of popular sovereignty, unity of state power and democratic centralism.

Thus the new stage of social development—the stage of the

construction of an advanced socialist society, characterized by radical changes in the foundation and superstructure of society, was bound to lead to corresponding qualitative changes in the state as well, as one of the major components of the superstructure. The elaboration of a new Constitution is simultaneously a prerequisite for the perfecting of the state and a part of the process that leads to this end. *For this reason the new Constitution of the People's Republic of Bulgaria became an objective necessity for our progress.*

What are the characteristic features of the Draft of our new Constitution?

The first feature of the new Constitution is its continuity with the 1947 Constitution. Both are constitutions of a socialist type reflecting the respective stages in the development of socialist society in our country. For this reason the new Constitution also preserves all the characteristic socialist principles that relate to the socio-political and economic structure of our country and the freedoms and rights of its citizens. Parallel with this, it also reflects the further evolution of these relations under the new conditions.

The second feature of the new Constitution is that its theoretical basis is the Program of the Bulgarian Communist Party. For this reason, the Constitution also reflects the results achieved thus far and formulates future trends and directions. In the hands of our people it will be a successful instrument for the implementation of the Party Program—the building of an advanced socialist society in Bulgaria.

The third feature is that the whole content of the new Constitution is imbued with the spirit of the basic goal of the Party Program: "Everything in the name of man, everything for the good of man!" This is a goal that can be attained only on the basis of the all-round progress of society as a whole.

The fourth feature of the new Constitution is that it reflects not only the state structure but also the unified system of social administration. An advanced socialist society can be built only if there is close and organized interaction among all the elements of the system of social administration. The Constitution thereby becomes the basis for a further improvement of social administration.

The fifth feature of the new Constitution is its scientific foundation and its conformity with the requirements and achievements of the Marxist-Leninist science of social administration. It reflects the achievements of socialist socio-scientific thought—political, economic, philosophical, sociological and legal.

The sixth feature of the new Constitution is its clear and consistent political purposefulness. As a socialist Constitution, it reasserts the principle that all power stems from the people, belongs to them and serves them, and that the Bulgarian Communist Party is the guiding force in society and the state.

These characteristic features make *the new Constitution a reliable political and legal basis for the further socialist development of the People's Republic of Bulgaria.*

The Draft of our new Constitution was made public and submitted to a nation-wide discussion nearly two months ago. Its stipulations were explained and documented at meetings held for this purpose, and through the mass media—press, radio, television, etc. Besides, at the plenary sessions of the Central Committee of the Bulgarian Communist Party held in July and November 1968, and subsequently at the Tenth Party Congress, the imperatives of the new constitutional principles were substantiated. *This is why it is not necessary to substantiate again the texts of the Draft in detail.*

I will dwell briefly only on the key elements of the Draft:

The Constitution starts out with the socio-political structure of the People's Republic of Bulgaria and the character of the state, indicating the main lines of our socio-political development—the further broadening of socialist democracy. This is the first time a constitutional text in our country contains the clear and categorical statement that Bulgaria is a socialist state and that its social composition comprises the working people from town and country, headed by the working class.

The principle of the sovereignty of the people is firmly established in Article 2, according to which all power in the Peoples' Republic of Bulgaria stems from and belongs to the people. The people implement this power through freely elected representative bodies or directly.

The definition of *the objectives, main lines and basic principles of the activity of the socialist state* constitutes an important element of the Draft. These principles have been confirmed by the practice of state building and are derived from the character of the socialist state.

On the basis of the principles adopted in the Constitution, the socialist state serves the vital interests of the people. It guides the nation's development and creates conditions for the improvement of the well-being of the people and for the free development of man. The main trend in the activity of the socialist state is to promote the creation of the necessary conditions for the evolution of socialist society into communist society.

An essential feature of the political organization of society in our country—reflected in the draft of the new Constitution—is that *the Constitution proclaims the guiding position of the Bulgarian Communist Party in the state and in society.* Thus a legal expression is given of the historical role and position that *the Party has won* in the process of its long struggle against capitalism and monarcho-fascism and for the building of socialism in our country—a role and a position that have asserted themselves for a long time now in the practice and the consciousness of our people.

In connection with the principle that the socialist state in the performance of its tasks relies increasingly on the *public organizations,* the Draft Constitution defines their place and the role within the system of social administration.

The public organizations as voluntary organizations of the working people express and defend their specific interests and strive to raise their socialist consciousness.

Under socialism the public organizations help the state to perform its functions and the state, on its part, can transfer to them, *with their consent,* the performance of specific state functions.

A separate text deals with the *Fatherland Front* as an embodiment of the alliance of the working class, the toiling peasants and the people's intelligentsia. Its role is stressed as a support of the people's rule, as a mass school for the patriotic and communist education of the population, and for enlisting the working people in the government of the country.

Obviously, it will be wise to make an addition to the Constitution. We have in mind *the Bulgarian Agrarian Union,* the Communist Party's loyal ally and co-worker in struggle and construction. The Party Program speaks of its role. I believe, however, that its status should also be reflected in the Constitution of the People's Republic of Bulgaria.

For this reason we should add a new (third) paragraph to Article 1, worded as follows:

"The Bulgarian Communist Party heads the construction of an advanced socialist society in the People's Republic of Bulgaria in close fraternal cooperation with the Bulgarian Agrarian Union."
The Draft Constitution states that *the People's Republic of Bulgaria forms part of the world scoialist community.* It is quite clear to all of us that this is one of the main conditions for the independence and all-round development of our country. The inclusion of this text in the Constitution once again expresses our loyalty to the principle of socialist internationalism and our profound conviction as to the indivisibility of Bulgaria's national and international interests. The trend of the further participation of our country in socialist integration is thus underlined.

The socio-economic structure of the People's Republic of Bulgaria is defined in the new Constitution in conformity with the vast changes in the development of the socio-economic relations in our country during the period of the building of a socialist society, with the complete victory of socialist relations of production in town and countryside! We are now fully justified in sanctioning the socialist character of our country's economic system in the Constitution. Our socialist economy is characterized by three features:

a) the complete domination of the socialist ownership of the means of production;

b) the complete elimination of the exploitation of man by man;

c) its planned and gradual evolution into a communist economy.

In the People's Republic of Bulgaria private ownership no longer has any place and never again will have. The means of production can only be socialist property. *State ownership*—the supreme form of socialist ownership—defines the socialist character of the other forms of public ownership: *cooperative ownership and ownership of the public organizations* which are sanctioned in the Constitution.

The forms of public ownership will develop and gradually draw closer in its evolution into a *single ownership by all the people.* In practice this evolution means the building of an advanced socialist society and the creation of the basic prerequisites for the transition to a communist economy. But this evolution can be achieved only through the development, improvement and interpenetration of the forms of socialist ownership through the extension of the public character of socialist ownership as a whole, and not by the underrating of cooperative ownership. This question was thoroughly discussed at the Tenth Party Congress, where it found a clear and correct solution.

I take pride in stressing that the discussion of the problem of ownership showed how far along our industrious people have come, how high their socialist consciousness has been raised. Our citizens unanimously and firmly came out in support of socialist ownership, of its further consolidation, extension and development, because it is precisely here that they see the foundations for the all-round progress of socialist Bulgaria—the basis for a continuous improvement of the people's well-being, personal welfare and happy life.

This high socialist consciousness of the citizens was also manifest in their attitude towards *personal property*—one of the forms of ownership regulated by the Constitution. I shall dwell briefly on this form of ownership since it gave rise to many questions during the discussion of the Draft.

The right of personal property affects primarily real property and the belongings that satisfy the personal needs of the citizens and members of their families. The majority of the citizens who participated in the discussion emphatically spoke in favor of preserving the purely consumer character of personal property, of creating conditions that would preclude its utilization for speculative purposes or for making unlawful profits.

Many citizens are alarmed by the manifestations of private property mentality. They suggest a restriction of the range of objects of this nature and their utilization. This concern is not unjustified; we should review our legislation and eliminate all possibilities of violating socialist principles of distribution based on work and socialist ethics. For this reason, the Constitution states clearly and unequivocally that citizens may not exercise the right to personal property to the detriment of the public interest.

Bearing in mind the decisive role of the socialist relations of production that fully prevail in our country, the Draft consolidates *the principle "from each according to his abilities, to each according to his work" as the basis for the distribution of material goods.* In addition to this, social welfare funds are acquiring an ever growing significance and help promote education, culture, and social security. The allocation of social pensions, scholarships, the extension of student hostels, the increase of children's allowances, are also to be helped by social welfare funds. In fact, these are the sprouts and seedlings of communism that will continuously develop in our land. The extension of public consumption also finds an effective expression in the Directives of the Tenth Party Congress on Bulgaria's socio-economic development under the Sixth Five-Year Plan, in which a considerable increase of the social welfare funds is envisaged.

The forms of ownership, the sum-total of social relations and the socialist character of our economy determine the nature and functions of the political superstructure. The economic, organizational and other functions of our state are fully reflected in the Draft Constitution. The state directly guides the development of the economy, culture, science and the whole social life of our country. For this reason, the Constitution regulates *the basic organizational forms and methods of economic management* and the activity of the socialist economic organizations, while reasserting the tested methods and means—the unified plans for the nation's socio-economic development, cost accounting, material incentives and moral stimuli, etc.

The concern for the promotion of science and technology is an important element of the Draft Constitution. The building of a socialist society is inconceivable without science and technology. For this reason, the Draft makes it incumbent on the state to create all the conditions necessary for their proper development. The introduction of the achievements of science and technology in production becomes an obligation under the Constitution, because we need science for practice, science to be applied to life—not science for the sake of science itself.

We can state with confidence that the socio-economic structure of the People's Republic of Bulgaria, sanctioned by the new Constitution, will contribute to the further development of the productive forces and of the socialist relations of production.

As a result of the victory of socialism in the socio-political, economic and spiritual life of society, as a result of the increased socialist consciousness of the working people, it has become possible in the Draft of our new Constitution to considerably extend the rights and freedoms of the citizens, to create new guarantees for their enjoyment, as well as to pave the way for their further extension and consolidation. The fact that over a quarter of the clauses of the Constitution precisely define these problems testifies eloquently to the endeavor to fully regulate the question of the citizens' rights and freedoms. Moreover, the section dealing with these problems comes immediately after the section dealing with the country's socio-political and socio-economic structure.

In this respect the Draft preserves and further develops the basic principles adopted in our first socialist Constitution.

Marxism-Leninism formulates quite clearly the range of man's rights and freedoms after his liberation from the exploiters' yoke and his advance into socialist society, in which his freedom, as Engels put it, turns into a conscious necessity.

The application of this principle in life also depends on the working people themselves, on the growth of their consciousness, on their active participation in socio-political life and on their contribution to the rapid increase of the economic potential of the country.

The salient feature of the citizens' legal status under socialism is their equal relation to the means of production, which are socialist property. On this basis the complete equality of all citizens before the law is proclaimed and guaranteed; and all privileges and restrictions on the basis of nationality, extraction, creed, sex, race, education and social and material status are illegal.

The socialist state secures the equality of the citizens by creating guarantees and opportunities for the exercise of their rights.

Our first socialist Constitution had the task of securing to women equal rights with men. We are now going a step further by proclaiming equal rights for women and men. In order to secure real equality, the Constitution confers certain specific and broader rights to mothers and guarantees these rights. The principle of equality in the Constitution also pervades the sections regulating the relations between husbands and wives, parents and children. The spouses have equal rights and obligations in marriage and in the family.

Young people are the future of every nation. Socialist society needs young people who are educated in a communist spirit, with high intellectual and moral endowments, physically strong and with sound work habits. For this reason the new Constitution gives special protection to youth and guarantees all the rights conducive to their harmonious development.

In what direction do we envisage an extension of the rights and freedoms of the citizens and guarantees for their exercise?

First, the citizens' right to work is recognized. Every citizen has the right freely to choose his own profession. The development of the socialist socio-ecomonic system is the most secure means for guaranteeing the exercise of this right. The Draft also confirms the socialist principle of remunerating work in accordance with its quantity and quality.

Second, the right to recreation is secured for citizens by reducing working hours without diminishing their pay, by an annual paid leave and through the establishment by the state and public organizations of a wide network of holiday houses, cultural clubs and other places for rest and recreation.

Third, the social rights of the citizens are considerably extended. The Constitution recognizes the right of all citizens to social security and assistance in case of temporary or permanent disablement, as well as in other cases established by law. Children, incapacitated citizens and old people, who have no relatives or have been deprived of the care of their families, enjoy the special protection of the state and society.

Fourth, constitutional conditions are created for promoting the nation's culture. The citizens are guaranteed the right to free education in all types and grades of schools and universities. All educational establishments belong to the state. The state creates the conditions for the introduction of secondary education for all——education based on the achievements of modern science and Marxist-Leninist ideology.

The Draft secures special protection for the rights of authors, inventors and rationalizers by making it incumbent on the state, economic and public organizations to create conditions for the promotion of creative activities.

The Draft also sanctions a number of other rights of the citizens, which have already been regulated.

It goes without saying that in our society the degree of satisfaction of the citizens' rights also depends upon us, the citizens of the People's Republic of Bulgaria. During the discussion of the Party Program, the Directives and the Draft Constitution, some people got the impression that a consumer era was about to begin. Of course, this is not so, and it could never be so. The further satisfaction of the consumer needs of the population is possible, but it will take place only on the basis of a growth of production and an increase in it efficiency.

For this reason, the rights of the citizens cannot be divorced from their obligations.

The first and sacred duty of every member of socialist society is to do socially useful work in accordance with their abilities and qualifications. The fulfillment of this duty is a matter of honor for the socialist worker.

The second and sacred duty of the citizens is to guard and increase socialist property as an inviolable foundation of our socialist system

The third and sacred duty of the citizens is to observe and abide by the Constitution and the laws of the country strictly and in good faith.

The new Constitution more fully and precisely defines the character and the structure of the state organs, of the whole state apparatus, in accordance with the Marxist-Leninist principle on the unity of state power and on the basis of the principle of democratic centralism. During the elaboration of the Draft and during its discussion particular attention was paid to the structure of the state apparatus. The efficiency of state administration as a whole depends largely upon a correct definition of these functions, the recognition of the degrees of competence and the interrelations among state organs. The normal functioning of the whole social mechanism depends upon the activity of the state organs.

The Program adopted by the Tenth Party Congress provides a clear line for the extension of socialist democracy. This means, above all, to enhance the role of the representative bodies of the state, directly elected by the people, the National Assembly and the People's Councils.

For this reason, the clauses of the Constitution define *the National Assembly* as the supreme representative body, expressing the will of the people and their sovereignty. The Constitution puts the National Assembly at the top of the pyramid of state bodies and paves the way for the elimination of all the vestiges of formalism in its work.

The principal elements that guarantee the enhanced role of the National Assembly are:

a) The National Assembly combines the legislature and executive functions of the state and exercises supreme control. Its ample and broad competence is the best proof of the supreme status of the National Assembly.

b) The status of the National Assembly as the sole legislative body of the People's Republic of Bulgaria is preserved. At the same time, the order of the drafting and adoption of laws is considerably improved and rendered more democratic. Under the new Constitution, the right of legislative initiative is vested not only in the Council of Ministers and in the Members of Parliament, as hitherto, but also in the State Council, the standing committees of the National Assembly, the Supreme Court and the Chief Public Prosecutor. The National Council of the Fatherland Front, the Central Council of Trade Unions, the Central Committee of the Dimitrov Young Communist League and the Managing Board of the Central Cooperative Union also enjoy the responsible right of legislative initiative on matters pertaining to their own activities. The broader range of those who have the right of legislative initiative will make it possible for the laws to express more fully and precisely the will and the interests of the working people. The improvement of legislative activity is also achieved through the adoption of bills by two series of votes at different sittings.

c) The National Assembly is recognized by the Constitution as the supreme organizer of the planned direction of social development.

The Draft Constitution provides for the establishment of a new organ of our state apparatus: *the State Council.* The establishment of this organ corresponds to the objective needs of our development. Until now the Presidium of the National Assembly was the supreme body representing the state in international relations, exercising fairly restricted functions of control.

Under the new Draft, the State Council is a qualitatively new organ that, in the exercise of its rights, combines the making of decisions, with their implementation. This defines both the scope and the character of its competence. The Draft Constitution defines the State Council as a supreme permanent body of state power. As the supreme body of the National Assembly, the State Council secures the combination of the legislative with the executive. It ensures the general guidance of the nation's domestic and foreign policy. The State Council has the right to issue decrees on matters of principle pertaining to the executive and administrative activity of the state. In exceptional cases the State Council has the right to amend or supplement individual stipulations of the laws by decrees.

It hears reports on the work of the Council of Ministers or of its members and takes appropriate decisions. The State Council is responsible to and reports to the National Assembly on its entire activity.

Modern government reveals the great importance of the *Council of Ministers* in pursuing state policy and in the normal functioning of the whole state apparatus. The new Constitution defines the Council of Ministers as the supreme executive and administrative body of state power. The Council of Ministers organizes the implementation of the home and foreign policy of the state; it directs, coordinates and controls the activity of the ministries and the departments; it draws up the drafts of the national socio-economic plans and the draft of the annual state budget and submits them to the National Assembly; it organizes the implementation of the laws, decrees and acts issued by it, etc. The Constitution secures the necessary conditions for turning the Council of Ministers into an operative body for the overall guidance of dynamic executive and administrative activity. The structure of its bodies and their functions have to be defined in accordance with these requirements; therefore it was not considered expedient to specify the ministries and departments in the Constitution. They will be constituted by decision of the National Assembly in accordance with the changing concrete conditions and tasks.

In the Draft of the new Constitution the question of the *place and role of the People's Councils* is regulated in accordance with the documents of the plenary sessions of the Central Committee of the Bulgarian Communist Party held in July and in November 1968.

What are the main features of the People's Councils at present? On the one hand, they are organs of unified state power and thus implement the policy of the state on their territory, engaging in activities aimed at the implementation of state tasks and deciding upon questions of local significance. On the other hand, they are organs of people's self-government through which the enlistment of the working people in government is organized.

The Draft preserves and further develops *the basic principles of the organization and activity of the courts and the public prosecutors' bodies.*

The courts in the People's Republic of Bulgaria are called upon to protect the state and social system established by the Constitution, as well as socialist property, the life, freedom, honor, rights, and legal interests of the citizens and the rights and legal interests of the socialist organizations. They should educate the citizens in a spirit of devotion to the country and the social cause, to labor discipline, to a conscious implementation of the laws and of respect for the rules of the socialist community.

The Draft determines the system of courts and sets down the major principles of their organization and activity. All judges and assessors are elective, have equal rights in hearing the cases and may be recalled before the expiration of their terms.

The supervision over the strict and equal application of the laws by all the state organs, the economic and public organizations and the citizens is implemented by the Chief Public Prosecutor. In the performance of their official duties the public prosecutors are independent and act only on the basis of the law.

Comrade MPs, during the discussion of the Draft of our new Constitution, the commission received a number of proposals for amendments and additions. Some of them refer to the content of the Constitution; some refer to the systematic arrangement of the texts; a third and very considerable portion is of editorial character. The expedient proposals have been reflected in the Draft, but a number of proposals were made that do not refer to constitutional matters or pertain to ordinary legislation, and these ought to be transmitted to the appropriate bodies for consideration.

Many of the proposals suggest that *our legislation should be brought into conformity with the new Constitution.* This makes it necessary, on the one hand, to review the present legislation in order to bring it into harmony with our new fundamental law. On the other hand, it is necessary to complete, within a short time, the process of renovation and refinement of the legislation that started after the July 1968 Plenum. Thus, for example, conditions have already matured for the National Assembly to pass a new Law on the People's Councils, a new Labor Code, a new Law on the socialist economic organizations, etc.

The Draft of our new Constitution has found a broad response abroad. It was received with great interest by Bulgaria's friends, by all progressive people. They see in it a new and brilliant demonstration of the socialist gains of the Bulgarian people, a broad new step in the development of socialist democracy. The Draft was particularly welcomed in the fraternal socialist countries, since it reflects the rich experience of our Party, of the People's Republic of Bulgaria in state building; while its creative approach to the solution of the complex and urgent problems of our times has found new ecpression.

Taking into consideration the proposals and recommendations of the working people and the theses of the Tenth Congress of the Bulgarian Communist Party on the broad extension of socialist democracy, on the development of the socialist state and of the whole system of social administration, the Draft Constitution Committee proposes to the National Assembly that it discuss and adopt the text of the Draft and decide to submit it for adoption by a nation-wide referendum.

The Constitution is the fundamental law of the People's Republic of Bulgaria. All our legislation is based on it; it determines the entire lift of our society; it directly affects all classes and social groups, every team of workers, every family, every citizen. For this reason the Draft was submitted to nation-wide discussion. And it is for this reason that it will be proper and necessary that the Commission, after the adoption of the Draft by the National Assembly, be adopted by the Bulgarian people—the only full-fledged masters of their destinies and the destinies of Bulgaria.

We are deeply confident that our people, who are heirs to great revolutionary traditions, who carried out the socialist revolution in Bulgaria and who are successfully building a socialist society in close and indestructible fraternal alliance with the Soviet Union and the other socialist states; our people, who adopted the Party Program for the building of an advanced socialist society as their own program, will vote unanimously for the new Constitution and in so doing vote for their own happy present and even happier future.

Thank you for your attention.

10

The Fatherland Front in the Building of an Advanced Socialist Society

Excerpts from a speech to the 7th Congress of
the Fatherland Front, April 22, 1972

I wish to dwell briefly on the problems that were discussed here: the character of the Fatherland Front, the forms, style and methods of its work at the present stage.

To begin with, I would like to express our profound satisfaction—my own and that of the comrades of the Politburo whom I have consulted—over the work of the present Congress, which we assess highly. The Congress is being held at a high political and business-like level and that does not surprise us since we know well what ardent and selfless patriots are now in the ranks of the Fatherland Front—patriots who are worthy representatives to this Congress.

This year we shall celebrate the 30th anniversary of the founding of the Fatherland Front. These three decades in our nation's most recent history are—and this should be stressed—closely and indissolubly linked with the existence and activity of the Fatherland

Front. Its significance and the part it has played during this period need hardly be emphasized to you. Let me just reiterate that the Fatherland Front was born under the most trying conditions of a life-and-death struggle during World War II and that it was set up on the initiative of our immortal leader and teacher Georgi Dimitrov in order to rally and unite all the patriotic forces in Bulgaria and to lead them in the struggle against the monarcho-fascist dictatorship and nazi occupation—for the political, economic and social liberation of our country. *Under Bulgarian conditions its establishment marked the culmination and triumph of Lenin's ideas on the alliance between the working class and all the working and progressive forces of the nation, the culmination and triumph of Georgi Dimitrov's ideas and struggles for a united and popular front.*

After the victory of September 9, 1944, in Georgi Dimitrov's time and under his guidance, the Fatherland Front began to reorganize itself into a mass and all-embracing organization rallying the efforts of the people in the building of a new social system, socialist Bulgaria. The road it has traveled since its creation to the present day most eloquently shows that it was, and still is, a vital necessity for our country. Only thus—as a historic necessity of the times—was it able within three decades to grow from small under ground committees into a mass nation-wide organization, embracing practically the whole conscious population of our country. Nearly four million individual members, such collective members as the Bulgarian Communist Party and the Bulgarian Agrarian Party, the Bulgarian Trade Unions and the Dimitrov Young Communist League, and other public, mass and cultural organizations and unions—today this is Bulgaria's Fatherland Front, an embodiment of the alliance and friendship, of the unity of purpose and aspirations, of the brotherhood and joint work of communists, agrarians and non-party people. It is a brilliant embodiment of the ideological, moral and political unity of the Bulgarian nation building a socialist society!

During these three decades our country made big strides in its political, economic and social development, so much so that there is no longer any basis for comparison between Bulgarian in 1942 and Bulgaria in 1972. Bearing in mind the new tasks facing our country at the new stage of development, the Ninth Congress of the Bulgarian Communist Party included in the agenda some basic problems of public administration. As we know, after the Ninth Congress the Central Committee worked out a number of problems pertaining to the further development of socialist democracy and elucidated the long-range functions and tasks of the public organizations.

Our Party also paid great attention to the problems relation to the development, functions and tasks of the Fatherland Front. After the July 1968 Plenum of its Central Committee, the work of the Fatherland Front began to be reorganized in conformity with the new stage in our country's development. At its Tenth Congress last year our Party again discussed the place and role of the Fatherland Front within the system of public administration. Both the Report of the CC of the Congress and the new Party Program formulated the basic principles defining the trends of development of this largest organization in our country; its place and role, the style and methods of its work. The decisions of the Tenth Congress are well known; they have been discussed here in detail and with a knowledge of its problems and tasks.

There is no doubt that after this Congress the Fatherland Front will have to complete its reorganization so as to keep abreast of the needs and requirements of our times.

Such is the imperative of our progress, comrades. As an ancient philosopher said some 2,500 years ago, "Everything flows."[1] Everything flows; everything changes. Conditions in Bulgaria 30 years ago or even 20 years ago were quite different from what they are now, when all our working people energetically, selflessly and very successfully are tackling the problems connected with the building of a developed socialist society in Bulgaria. It is obvious that the Fatherland Front as a socio-political organization of the Bulgarian people is also subordinate to the laws of dialectics, the laws of social evolution.

Just recall those distant days immediately after September 9, 1944. Remember how all-important was the so-called FF

---

[1] the Greek philosopher *Heraclitus* (c. 540-480 B.C.).

certificate[2] at that time, how many things it was needed and used for? Without an FF certificate one sometimes could not even buy a pair of rubber sneakers. The issuance of the certificates at the time was part of the activity of the local Fatherland Front committees; times were such that even minor things had a major political significance. Or let us take yet another Fatherland Front activity: the readers' groups. They were meant to play, and they did play, a major role at that time, bringing scores and hundreds of thusands of working people into contact with the world of literature.

What is the situation now? *At present there are no illiterates in Bulgaria;* the overwhelming majority of young people have graduated from secondary schools; books are published in thousands of copies and are found in growing numbers not only in state and public libraries but in private homes as well. Formerly, wireless sets were few in number and TV sets were nonexistent. Today radio broadcasts are received in every home and millions of spectators gather in front of the TV sets. And over the radio one can listen to poems which are much better read than ever before, to short stories and even to entire novels. The readers' group activity of the Fatherland Front has diminished and will soon end, since no one would want to eliminate from our life such strong competitors as education, TV and radio broadcasts.

Naturally, comrades, the examples of FF certificates and readers, groups are just curious examples that affect subsidiary aspects of the vast and multiform activity of the Fatherland Front. The big, major problems related to its character and its activities stem from the fundamental changes that have taken place in our country.

What do I have in mind?

I have, above all, in mind the changes in the sphere of our public and political life. During the years of the resistance movement, the Fatherland Front rallied primarily public and political figures. After the victory of the revolution it gradually became a mass organization built on clearly defined political lines in the struggle against domestic and foreign reaction and against the disruptive activity of the

[2] *FF Certificates,* documents issued by the Fatherland Front Committees on various levels after the victory of the September 9, 1944 socialist revolution in Bulgaria. These certificates were tools of class struggle to deny the old ruling class access to certain sources for counter-revolutionary activities, as well as assist the new state structure to regulate the distribution of goods and services among the people.

anti-popular opposition. At that time the question of "who will prevail" was being decided in Bulgaria's political life. Substantial political forces were combating Fatherland Front rule and quite a few people were under the influence of the enemy's demagogic propaganda.

What is the situation today? It is superfluous to talk at length about it. The bulk of our people stand on clear-cut Fatherland Front and socialist positions. If once there was a considerable difference between Fatherland Front members and non-members, a difference that ranged from political indifference through wavering to outright hostility to socialist ideas and plotting against them, no such difference exists today. I am speaking of the nation as a whole. Those who do not accept socialism and will die with their hatred of the working people are so few that they play no role whatever in the political balance of forces in our country.

Impressive changes have also taken place in the economic sphere and in the structure of our society. We have established cooperation among our farmers and have built a highly developed, modern socialist agriculture. We have created a sound socialist industry. The bourgeoisie no longer exists as a class. There exist only friendly classes of the workers and cooperative farmers, as well as a large detachment of people's intelligentsia devoted to the cause of socialism. Today the working class, the mainstay of the socialist system, is the most numerous section of the working people. As a result of the further reform of agriculture, the working class in agriculture—I have in mind the machine-operators—is steadily growing. At present the Bulgarian trade unions are the most powerful organizations of the working people. Here again our experience under the traditions prevailing in the People's Republic of Bulgaria eloquently confirms Lenin's forecast about the transformation of the trade unions into an all-embracing organization of the working people. This is of great historical significance to our socio-economic development, and our Party highly values the role which the Bulgarian trade unions are playing and will increasingly play in the economic sphere and in all other walks of life.

The victorious advance of socialist construction paves the way for an extension of socialist democracy; at the same time, it necessitates an ever broader involvement of the population in the administration. It is precisely for this reason that in the past few years our Party has been paying particular attention to the problems of public administration. Further promotion of the role of the public organizations in public administration, and the extension of democracy in the work of the state bodies—this is the basic trend in the development of socialist democracy in our country.

In our efforts to improve public administration, we must find a proper place for each of the organizations, define their character, functions and tasks, achieve coordination and purposefulness in their work. Apart from the Bulgarian Communist Party, the Bulgarian Agrarian Party and the Fatherland Front, quite a few other mass organizations and movements exist—the Trade Unions, the Komsomol, the Women's Committee, the National Committee of Bulgaro-Soviet Friendship, the Bulgarian Union of Physical Education and Sports, the Bulgarian Red Cross, the Hikers' Union, the scientific and technical unions, the cultural unions, and so on. If our whole system of public administration is to function properly, each of these organizations must find its proper place, and their activities must be duly coordinated. Precisely for this reason our Party paid attention to these problems at the July 1968 Plenum of its Central Committee, at the Tenth Congress, and in the Program for the building of a developed socialist society in our country.

What is the place of the Fatherland Front within the system of public administration at the present stage—that of the building of a developed socialist society?

Briefly, as the Party Program puts it, the Fatherland Front will develop as the largest all-embracing socio-political organization and nation-wide movement; as the embodiment of national unity; as the largest social mainstay of the Party and the people's government; as a school for the communist, patriotic and internationalist education of the working people and for the involvement of the working people in public administration.

Obviously, the Fatherland Front will not be able to accomplish its important tasks successfully if it attempts to preserve old organizational features and fails to apply the forms of work proper to a nation-wide movement. The more it opens its doors to the public expression of all the strata of the population, of all our citizens, the greater will be its role in the extension and practical implementation of socialist democracy. For this reason, the July 1968 Plenum provided a new orientation to Fatherland Front work, i.e., to apply the methods and means proper to a nation-wide movement. Or, as someone has said, the Fatherland Front should gradually evolve from an organization into a movement and from a movement into an organization. Of course, this does not mean tilting at windmills; it means that we have to work in a flexible and comprehensive manner, overcoming the rigidity of organizational features and self-containment and doing away, in practical activity, with the distinction between the members of the organization and the remaining portion of the population. In the final analysis, this means that we have to promote the role of the Fatherland Front in our nation's multiform life.

In the future the Fatherland Front will continue to be the organization in which the Bulgarian Communist Party, the Bulgarian Agrarian Party, the Bulgarian Trade Unions, the Dimitrov Young Communist League, the mass organizations and movements, the unions of scholars and men of arts, will participate as collective members. It will therefore unite them and "sum up" their efforts, if I may put it that way. As you see, the Fatherland Front will continue to be a very important forum of the socio-political forces in our country.

As the broadest mainstay of people's rule, the Fatherland Front will even more closely link its activities with that of the state bodies. We have corrected the old concept that existed prior to the April 1956 Plenum of the Central Committee, according to which the Fatherland Front was to become some sort of a subdivision of the People's Councils. Obviously, this was incorrect. Still, the Fatherland Front must be closely connected with the work of the central and local state organs. Otherwise we shall not be able to create conditions under which all its members and the whole active population will fully participate in the administration of the country, in economic activity, in the different undertakings and activities of the authorities.

Whenever problems of vital importance for the whole country, or for a given region or settlement, are being discussed and solved, the Fatherland Front must be in the lead. No undertaking, provided it is of general interest, reasonable and expedient, will fail to gain broad support among the people. In such cases, it is the Fatherland Front's task to take the lead in the movement, to convince people, to mobilize them and help them move. Last year, when organizing the Referendum on the new Constitution and the elections to our National Assembly, we were all able to realize the importance of the Fatherland Front and to see what it can do in such cases. At this Congress a number of comrades spoke of local campaigns in which the Fatherland Front had mobilized not only its members but the entire population as well.

In other words, there is no reason to fear that the elimination of the internal organizational self-containment will reduce the role of the Fatherland Front. On the contrary, the holding back of this imperative process, which consists in eliminating old organizational features and self-containment, can only restrict the role of the Fatherland Front.

Such is the stage of development at which our country finds itself at present. We are building a mature socialist society. The prerequisites for gradually overcoming class differences and forging a homogeneous society are increasing. The changes in the character of our society also raise the question of the changes in the character of its largest socio-political organization: the Fatherland Front.

Nobody can doubt our devotion and love for the Bulgarian Communist Party. Bulgarian communists have paid for this love with their lives. Nevertheless, we know that the working class and its Communist Party are not eternal. The historic mission of the working class is to put an end to bourgeois rule and to build a classless communist society. The historic mission of the Party is to be the leading detachment, the militant staff, the leader of the class in the fulfillment of its mission. The time will come when both the working class and the Communist Party will have accomplished their tasks and cease to exist. Naturally, this will be a long historical process, but it is inevitable. And we communists are doing all that is necessary for the advent of that moment and are proud that we are a party of a class that is the only class in the history of mankind which does not fight for the perpetuation of its class rule but for the abolition of the class division of society!

There was a time when the question of whether one stood for or against the Fatherland Front was equivalent to the question of whether one stood for or against Bulgaria's development along a socialist path. This question was settled long ago. Once the term "Fatherland Front Bulgaria" was a mere wish, a dream of the working people, a political slogan. At present Bulgaria is a Fatherland Front Bulgaria in the full sense of the term. Today there is no Bulgarian citizen, statesman, political or public figure; there is no politically literate man on earth, who does not know that socialism has completely and irretrievably triumphed in Bulgaria; that Bulgaria is a prospering socialist country firmly linked with the Soviet Union and confidently and rapidly striding towards its communist future.

Such is present-day Bulgaria, Fatherland Front Bulgaria, Socialist Bulgaria. And no power on earth can drive us back and divert us from our path, the path of fraternal friendship with the Soviet Union, the path of construction and of struggle for the complete triumph of communism in our country and in the world!

11

For a Radical Improvement
in the People's Living Standards

Excerpts from a report to the Plenum of the Central
Committee of the Communist Party of Bulgaria,
December 11, 1972

The present Plenum of the Party's Central Committee is to discuss a very important question of Party policy: the implementation of the decisions of the Tenth Congress of the Bulgarian Communist Party on the improvement of the living standards of the
people.

*Concern for man always has been, is now and will be the basic
content of our Party's policy.* It is the meaning and the supreme goal
of its varied activity. It was its chief guiding principle when it fought
against fascism and capitalism, when it prepared and carried out the
September 9, 1944 uprising, when it effected profound quantitative
and qualitative changes during the transition period and when it
ensured the victory of socialism in our country.

*Concern for man is also the chief guiding principle of our Party
now that we are building a developed socialist society.* This is con-

149

ditioned by the very nature of socialism. *The fuller satisfaction of the growing material and cultural needs of our people is a fundamental law and the supreme goal of socialist production, of the development of the new social system.*

The April 1956 Plenum of the Central Committee played a major role in the Party's policy of raising the general living standards. Restoring the Leninist principles of leadership and releasing the creative forces of the working people, the April Plenum paved the way for the accelerated development of Bulgaria's productive forces and for our socialist cultural revolution. This made it possible to improve the material and cultural standards of the people steadily and rapidly.

The July 1968 Plenum of the Central Committee and the Tenth Congress of our Party mark the beginning of a new stage in the implementation of this policy. The Program of the Bulgarian Communist Party adopted by the Congress not only elucidated the nature of the developed socialist society but it also outlined the chief trends of this development in our country. At the same time, it elaborated the main problems related to the life of the people, with the further improvement of their welfare, revealing and substantiating the necessity for a new approach to their solution.

However, in order to be able to apply this approach consistently our Party must possess a concrete and comprehensive program for the improvement of the living and cultural standards of our people not only under the Sixth Five-Year Plan but also during the coming years.

The need for such a program stems both from the decisions of the Congress and from a number of important political, economic, social, ideological and international considerations.

—*politically,* the elaboration of such a program is related to the general stragegy of the development of our country at the present period. It will contribute to the development and extension of socialist democracy; help enhance the political activity of the people and further promote their political consciousness; and it will further strengthen their moral and political unity. It will even more clearly reveal the advantages of the socialist system.

—*economically,* it will contribute to the establishment of a structure and of production proportions under which it will be possible to bring production and consumption into greater harmony, to speed up the development of the productive forces considerably, and to reveal the action of the fundamental economic law of socialism more fully;

—*socially*, it will make it possible to adopt a comprehensive approach to the satisfaction of the material and cultural needs of our people, to solve, correctly and promptly, the problems that are of the utmost importance for the life of the millions of working people in town and village—bearing in mind both the changes that have taken place in consumer demand and the real possibilities of our society to meet the demand;

—*ideologically*, it will create more favorable conditions for the communist education of the people and for the promotion of their socialist conscience; for a more creative atmosphere in all spheres of public life; for man's many-sided development; for a greater self-confidence of the working people as dedicated fighters for the triumph of socialism and communism;

—*internationally*, it will further raise Bulgaria's prestige on the international scene and will augment the contribution to the power of attraction of socialism and of its influence upon the development of the world revolutionary process.

What should such a program for the improvement of the living standards of the people represent?

This question calls for a certain specification. On the one hand, it should be borne in mind that the programmatic principles in the sphere of material and cultural standards have already been worked out in the Party Program. On the other, the comprehensive program for the improvement of the people's well-being should not and must not be reduced to concrete operative measures in this field. The mapping out and implementation of such measures is a task of the Council of Ministers, the individual ministries, government offices, economic organizations and enterprises.

Obviously, the task of the present Plenum is to work out and approve a comprehensive program that will clarify the approach, the pace, the ways and means, and the chief forms *for the implementation* of the fundamental principles in the sphere of the improvement of the general living standards, as formulated in the new Party Program.

This program must provide an answer to the following question: *how and under what conditions* shall we be able to solve the pressing problems of the material and cultural welfare of our people radically, bearing in mind both the present needs and possibilities and their future development? Because of its character, this program cannot and should not be confined to the Sixth and Seventh Five-Year Plans. On a number of problems it will have to embrace a longer period.

We fully realize that the elaboration of such a program is a complex, difficult and responsible task that does not depend solely upon good will. It requires the presence of certain objective conditions which have not so far been fully available. But these conditions are already at hand or will soon be created.

In the first place, we have a clear strategy about the building of a mature socialist society and about the main trends of Bulgaria's economic and cultural development over a longer period.

Second, Bulgaria possesses an economic, scientific and technological potential that allows us to solve the pressing social problems on a much larger scale.

Third, Bulgaria's fraternal economic, political, cultural and all-round cooperation with the USSR and the indestructible friendship between our people and the great Soviet people are increasingly developing, strengthening and deepening as a powerful motive force of our development. Bulgaria's participation in the international socialist division of labor is extending and strengthening on the basis of the Comprehensive Program for the promotion of socialist economic integration among the Council for Mutual Economic Assistance (CMEA) member-states.

Fourth, our Party has now acquired more theoretical and practical experience in directing all the processes of socialist construction and in implementing its policy of meeting the material and cultural needs of the people ever more fully.

At the same time our Party relies on the immediate and growing support of the working people, on their greater socialist consciousness, on their skill and selfless labor, on their readiness to make this comprehensive program their own concern.

In this sphere, too, we make use of the experience of the fraternal parties in the socialist states and, above all, of the rich experience of the Communist Party of the Soviet Union, of the USSR, where the general laws of the already established mature socialist society are most clearly manifested.

All this enables us to elaborate a program that best conforms to the requirements of the objective laws of socialism, to the heightened role of the subjective factor and to the international conditions under which our country is developing.

I. A NEW APPROACH IN THE IMPLEMENTATION OF THE PARTY'S POLICY OF IMPROVING THE GENERAL MATERIAL AND CULTURAL STANDARDS

Comrades, before proceeding to the elaboration of the different problems connected with the implementation of the decisions of the Tenth Party Congress on improving the general living standards, we must clarify two questions of principle.

The first question refers to the degree, the level of the people's welfare. What living standards are we to attain in the coming years?

Until now we assessed our successes in raising living and cultural standards by comparisons with the past, when our people had poor living standards, in the true sense of the word, or with neighboring backward countries. Now, proceeding from the available objective conditions and from the requirements of mature socialism, we need another yardstick, another criterion. *The science-based nutrition norms, the rational norms for meeting the needs of the working people in housing, clothing and footwear, their cultural and other intellectual needs must become the criteria of their living standards.*

The second question refers to the approach to the problems related to the people's welfare. What has it been and what should it be?

During all the stages of the socialist construction of our country we have been guided by the imperative: Everything for man, everything in the name of man. In the past five years, however, we also realized that if we want to respond to this imperative more fully, we must develop Bulgaria's productive forces, as well as create and consolidate a corresponding material and technical foundation to ensure the necessary resources. We therefore consciously stressed that the main and immediate task was to build the material and technical foundations of socialism. This concept was reflected in the distribution of our national income, in the proportional rates of our economic and social development.

Thanks to the accelerated development of the productive forces, we succeeded within a short period of history in establishing a relatively strong production base as a prerequisite for rising living standards.

Under present conditions we not only can but must adopt as the main and immediate task of the development of social production and of the general development of our country the attainment of a *specific degree of satisfaction of the material and cultural needs of our people.*

What does this call for?

1) to set the problem of meeting the material and cultural needs of the people as a starting point when elaborating forecasts and plans for our socio-economic development. It is particularly important to determine these needs according to science-based norms of consumption;

2) to consciously and purposefully change the structure of consumption, organically combining the material and cultural principles of the life of people;

3) to direct our efforts not only at increasing material wealth but also at creating better conditions for the enjoyment of this wealth by the population;

4) to adopt a comprehensive approach to the problems of living standards and solve them in such a way that every individual step forms part of our general conception of our over-all program for the improvement of the life of our people.

In this approach, the tasks of the present and of the future are closely intertwined. It requires that we strictly bear in mind the whole complexity of conditions that, in their totality, determine living standards, their level and quality. It goes without saying that the new approach should be based on accurate socio-economic analyses at every stage of our development and on the conditions, interests, sentiments, aspirations and daring of the different categories of working people in our society. The drive to attain a specific degree of satisfaction of people's needs calls for an accurate assessment of them as developing individuals, of their present and their future.

Need we demonstrate the great importance of this approach? It is conditioned by our achievements and by objective necessity. Moreover, if we continue to stick to the old approach and fail to consider the problem of the needs of our people as a starting point in elaborating the forecasts and plans for our country's socio-economic development, the development of the productive forces and the construction of the material and technical foundations of socialism will be slowed down.

Naturally, this approach has nothing to do with theories about so-called "consumer socialism," because it does not imply a slighting attitude towards production nor does it mean to educate man in a parasitic and philistine spirit. The Party and the people are well aware that one can distribute and consume only what has already been produced. This is an elementary truth. The fact that production relies on us, on our own skill and efforts, on our knowledge and discipline, is likewise an elementary truth. The more commodities of higher quality and lower cost we produce, the more goods we will have and the better we will live.

We also strive to organize our whole further economic activity *so as to produce not just anything*, no matter how and when, but to produce in order to ensure the ever fuller satisfaction of the needs of our people.

Therefore, the present approach, far *from repealing the determining role of production, re-asserts it* by making the improvement of living standards the main and immediate task of its further development.

This approach has nothing to do with various views now current in the bourgeois world about the so-called "mass consumption society," the "affluent society," the "streamlined consumer society" and the like. The bourgeois ideologists are out to "prove" that capitalism is undergoing a process of transformation; they attempt to conceal the fact that the social and class clashes are getting more acute, and that unemployment and poverty are rampant behind the facade of "welfare" in the capitalist world.

We must point out that the efforts of our Party to improve the living and cultural standards of our people have nothing to do with the philistine views about a material well-being devoid of ideals. We have always regarded man as an intricate entity of material and spiritual needs. Naturally, we assess the role of the worker's material interest in the results of his labor according to its merits. Our Party has invariably pursued a Leninist policy of most closely linking the personal and public interests in the drive for socialism. Yet we realize that material welfare as such is not the sole criterion of human happiness. As communists we have always attributed great importance to man's intellectual life, to his cultural interests, his daring and ideals. Our heroic history abounds in examples of selfless service to the people and the country, regardless of privations and adversities.

For this reason, when we set ourselves as our immediate task the ever fuller and more complex satisfaction of the needs of the people, we have in mind the harmony of the material and spiritual needs of all the members of our society, which will contribute to the all-round and harmonious development of the individual, to everything that is positive and valuable and inherent in man. Along with the satisfaction of material needs with regard to food, clothing, housing, etc., we shall, therefore, attribute a growing importance to the efforts to create a social ambiance, a milieu for man's existence and development in which he will be able to satisfy his multiform spiritual interests fully — his needs with regard to education, cultural recreation, etc. Ethical human relations and the respect of human dignity in all spheres of our socio-political, economic and cultural life should dominate in our society. The role of the moral and other intellectual incentives will increasingly grow in the production and all-round activities of the working people. The sense of one's well-performed public duty, of one's personal contribution to the progress of socialism and the prosperity of our nation will become an ever more important factor in their activity.

All this means that the problems connected with the improvement of living standards and with the satisfaction of the needs of the people at the present stage will have to be solved in a new way and not only on the basis of the dynamics of our development, not according to subjective assessments, not piecemeal or in part. We need a comprehensive approach to the pressing social problems, to the study, planning, programing and solution of the problems upon which the increase of the degree of satisfaction of popular needs depends.

When speaking of a comprehensive approach in carrying out our Party's policy of living standards, we have in mind not only the sphere of services or the production of consumer goods. This would be a one-sided and erroneous placing of the problem. Once we accept that the satisfaction of the needs of our people is the immediate goal of social production, we must also subordinate to it all our efforts aimed at developing metallurgy, power production, the chemical industry, construction work, transport, etc., i.e., our efforts in all spheres and phases of the process of reproduction.

This approach will have to be the guiding principle in our work not only under the Sixth Five-Year Plan, but also throughout the building of a developed socialist society. It requires that we continue to pay attention to the further development and modernization of the material and technical foundations of socialism and, more particularly, to the following questions:

a) all-round intensification,

b) acceleration of scientific and technological progress,

c) rapid increase of the social productivity of labor,

d) attainment of the world indicators in quality and the technical level of production.

It is obvious that unless we solve these key problems of our economic policy, the decisions to raise the living standards of the people and to have more goods of high quality on the market will remain pious wishes, will turn into subjectivism, daydreaming and empty demagogy. For this reason, the Party's Central Committee warmly greets and backs the initiative of the working people in our country in working out their own local "greater achievement" plans, aimed at securing not only the fulfillment but also the overfulfillment of the Sixth Five-Year Plan. Actively involving the working people in the efforts to tap and use the reserves of our socialist economy fully, as well as those of the socialist form of management and administration and, generally speaking, of the socialist mode of production—this policy should become a firm, stable and irrevocable law in our work, because it corresponds to the vital interests of the working people and to the general interests of the socialist system.

The consistent application of the new approach affects the many-sided activity of our Party in all spheres of our domestic and foreign policy, as well in the problems of international socialist integration. Obviously, it is beyond the powers of a single plenum to embrace all of these problems at once in their multiformity. A large part of them will have to be borne in mind in the elaboration of the long-range plan up to 1990.

We therefore propose that the present Plenum of the Central Committee focus the attention primarily on the pressing problems that can and should be solved under the Sixth and Seventh Five-Year Plans.

What are these problems?

1) Specification of our policy in the sphere of raising the incomes of the working people;

2) determination of ways and means of overcoming the shortage of various commodities on the market and of improving the structure and the quality of commodity stocks;

3) problems connected with the development of housing;

4) problems related to the social condition of the working people, the length of working hours and leisure time, and the improvement of the sphere of social service;

5) problems connected with the necessity of ensuring unity of social, collective and personal interests, on the basis of a consistent application of the economic mechanism and the improvement of planning and planned economic management;

6) problems of social democracy, the defense of the interests of the working people and the further promotion of the creative efforts of the masses, so that the people may fully reveal themselves as masters of production and public affairs, as masters of their country.

The Politburo considers that these are the most burning and pressing problems and that we must not only adopt conceptions for their over-all solution but also outline practical ways and means of turning these conceptions into living reality. In this respect, our decisions will become a practical program for the realization of the comprehensive approach to the solution of the pressing problems related to the welfare and the life of the working people of our country.

The elaboration of these problems and the decisions that the

Plenum of the Central Committee will adopt will have the immediate task not only of ensuring a better life to our people but also of contributing to a still more rapid increase of labor productivity and to raising our national production, as regards quality and technology, to a world level; and to speeding up the over-all socio-economic development of our country. In the final analysis, this will also be the most secure guarantee of a steadfast implementation of the Party policy of continuously and ever more fully satisfying the growing material and cultural needs of the working people.

II. THE PARTY POLICY IN RAISING THE REAL INCOME OF THE WORKING PEOPLE

Comrades, the question of *the dynamics, size, structure and mode of formation of the nominal and real income of the working people* ranks first within the sum-total of measures aimed at raising the living standards of our people. We must, therefore, pay special attention to it and promptly solve some important problems in this sphere.

Formation and Regulation of the Income of the Working People

The policy of steadily raising the population's income has been established in our country during the years of the people's rule. Income has been showing a particularly upward trend during the period after the April 1956 Plenum of the Central Committee.

On the basis of the growth of our national income, the per capita nominal income rose from 370 leva in 1952 to 1,117 leva in 1971.

The changes in the structure of industrial and office workers according to the size of their nominal wages or salaries are particularly indicative. Whereas, in 1957, 45.6 per cent of industrial and office workers received salaries of up to 30 leva and only 1.8 per cent salaries above 150 leva, in 1971, there were no industrial and office workers getting salaries below 60 leva, only 12.5 per cent of the total getting salaries between 60 and 80 leva and 24.7 per cent above 150 leva.

The task now is not only to consolidate our achievements but also to open up new possibilities for further quantitative and structural changes in the pattern of incomes of the working people and to adjust them to the new conditions and requirements as regards size, structure and mode of formation.

In this connection, under the Sixth and the next Five-Year Plans we must increase the growth rate of the population's income and solve in good time a number of pressing problems in the sphere of the policy of the formation and regulation of income, problems that now acquire particular importance.

What are these problems?

First. *The problems of working out a new conception on the minimum size of the income of the working people.* We have in mind the correct fixing both of the minimum wage, corresponding to the lowest qualified labor, and the size of the minimum income from the social welfare funds through which the low-paid working people and their families are guaranteed minimum means of subsistence.

The profoundly humane character of our society makes it necessary, in the further over-all increase of the income of the population, *to lay emphasis on an increase of the income of precisely these categories of working people.* Other pressing problems in this field will also have to be solved at a later date.

In this connection, by 1973 the minimum wage should already be raised to 80 leva.

The salaries of teachers, doctors and other medical categories, as well as of the lecturers at the higher educational establishments, etc. will have to be increased at the beginning of 1973.

We must increase the salaries of the miners working underground and of the workers and experts who practice their professions under extremely difficult conditions. It is also necessary to increase the remunerations of those who work on night shifts.

The second question refers to the need to make greater use of the growing possibilities *in order to increase the pace of raising the real income of working people* as one of the most general and important indicators, characteristic of our policy of improving the living standards of our people.

In this connection, the trusts and the agro-industrial complexes, the enterprises and cooperative farms should be granted the right to carry out a number of social undertakings: to assist large families and school children with clothing and food; to set up boarding schools and other children's establishments; to aid old-age pensioners who have worked all their lives in a given enterprise, etc.

Bridging the Gap Between the Income of Workers and Cooperative Farmers and Remuneration Based on Work

When speaking of the Party policy of raising the living standards of the people, we have in mind the care taken of *all* the members of our socialist society. In this connection, we must extend the scope of our policy of bridging the gap between the living standards of cooperative farmers and those of industrial and office workers. This is a major problem of the Party's policy in the sphere of incomes.

As we know, after adoption of the April 1956 line, a policy of sharply raising the income of the cooperative farmers was pursued. As a result, the absolute size and the ratio between the nominal incomes of these two social groups have changed as follows:

	1956	1957
	(in leva)	
Industrial and office workers	462	1174
Cooperative farmers	275	995

During that period, the real income of workers has grown by an annual average of 5 per cent and that of the cooperative farmers by an annual average of 7.2 per cent.

The further bridging of the gap between the living standards of workers and farmers is connected with the solution of a whole range of economic, social, cultural and other problems. The material base of this process is *the development of the productive forces and the introduction of factory farming.* The main trends in developing agriculture by means of industrial methods were worked out by the April 1970 Plenum of the Central Committee of the Bulgarian Communist Party. The task now is to adopt practical measures for their application.

I shall dwell only on a few social aspects of the problem.

First, the main trend in reducing the difference in the income of industrial and office workers, on the one hand, and of the cooperative farmers, on the other, should be a still more rapid increase of the income of cooperative farmers from the public farms than that of the income of industrial and office workers.

Second, the measures envisaged in the Decree of the Central Committee and the Council of Ministers on the consistent application of the economic mechanisms in agriculture are of great importance in this area. We must secure the necessary conditions for the introduction, as early as 1973, of an non-taxable minimum labor remuneration for cooperative farmers, increasing incomes for most of them.

The correct regulation of the level and growth of incomes of individual agro-industrial complexes and cooperative farms, from the point of view of the differential rent, is also important. In this connection, it is necessary to level the remuneration of labor in the cooperative and state farms gradually by introducing labor quotas differentiated according to the conditions of production, etc.

Third, the introduction of industrial methods and the changes in the internal class structure of the cooperative farmers will be of particular importance for the growth of income. The number of people engaged in manual and unskilled work in agriculture will diminish further and the number of machine operators, experts and skilled workers will grow. This will lead not only to further social and class changes but also contribute considerably to an increase in the nominal income of farm workers.

Fourth, the bridging of the gap between the real income of cooperative farmers and that of industrial and office workers also calls for a new approach to the utilization of public funds. In this respect, even now, under the Sixth Five-Year Plan, it is necessary to solve certain problems connected with granting the same rights to cooperative farmers that industrial workers already enjoy with respect to old-age pensions, social security, children's allowances, etc.

Fifth, the process of the migration of manpower from agriculture to industry should be put on a new basis. Special attention should be paid to the establishment of systems of settlements in which the utilization of the bountiful housing fund should be combined with the favorable conditions of village life and the proximity of the town. Many of our villages are able to retain a substantial population in permanent residence, with some of the members of the peasant families having employment in industry in the towns. Such a solution of the problem will speed up the bridging of the gap between town and countryside and will pave the way for a more rapid increase of income for the peasant population.

We must also speed up the establishment of nurseries and kindergartens, the building of the road networks and the availability of health services in the rural areas, so that the cultural, communal and living conditions in the villages rapidly catch up with those in the towns.

Real Income and Retail Prices

The fluctuation of retail prices is yet another key problem in the policy of the Party which determines the real income of the population. Under the Sixth Five-Year Plan, prices are to be kept stable. The prices of some commodities will even be reduced, depending upon the lowering of production costs, the availability of commodity stocks, consumer demand and the specific place of individual commodities in meeting demand.

The Central Committee considers that under the Sixth Five-Year Plan it might be possible *to reduce the retail prices of a number of goods.*

The policy of price reductions does not mean that there will be no luxury goods at higher prices on the market. Such goods are needed because they meet specific needs of those working people who are ready to pay a higher price for goods and services of higher quality. We should, therefore, develop more extensively the production of such goods and services.

In the sphere of our price policy, we should take a closer look at the problem of *raising average prices as a result of the change in the range of commodities.*

Bearing in mind the fact that we are developing as a land of international tourism, we must not allow too substantial a reduction of the retail prices of consumer goods. In the future, the improvement of the living standards of our working people should be chiefly the result of higher wages. In this way the promotion of tourist trade will not entail losses for the Bulgarian nation.

Taxation

The material welfare of the population also depends upon the taxes that it pays. At present we have an income tax, a tax on real estate and personal property and a bachelor tax.

What should the Party's policy in the sphere of taxes be?

The problems connected with income tax deserve our utmost attention. At present there is a substantial difference between the taxes paid by industrial and office workers and those paid by cooperative farmers. The Central Committee and the Government have decided to bring unity into this area as well. In the future, cooperative farmers will pay a tax on their income from the work they have invested in public property in the same way as do industrial and office workers. This will increase the income of cooperative farmers whose income is equal to the minimum monthly wage. Like the industrial and office workers who get such a wage, they will not pay an income tax.

Moreover, it should be noted that the present income tax scale is obsolete. A great number of industrial and office workers fall within the higher brackets. This makes it necessary to improve taxation by increasing the untaxed wage to the planned minimum and by properly spacing the difference between the rates. At the same time, we should proceed to the gradual abolition of income tax upon the wages of working people engaged in social production. This will contribute to a consistent remuneration according to the quantity and quality of work.

In this connection, it is necessary to work out, right now, a special program and a mechanism for the practical solution of the problem of gradually abolishing the tax on wages, starting with the beginning of the Seventh Five-Year Plan period.

Development and Utilization of Social Welfare Funds

After the victory on September 8, 1944, the aim of our Party's social policy has been to secure free medicare, free education, social security for all working people's system of social assistance, access of the broad masses to culture, artistic values, sports, etc. Thanks to the efforts of the whole Bulgarian nation, these ambitious tasks were successfully implemented by the people's government in an incredibly short time.

The growth of the real income of the population will more and more depend upon the social welfare funds. Its cultural and social needs will be met from these funds more and more fully.

Parallel with this, we must put an end to leveling in the utilization of the social welfare funds, seeking possibilities of combining the social and economic criteria. This can be done, for example, by giving a certain preference to the best industrial and office workers and cooperative farmers in the utilization of the social welfare funds, by making the various types of social security directly dependent upon the individual results of work, by offering certain material goods on economically substantiated terms, etc.

The problem of the support of the growing generation holds a central place in our social policy and in the utilization of the social welfare funds. Part of the support of children has already been assumed by society under different forms.

We must adopt a policy of having society gradually assume the entire support of the growing generation.

In the next few years we must take more effective steps to increase the birthrate and to improve the conditions for the upbringing of children. What should these steps be?

We believe that henceforth the birthrate should be promoted not by raising children's allowances but by rapidly extending the network of children's establishments so as to include more children; by extending housing, giving priority to young and large families, and by increasing the production of baby foods and of goods connected with children's upbringing. The paid leave for the upbringing of small children should be extended.

We must also extend the non-paid leave for the rearing of young children, say, until the age of three, with the mothers keeping their jobs during that period of leave.

Life within the work force today depends to a large degree on the requirements of scientific and technical progress. Accordingly, the further development and improvement of the work forces should follow the line of securing *conformity between the level of scientific and technical progress and the organization and activity of the work force.*

The rising technical standards and the emergence of new skills and professions place the workers in a better creative atmosphere, requiring them to possess universal habits and polytechnical training. As Karl Marx had foreseen, the worker, these days, increasingly keeps abreast of the process of production. This means that the main line in further improving the work force should *be to expand the sphere of action of collective labor.* The collective forms of labor organization help to broaden the workers' horizons, enhance the mutual responsibility and the significance of collective opinion in solving the general problems and improving the over-all result of the work done by the economic organization.

The construction of a developed socialist society calls for a drastic *improvement in the qualification standards of the work force and for a rise in the workers' educational level.* Formerly, the character of the production required between 35 and 57 per cent of the workers to be nonskilled, and between 4 and 8 per cent to have secondary education. Mechanized production has changed the picture radically. It requires approximately 20 per cent skilled workers, and 40-60 per cent of people with secondary and secondary vocational education. This trend is already apparent in individual plants and factory shops. Under the next five-year plan, and especially in the period up to 1990, it will become manifest everywhere. This calls for the elaboration of a broad program to bring the qualification and education standards of the working people speedily in line with the requirements of the scientific and technical revolution. No rapid advance is possible without it.

Social planning is of key importance for the development and improvement of the work force. The present plans for the social development of work forces are too primitive. They do not secure a *comprehensive approach,* nor do they properly regulate the processes and factors on which the maturity of the work force and the full expression of its potentialities depend.

When speaking of social planning, we have in mind not only the social plans of state trusts, agro-industrial complexes, plants and factories, cooperative farms, etc. What we also need is a *uniform system of society planning from top to bottom.* This means that the task of developing and improving the work force should be not only the concern of grassroots planning but also the object of the *comprehensive state plan.*

The plan should have a special chapter and a system of indicators and norms which secure the planned regulation, development and improvement both of production relations in their unity and the basic cell of these relations—the work force.

No complete expression of the work forces or further development of the creativeness of the masses in the implementation of the Sixth Five-Year Plan is possible without an *ever broader deployment of the nation-wide socialist emulation drive.* On this point we have made new detailed surveys. The task now is to wind up the job of introducing a new approach in the organization and management of the emulation drive. In this connection we should look at the following points of principle:

1) *The nation-wide emulation drive should develop from top to bottom as a component of the over-all system of planning and planned management.* All our plans should be prepared in such a way as to take into consideration the revolutionizing role of the emulation drive, and to secure the conditions for its development through every section of the plan and through the entire system of norms and indicators. What is more, we should finalize the concept of the emulation drive as a *basic factor in the fulfillment of plans through the working out of local "greater achievement" plans by the millions of working people.*

This requires the planning organ, the ministries and the state trusts to provide, right now, in specifying the 1973 plan, the conditions for a new upsurge of the nationwide emulation drive.

2) The emulation drive should be further developed as part of a *broad integration of the advantages of a socialist system* with the contemporary scientific and technical revolution, and the extensive use of the modern methods and means of management and ad-

ministration. *The main criterion* in the development of the emulation drive should be: the work forces' contribution in raising *the people's living standards by means of a rapid increase in labor productivity and bringing the technical aspect of production up to the world level.* In this respect. every work force should have a concrete program of action as of January 1, 1973 and up to the end of the Sixth Five-Year Plan.

3) The further development of the emulation drive and the active participation of the working people in socialist construction *call for the system of moral incentives adopted by the Politburo to become effective as a matter of urgency.* The use of moral stimuli should be organized on a broad scale, and a statute should be worked out for their full utilization.

4) The steps we have planned — to increase incomes, to reform the wage scale, to make a transition to a five-day working work, etc. — require us to encourage, popularize and broadly unfold some *nationwide initiatives.*

The drive to fulfill and overfulfill the local "greater achievement" plans by every state trust, agro-industrial complex, factory, state farm, cooperative farm, and others, based on the spread of patriotic initiatives, is a national imperative and the major factor for the contribution of every work force to the fulfillment and overfulfillment of the Party's social program.

As you see, implementing a new approach to raise the general living standards is a complex political, economic, social and ideological problem. It calls for the efforts of the whole Party, of the entire people.

The program worked out on how to implement the decisions of the Tenth Party Congress on raising the living standards should become a powerful means of mobilizing the people of town and village for a more effective management of the economy, for a fuller use of socialism's advantages in developing the productive forces and in steadily raising the people's prosperity.

This is their own program; its destiny is in their hands. It can be put into practice only with the joint efforts, skill and creative daring of the working class, the cooperative farmers and the people's intelligentsia, who have always responded with readiness to the appeals of the Bulgarian Communist Party.

It must become the cause of the Fatherland Front, the Komsomol, the trade unions, all public bodies and organizations, the ministries and departments, the state trusts, the agro-industrial complexes, the trade organizations, the scientific institutes, and of all Party, state and economic executives.

We are confident that the Bulgarian Agrarian Party and its members will spare no effort for the implementation of the humane and progressive social tasks that have been mapped out, because we are fighting together for the same goals and the same great ideas—for the building of socialism and for the progress and might of our nation.

The tasks posed by this Plenum could be successfully solved if they are immediately tackled by all Party bodies and organizations, and communists from all sectors of life. There has never been a Party undertaking, no matter how complex or difficult which has not been realized in practice when it has been tackled by the Party bodies and organizations and when Party members have set personal examples. In this case, too, they should be the organizers of the fight for more popularly priced products of better quality, for a higher productivity of labor, for a fuller satisfaction of the material and cultural requirements of the working people. In this case. too, the Party bodies and organizations and the communists are called upon to be *the motive force* of this all-national drive, and to play a decisive role in implementing the Party's social program.

Owing to the complexity and diversity of the problems under discussion, a number of them need additional elaboration and specification by the Party's Central Committee, as well as by the State Council and the Government. To make it possible for the problems posed by this Plenary Session to be tackled on time along state and economic lines, it would probably be expedient to *set up a special government commission at the Council of Ministers on the problems of living standards. This commission, proceeding from the decisions of this Plenary Session of the Central Committee, would make sure that the problems get further treatment and specification, and would direct the over-all process of implementing these decisions.*

Undoubtedly, the complex issue of raising the general living standards should be linked directly with the further development of the productive forces, with the Party policy of quickly raising labor productivity, with the broad development of integration with the other fraternal socialist states, especially with the Soviet Union. The elaboration of a long-term plan up to 1990 and the Seventh Five-Year Plan, too, should be subordinated to this goal.

The chief guiding principle in the further implementation of the Party policy in that domain should be: *care of man through care of the entire society, and care of society through care of the individual man.*

Comrades, a few days from now the Soviet people, together with the Bulgarian people and all of progressive humanity, will mark the 50th anniversary of the foundation of the great Union of the Soviet Socialist Republics.

It is a telling fact that the Central Committee of our Party discusses the problems of raising the material and cultural standards of the people on the eve of this great date. There is something deeply symbolic in this.

Because the USSR, born during the Great October Socialist Revolution, was not only the first state of workers and peasants in the world, but also the first state to point to the genuine path to the people's welfare, happiness and prosperity.

Because the USSR is an example and an inspiration to us, it is our mainstay in the building of the new life.

Because the experience of the USSR in raising the material and cultural level of the people is of world-historic significance, from which we have learned and will continue to learn.

Because our social program, which further elaborates and renders more concrete the decisions of the Tenth Party Congress on raising the people's prosperity, is, in the full sense of the word, an expression of the profoundly humane principles of the Great October Revolution.

We are confident that this Program will be put into practice. Its implementation depends on the work and creative efforts, on the conscientiousness and discipline of the people. It depends on the ever growing cooperation with the Soviet Union and the other socialist countries. This is the reliable guarantee for its successful implementaion in life.

Raising Living Standards is a Nation-wide Cause

Comrades, the problems we are discussing today affect the life, the interests and the fate of millions of builders of socialism, and their implementation should become the personal concern of everyone of them. All the nation's forces should therefore be mobilized in such a way as to induce *every worker, every cooperative farmer, every employee, to become an active and conscious fighter for the implementation of the decisions of this Plenary Session.*

We must complete the process of *enhancing the role of the work force in socialist society*—yet another major question of principle, an issue of our advance to communism—to enable the Party Program for higher living standards to become more directly connected with the daily work and efforts of the working class, the cooperative farmers and the employees.

In this direction, quite a bit has been done this year along Party, trade union, economic and administration lines. But it is still only the beginning of that major reconstruction dictated by life.

What should be given special attention now so as to raise the role of work forces to the level of the tasks that will be posed by this Plenary Session?

1) The main functions of every work force should be developed to the utmost.

The main function of the work force is to implement effectively the production tasks and to improve constantly the organization of work through firm self-discipline. The work force should be guided primarily by the interests of society and should endeavor to make a maximum contribution to socio-economic progress and to the rapid growth of labor productivity.

The other essential functions of a work force are *social and educational.* They should be directed at perfecting relations within the work force proper: its consolidation as a close-knit working family; creating a psychological climate of genuine friendship and comradely relations; educating creative personalities, people with communist ethics and morality. On the other hand, by improving the workers' working and living conditions and raising their professional skill and cultural standards, each man's contribution to the collective is augmented.

2) To further enhance the role of the work forces, we should constantly see to their development and improvement. There are many problems to be solved in this respect. I will dwell on only some of them:

a) The Party, state, trade union and economic organs should properly regulate relations within the work forces. Relations among people in a work force depend on the technology of production, the labor norms and the system of incentives; the plan targets, the results of the work, the administrative directives and the internal regulations; the work done by the Party, trade union and Komsomol organizations. Apart from this, in a work force there also exist relations of an ideological, ethical, social, psychological and other character.

It goes without saying that the state of a work force, the psychological relations within it, will be better where work is organized with precision, without breakdowns, where science-based labor norms exist, and where internal regulations are correctly worked out and applied. When there are flaws in the organization of production and labor, there can be no sound work force but only tension and discontent which have an adverse effect on the psychological relations between people and on the entire work force.

All this goes to show that if we want to develop, strengthen and promote the role of the work force we must constantly see to it that relations within it are strengthened and improved.

3) *The third major problem upon which the code of labor should dwell is setting the rules for relations between managers and operators, between the work force and the individual worker, between the factories and the workers.*

4) *The fourth problem to be dealt with in the code is concerned with the working people's participation in the management of production: in what direction should it be improved?*

The drafting of a new labor code should proceed from the decision of the February Plenary Session of the Central Committee as to *the functions and the role of trade unions during the period of building a mature socialist society.* This calls for the new code to provide legislative endorsement for the rights and obligations of trade unions today. Particular attention should be paid to the precise formulation of all powers granted to trade unions in drafting, applying and exercising control over labor legislation and protecting the rights of working people.

It would be correct to draft, simultaneously with the labor code, a comprehensive social *security and welfare law*. This is also necessitated by the fact that social security is going to develop and become *security for all*.

For an Improved System
of Planning and Planned Management

Comrades, the comprehensive solution to the problem of providing more fully for the working people's material and cultural needs calls for perfecting the system of the planned management of socio-economic development. The current system of planning does not fully correspond to the new tasks connected with the attainment of the main objective of our socio-economic development: the care of man, higher living standards of the people and the versatile development of the individual.

The principal shortcoming in planning consists in applying the branch approach to almost all problems, the method of determining the dynamics of growth rates *of individual branches*. The program objective and the *comprehensive* approach still find no place. This affects all indicators of our economic development adversely.

Our economy is a complex dynamic system with numerous sub-systems. A large portion of these sub-systems are objectively existing *economic complexes*. At the present stage of the scientific and technical revolution, these economic complexes assume a key role in shaping proportions, raising the efficiency of production and achieving the main objective of our economic development. *The narrow branch approach* tends to impede the establishment of new proportions and of a highly effective structure of the national economy, as well as a comprehensive solution of social problems.

Planning should be further improved along the following main lines:

First. The job of modifying the character and content of the plan should be completed. In line with the decisions of the July Central Committee Plenary Session and the Tenth Party Congress, the plan should actually become a comprehensive socio-economic development plan. It should enable us to direct the development of both the economic and the social processes in our society.

The main objective of the plan should henceforth be to secure a rising living standard for the people, based on the continuous development of socialist production and growing labor productivity.

Second. The main approach in planning should be of the program-objective type. This means that the crux of the matter in drafting the plan should be *to base and formulate the chief aims of economic and social development for the forthcoming planned period scientifically.* The effective development of the economy should be subordinated to them. Every complex, every branch should have such objectives. But, in their totality, all specific and concrete objectives should be subordinated to the chief plan target: the care of man.

Third. The entire system of planning should be based on the principle of a comprehensive examination, planning and solution of the problems, without underestimating the branch cross-section of the plan.

Fourth. As the process of drafting the plan and its realization are closely connected, changes ttat occur in the situation after the adoption of the plan should be promptly taken into account.

Scientific, technical and social progress leads to an ever closer interplay of political, economic, social and technical factors of social production.

This, of course, does not imply a departure from stability in plans and state norms. We shall not deviate from this principle. *It is of importancefor us to set up a system of reserves and to apply it effectively to planned management.*

The indicated chief trends of introducing ways of perfecting planning in their totality boil down to the consistent introduction of the program-objective and comprehensive approach.

In working out the Sixth Five-Year Plan, we endeavored to apply these methods. Experience so far has shown them to be correct. The task now is to bring these efforts to conclusion.

Above all, we should introduce clarity into the issue as to what are the comprehensive programs.

A point of departure in drafting a comprehensive program should be to work out a modern conception of how to develop a given complex. This conception should clearly outline the aims that we set ourselves. It should also include an analysis and an assessment of the present state and the trends of development in the most advanced countries. In this undertaking, we should chart the main directions of our development in the long run and the basic means of achieving this advance. On the evidence of all these facts we should work out a comprehensive program *containing all the necessary economic, social, technical, productive, organizational, scientific and technological measures leading to the attainment of the pre-set objectives.*

The objectives of individual complexes stem from the general objectives of social development; they take into consideration the level attained by the productive forces and at the same time chart new directions for their development. These objectives should correspond to the main trends of the present-day scientific and technical revolution.

This means that the comprehensive programs should be made not for individual kinds of production, not for semi-finished or total production, but for the final products with which a certain complex takes part in the over-all process of reproduction.

The separate national program or groups of programs should be elaborated for large complexes, including interrelated branches and lines of production, whose development is comprehensively coordinated by these programs. It should be noted that complexes of this kind *exist objectively* in the national economy.

The task now is for them to become the basis of comprehensive planning and management.

Several interbranch economic complexes (though not organizationally constituted), united by a common objective, by homogeneous production or by close cooperation in their production processes, have already taken shape in our country. The steam-power generating complex, the petrochemical, metallurgical, transport, construction and other complexes of interrelated branches are typical examples.

The need arises for the formulation of criteria enabling us to classify a certain branch under this or that complex. Evidently, the main guide line should be the final result that unites many production lines of various branches into one production cycle and hence into one production complex, as well.

The emergence of distinct large complexes permits us to transcend the narrow framework of branch planning, to chart the most effective ways of solving the important economic problems on which the successful development of the entire economy depends.

The programs for the development of individual complexes should be long-range in character, i.e., covering the entire time limit for achievement of the goal set before a complex.

The inclusion (in toto or in part) of different economic branches, sub-branches and activities into interbranch national complexes *predetermines the key role of the economic methods of guidance in planning and management, and it considerably restricts the administrative methods based on the branch or departmental character of planning and management.* The connecting link in the economic relations of all subdivisions in a complex is cost accounting and the material interests of the work forces employed in the branches, sub-branches and activities of a certain complex. Of course, here again the role of moral incentives should not be under-estimated.

Naturally, the comprehensive activity of all complexes is based on centralized planning. This has always been a settled matter with us. Proceeding from the objectives of social development, the central organs of planning *should establish limits* for the fundamental resources (including centralized capital investments) which are necessary for the development of interbranch complexes, as well as the foremost guiding indicators in kind and in cash for the manufacture of the final product. At the same time, the organs for the management of complexes should be empowered to maneuver with the resources so as to be able to use them reasonably in implementing the adopted programs most effectively.

The importance of the program-objective and comprehensive approach to planned management in our country calls for the formation of a strong team of scientists and experts of the Bulgarian Academy of Sciences, the Academy of Public Administration, the higher educational establishments and the organs of planning. The team should work out the theoretical and methodological problems of the application of this approach. This should be done within reasonable time to ensure that it is fully applied to the elaboration and implementation of the Seventh Five-Year Plan and the long-range plan up to 1990.

The questions of further *improving the structure of the population's income* acquires great importance at the present stage. We must devise a correct policy from the point of view of the ratio between the size of the income received from labor in the sectors and activities of social production and the size of the income received from social welfare funds, on the one hand, and, on the other, between the size of the income from social production and that of the income from the personal farms.

In this connection, we must substantially improve the whole practice of planning and regulating the structure of the working people's income.

The structure of our national economy and the distribution of labor resources by sectors directly influences the size of the population's income. For this reason, already under the Sixth, and especially under the Seventh Five-Year Plan, we must work out a special program for the improvement of the structure of employment and of the influence of this process upon the rise of the real income of the working people.

Rise of Wages and Intensification of the Stimulating Role of Remuneration According to Work Done

Under the Sixth and the Seventh Five-Year Plans wages will continue to be the basic lever in economically stimulating the working people to a more active participation in social production and to raising the social productivity of labor.

In this connection, a series of problems will have to be consecutively solved.

First, a new conception on wage raises will have to be worked out.

If we want to stimulate a rapid rise in labor productivity, the average annual growth rate of the wage must be higher than the present one.

The second major problem connected with the increase of the role of wages and of working people's income is to create *a new and more effective method of regulating the basic wage.*

What are the main goals which this reform should pursue?

1. We must create better unity in the evaluation of types of work according to complexity, strain and the conditions under which they take place.

2. *We must create prerequisites for the elimination of all elements of wage-leveling.*

Our task now is more precisely to reflect, through the wages, the differences in the complexity and the conditions of work, securing higher wages for those who have higher qualifications.

3. *The basic wage should become a sufficiently flexible mechanism for the evaluation of the individual abilities of the working people.*

4. The last but not least important task of the forthcoming budget and rates reform is to link the growth of the basic wage to the results, to the social productivity of labor, most closely.

Under the Sixth and the Seventh Five-Year Plans, the network of hostels and boarding schools should be extended. The problem of school canteens and refreshment counters, to be supplied with the necessary quantity of suitable warm foods and fresh snacks, should be solved. District, urban and village People's Councils and our whole public should pay particular attention to this problem and resolve it.

All children attending the elementary schools should be granted textbooks free of charge as of the 1973-74 school year.

The children of mothers who are university students and who do not have adequate housing facilities should get priority in children's establishments.

The plan for the construction of student hostels should annually comprise a larger number of family dwellings for the accommodation of student families.

The executive committees of the People's Councils should annually set aside 30 per cent of the newly built state housing for the accommodation of needy young families.

The problem of pensions is an important one for our social policy. We should pursue a line of gradually granting cooperative farmers the same pensioning conditions as industrial and office workers, and of adjusting the old pensions to the changing socio-economic conditions.

It may be possible, as early as 1975, to grant cooperative farmers the same pensioning conditions as industrial and office workers. The discrepancies between old and newly allotted pensions is a major social problem. It would be proper under the Sixth Five-Year Plan to update all the pensions allotted under the Pension Law prior to December 31, 1970. After 1975 the leveling of old pensions should be periodically (under every five-year plan) attuned to the new ones, depending on the changes occurring in the labor income of the active population and on our possibilities.

All these measures are objectively necessary but they require quite a lot of money. The question arises: what should be done to cover the expenditure needed to raise pensions? There can be only one answer: *through the legislation on pensions we must increase the national fund of working hours and achieve a higher effectiveness of labor which, in the final analysis, will contribute to an increase of our national income.*

The improvement of pensions should go hand in hand with improvements in the sphere of *temporary disability indemnities.*

More attention should also be paid to the problem of *vocational rehabilitation, qualifications and re-qualification of persons with an impaired capacity for work. This too is a major social problem.*

It is also urgent that we solve a number of problems in the sphere of social welfare. As early as 1973, we should introduce *social pensions* for people over 70 who are without an income and for people who have been invalids from birth or from childhood; we should also increase the monthly allowances to those entitled to social assistance.

Another task in this sphere is the development of the *social welfare establishments* for people unable to get along in society by themselves or with the aid of their relatives. They should be divided into several major groups: institutions for the aged, for invalids and people suffering from chronic diseases, and for physically or mentally handicapped children and adolescents.

In view of the continuous increase of the percentage of persons who are no longer able-bodied, the high employment of the active population and the formation of separate households of workers and their families, the problem of the care of the aged becomes extremely pressing. The network of social institutions of this nature should be considerably extended during the forthcoming five-year periods.

III. FULLER SATISFACTION OF EFFECTIVE DEMAND FOR CONSUMER GOODS

Comrades, the satisfaction of the effective demand of our people for consumer goods and services is yet another major problem in our social and economic policy.

The problem of the ratio between monetary income and the supply of consumer goods is not only an economic one. *It is also a political, ideological and social problem. Many aspects of our general policy touch upon it.*

The task of adjusting the volume and the structure of the supply of consumer goods to the effective demand is obviously a complex and difficult one. It calls for much time and for considerable funds. On the other hand, a comprehensive approach to raising the general standard of life presupposes in essence a new conception in this sphere as well.

The main elements of this conception are to be found in the decisions of the Tenth Congress and in our Party Program. The task now is to specify and approve the ways of its implementation as of 1973. What should be the pith and marrow in the solution of this problem?

1) Greater production of consumer goods should become a nation-wide task. The local "greater achievement" plans should also be subordinated to it. Every state trust, enterprise, agro-industrial complex, cooperative farm, every work force should strive to tap new reserves so as to sharply increase the production of consumer goods and services in 1973.

The development of production is not an end in itself, and we must get rid of this notion. In principle, the content, volume and structure of the production of consumer goods must be determined by the structure, volume and effective demand of the population. The activity of the other sectors of our economy must be subordinated to this.

In this connection, we should work out and adopt a comprehensive system of dynamic consumption norms, *corresponding to the degree of satisfaction of the needs of our people, as specified by the central organs, and corresponding to their purchasing power.* We do have certain norms at present, but they are now inadequate.

The task now is to establish norms of consumption *which will correspond to effective demand and will serve as a starting point in the planning of production and in the orientation of the sale of the output.* Once we have decided to increase the purchasing power of our people, we must first of all, on the basis of these norms, plan the *necessary* resources fully to balance this purchasing power. The distribution of our national income, accumulation and consumption, the distribution of capital investments by branches and sub-branches should also be subordinated to this requirement. This is a key problem!

When speaking of the global criterion in our policy on living standards, we have in mind, above all, *the creation of conditions which will help prolong the life of people to the natural limits, preserving their intellectual and physiological forces to the maximum until old age.* We must, therefore, pay particular attention to the elaboration of consumption norms. It is not sufficient to have more goods on the market; our purpose is to put both nutrition and the life of our people, their living conditions, on a scientific base.

We must clarify our conception of the development of the production of capital goods (group A) and the production of consumer goods (group B) in industry. Both our policy in the sphere of export and import and the satisfaction of the population's needs in consumer goods depend upon the ratio and the growth rate of these two groups.

Our Party stands on Marxist positions as regards the growth rates of these two groups. The priority development of the production of capital goods finds its economic justification in the increase of the technological level of production and labor productivity as the necessary bases for improving the general living standards. This does not imply, however, a widening of the gap between the growth rates of Groups A and B. On the other hand, it would not be wrong for the growth rate of the production of consumer goods to overtake that of the production of capital goods in some years, depending upon the needs but without this necessarily turning into a steady trend.

Bearing in mind this principle about the ratio between the growth rates of groups A and B, we consider that it would be correct, even under the Sixth Five-Year Plan, to seek ways and means of increasing the production of consumer goods by utilizing most effectively the available capacities, by regularly supplying the necessary raw and prime materials and steadily improving the organization of labor and production.

When we want to extend the range of goods, we must not turn production costs into a fetish. In some cases it might be necessary to increase production costs when introducing the production of new goods with new quality indicators and when improving the quality of the existing goods.

Naturally, society does not suffer losses as a result of these higher production costs, because higher consumer values are created, leading to a saving in raw and prime materials and labor.

We should reassess our conception of the quality of goods for export and for the domestic market. Both should be of high quality—and this has not always been the case. *In the future we should have a single standard and the same conditions for the production and acceptance of consumer goods, both for the domestic and for the foreign market.*

When speaking of the quantity, quality and range of goods, our attention should be focused on the conception of the *popular type of commodities.* Our Party worked out this highly important problem in good time. Unfortunately, neither in planning nor in production and trade, have measures been taken to ensure its adequate solution. As a result, the range of popular type commodities on the market is very small indeed. No one can object to the increase of the production of luxury, fashionable and expensive goods. Once we have a differentiation in incomes, these goods, too, should be on the market. The care of man however, means, above all, the care of the needs of the millions of working people. For this reason, both production and trade should give priority to augmenting the quantity and improving the quality and variety of the popular-type goods.

In this connection, we must introduce an obligatory minimum of the types of goods that the enterprises should produce, and an obligatory minimum range in all the warehouses and shops. This calls for a new system of planning and management of the range of the popular-type goods.

I believe that it would be appropriate to entrust the Ministry of Home Trade and Services with the planning and the regulation of the range of popular-type goods.

We must also change our attitude towards the Plovdiv Trade Fair[1] and the model exhibitions at which we display consumer goods. Most of them arouse in all of us pride and satisfaction at our potentialities and skill. It has now become a vicious practice, however, that very little of what is shown at the Fair appears on the market. This should no longer be tolerated. Henceforth, even during Fair time, *the state trusts-producers, together with the trading and supply organizations and the planning organs,* should work out measures for the introduction and mass production of the exhibits shown at the Plovdiv Fair and the specialized exhibitions.

The problem of maintaining a permanent balance between the production of consumer goods and the effective demand for such goods makes it necessary not only to increase production *but also radically to improve the forms and the ways of linking production with trade.*

Comrades, the population's demand for consumer goods cannot be met fully on the basis of domestic production. This is proved not only by our own experience but also by the experience of all advanced countries. Unfortunately, in a number of places there is still theorizing, slackness and hesitation with regard to this problem. Some people would like to solve it only on the basis of our national production. Others consider the extension of the import of consumer goods as a "heresy" and a "consumer approach"; as a result, imported goods in our country account for a mere 6 to 8 per cent of our trade, while in the other socialist countries this percentage is between 13 and 17 per cent.

The current Plenum must resolutely oppose these erroneous views and adopt an extensive program for the development of integration in the sphere of the production of consumer goods. Where

---

[1] *Plovdiv Trade Fair:* traditional trade fair that began in 1892 in the town of Plovidiv, which now has become a large, international annual event.

should we now place the emphasis, what conception should we adopt with regard to the different problems so that integration might contribute to the utmost in an improvement of the general living standards under the Sixth and especially under the Seventh Five-Year Plan?

First. The further development of integration should not be confined to increasing the export of consumer goods and to checking on the expansion of the country's commodity stocks.

The main elements in integration should be the joint or independent building of large capacities on the basis of the specialization per types of production; the joint solution of the problems of the technical level, the raw materials and the purchase of licenses. On this basis we must secure conditions for a rapid growth in volume, an extension of the range and an improvement of the quality of consumer goods. There is and there can be no other criterion.

The further development of integration in other spheres as well should be subordinated to this guideline — in machine building, the chemical industry, metallurgy, etc. Particular attention should be paid to the increase of the resources for export in group A, both for the socialist and non-socialist countries, in order to reduce the export of consumer goods in exchange for capital goods.

Special attention should be paid to cooperation and collaboration with the developing countries. Against the export of complete plant, machines and services, we can get from them much greater quantities of raw materials for light industry and manufactured goods of the light and food industries.

Second. We must introduce a new conception on the import of consumer goods. In the future we must pursue a policy of reducing the export of consumer goods, in which the domestic demand is not fully met, against the import of capital goods. We must increasingly acquire the latter by exporting capital goods. Within the framework of socialist economic integration we must pursue a policy of increasing the export of consumer goods, for the production of which our country possesses sufficient raw materials and for which domestic demand has been met.

In the future, exports above the plan are to be made only with the permission of the Ministry of Home Trade and Services. On the other hand, as of 1973, we must forbid the export, above the plan, of consumer goods that are in shortage.

Third. The system of cooperation, both with the socialist and the non-socialist countries, on *the exchange of the range of goods should be decisively improved and in such a way as to prevent, in the final analysis, a reduction in the volume of the commodity stocks, while simultaneously increasing the range of goods on the domestic market.*

The system of exchange should not have an ad hoc and accidental character, but should become a component of the import-export plan.

Other forms of cooperation should also be used. Thus, for example, the opening of a network of stores on a reciprocal basis in our country and in other countries for the sale of goods typical of each country should help broaden the range of goods.

These conceptions should be applied gradually in specifying the 1973 plan and then the 1974 and the 1975 plans. Undoubtedly we shall encounter difficulties, since contracts have already been signed. By compensating with other goods, however, we must reduce the export of goods that are in great shortage on the domestic market. In order to maintain the currency balance, the Ministry of Machine-Building, the Ministry of Heavy Industry and other ministries and corresponding state trusts should take measures to increase through their local plans the production of goods in short supply in the first place.

On the basis of all these steps, we must ensure that the relative share of imported goods on the domestic market attains 10 per cent in 1973 and 15 per cent in 1975. During the period covered by the Seventh Five-Year Plan this percentage should be between 20 and 25. In the future these indicators should be planned, controlled and accounted for like the other indicators of the plan.

IV. THE POLICY ON THE HOUSING PROBLEM

Comrades, the housing problem is one of the most acute social problems not only in Bulgaria but all over the world. All countries are tackling this social problem that faces contemporary mankind.

Throughout the period of socialist construction, in spite of the poor legacy we received from bourgeois Bulgaria, our Party and the people's government have been paying attention to housing construction and creating conditions for its development. Over the 1945-71 period, some 1,403,000 dwelligs were built in the country, with 62 million square meters (sq.m.) of floor space. Sixty per cent of the nation's housing stock has thus been renovated.

Housing construction is one of the key problems in raising the general living standards. In Bulgarian towns, 1,350,000 families live in 1,101,053 dwellings.

The Party's strategic target in the field of housing is a separate, comfortable and well-appointed dwelling, measuring up to the standards of the developed socialist society, for every family, and a separate room in the house for every family member.

The greatest efforts have to be made in this connection so as to *increase the number of dwellings* under the Sixth and Seventh Five-Year Plans.

As early as 1970, the Politburo of the CC adopted a program for a radical solution of the housing problem in the next ten to fifteen years.

What should be done to solve this problem?

First, the task now is to overcome shortcomings and to make up the time lag. The building of the planned number of dwellings should by all means be ensured under the Sixth Five-Year Plan, on the basis of *the introduction of new technologies in construction,* and ways and means should be sought to overfulfill the plan.

While drafting the Seventh Five-Year Plan now, funds and capacities should be ensured by the introduction of new technologies for the building of 600,000 dwellings.

Second, the question of the size of a single dwelling should be solved. This is quite a complex problem. Account should be taken of both the present and future housing needs. It would be right under the Sixth Five-Year Plan to build dwellings of an average size of 80 sq. m. of floor space, with the funds set aside for the purpose. Under the Seventh Five-Year Plan the size of dwellings should be increased, fixing the average floor space at 85 sq. m.

The furnishing of the dwelling should be in close functional connection with its plan and should contribute to its beauty and comfort. All dwellings should be built and delivered complete with basic interior decoration even during the current five-year period, and especially during the next one.

Third, another essential in the solution of the housing problem is the use of a comprehensive approach in the building of new residential areas. At present we are stepping up the construction of a number of new housing districts, while lagging behind, quite seriously, in the building of sanitation and other facilities.

The new housing construction should meet all needs of public life, now outstanding, and should become a basis for the gradual establishment of a communist way of life. Regardless of its scale, the new housing construction should be adapted to the whole complex of external conditions, to the necessary system of providing services to the population. It is necessary to plan the best location of all public establishments and their optimum combination for servicing the population.

Fourth, the solution of the housing problem should be based also on the new practices in the deployment of productive forces on the country's territory. We have large reserves of housing in the villages. Ways and means should be sought for the fuller use of that dwelling stock. On the other hand, wherever feasible, various activities should continue to be moved out of towns with a housing shortage, or new production capacities should be created where the dwelling stock is not being used well enough.

Fifth, this is the problem of the sources of funds and the ownership of dwellings. Proceeding from the conditions prevailing in Bulgaria, the Politburo of the CC considers that the savings of the population should continue in future to be used for housing construction. On June 30, 1972, the number of those saving for a home was 359,082, with 1,065.9 million leva saved, including 99,107 persons with 287.7 million leva for Sofia.

On the other hand, it is necessary to conduct a strictly defined policy in the building and allocation of state dwellings.

Sixth, greater social justice should be established in the renting out of the existing privately owned dwelling stock. The speculative approach to the setting of rents and the sale of real estate must be stopped. In cases of abuse, confiscation of the dwelling and eviction of the offenders should be carried out.

Parallel with the accelerated construction, serious attention should be paid to *the provision of housing with sanitation and other facilities; the equipment of dwellings with furniture and consumer durables and the system of repairs and maintenance of the dwelling.*

V. WORKING HOURS AND IMPROVEMENT OF CONDITIONS OF WORK

1. *Towards a Shorter Working Week*

Comrades, with the victory of the socialist revolution, our Party has already firmly pursued the policy of establishing an eight-hour work day, and subsequently reducing working hours on night shifts for those working in hazardous conditions and for workers under 18 years old. The working hours on Saturdays and days before holidays were reduced by two. While all this was being accomplished, the wages of industrial and office workers were maintained intact.

The problem of the duration of work time is a large and complex one. It has to do, first of all, with the national fund of working time in the course of the year. In this way it is organically connected with the volume of output and of all types of activities that should be performed within the limits of that fund. It is also closely linked to the problem of labor productivity, and the intensity of labor. The ratio between working time and free time is an important index of people's living standards. It is a well-known Marxist formulation that the wealth of society is measured in terms of the amount of free time of its members.

The Tenth Congress of the Party pointed out that if we create the necessary conditions we can go over completely to shorter working hours, even under the Sixth Five-Year Plan.

What should be done to reduce working hours? How should we accomplish this difficult undertaking without allowing any hitches in the progress of the economy?

First, it is necessary to prepare the proper production and technical conditions; to guarantee a transition to a five-day week while the local "greater achievement" plans will be fulfilled in volume, nomenclature, range of goods, labor productivity and quality of output.

Second, the switch-over to a five-day week should not be allowed to be accompanied by a wage reduction or an increase in the number of industrial and office workers.

Some disregard of this principle may be allowed in certain branches of the service industry only (transport, trade, public catering and others).

Third, the switch-over to a five-day week calls for a thorough preliminary preparation for a transformation of the internal organization of work in the enterprises. In this connection, one of the crucial problems is the abolition of overtime.

Fourth, workers in all branches of material production (excluding agriculture) and in the nonproductive sphere (excluding education and public health) will change over to a five-day working week.

Fifth, the transition to a five-day working week will be done in stages by districts on the basis of a special plan and timetable adopted by the Government.

It is proposed that the five-day week have 42.5 hours, and the duration of the working day will be established according to the corresponding timetable.

The reduction of working time does not always entail an increase in free time. The real free time depends on social and personal organization, on the existing conditions for the proper performance of activities characteristic of the time outside working hours. It is in this direction that we have many and varied problems awaiting solution.

The first one is the large amount of time spent in household work; and too much time is still lost in commuting to one's place of work.

The task now is *to take measures not only to increase the amount of nonworking time, but also of the real free time of people.* From that point of view, all irrational use of free time should be firmly cut down. The most effective use of nonworking time and increase of the proportion of real free time depends primarily on the sphere of the services. The transition to a reduced working week and the rational use of free time bring to the fore another major social issue: *the radical improvement of holiday arrangements.*

A fundamentally new concept of the working people's recreation should be worked out: holiday houses should be built in a new way; mountain villages, now practically deserted, are especially suited for recreation and tourism, as well as for setting up child-care establishments. They should be used on a more massive scale, and public villa construction should develop more widely.

It is necessary to create new forms of recreation, weekend and weekly. It is time to streamline the management of the holiday system by the gradual concentration and integration of its administrative and economic functions: supply, transport, servicing, etc. A new policy is also needed in the construction of new facilities.

Measures to reduce working time, changes in the pattern of work and leisure time, reduction of the ways of spending non-working time that are not rational from a social point of view, lengthening free time and organizing recreation, should become important components of the nation's plan and of the social development plans of communities. These plans should be elaborated and implemented with the active participation and control of the working people. In this connection, the question of the protection of the natural environment will increase in importance.

2. Improvement of Labor Conditions and Refinement of Man-Machine Relationships

Along with the reduction of working time and the increase of real free time, decisive measures should be taken for a further improvement of labor conditions. The scientific and technical revolution, the wide use of automatic systems for management and production and other means of cybernation and automation make it now necessary to specify what development the man-machine system should undergo in the next few years and how in its practical activity the Party will use the *law on the gradual and consistent transfer of production functions from man to technical devices under the new conditions.*

As we know, many technical devices have greater "physical" and "intellectual" capacities than an individual. For that reason contact with them creates great tension in man, requires a reorganization or other changes in the rhythms of his life, and leads to great fatigue.

All this necessitates keeping close watch over the process of technical re-equipment of production, so as not to allow man to become an appendage of the new devices.

It is also necessary to continue efforts to optimize the rate and rhythm of the working process, to adapt places of work to man's anthropometric characteristics, and evolve science-based patterns of work and rest.

For us, as builders of the most humane society, these questions are of first-rate political and social importance. We should set about their solution with the utmost vigor.

What is necessary in this respect?

First, to change the setting of the problem. One can no longer talk about safe labor conditions when only individual pieces of machinery and equipment are made safe. At the existing level of production it is necessary to *optimize all parameters of the working environment.*

Second, to raise the level of labor safety and sanitation should be one of the main tasks of designers and engineers. *Machines, equipment, apparatus and instruments should be designed and manufactured in such a way as to ensure safe and sanitary labor conditions when working with them.* This refers both to Bulgarian-made machines and to those we import.

Third, an important prerequisite for the improvement of labor conditions in newly built and operating enterprises is the availability of the necessary kinds of *highly effective technical equipment and material for optimizing the working environment, means of protection and special working clothes.* The supply of technical means and material for the optimization of the parameters of the working environment and of the equipment for the worker's personal protection is a task of prime importance. Its over-all solution should be ensured step by step during the 1973-75 period.

In the complex of changes associated with the introduction of ergonomics, for observing standards of sanitation and labor safety, *the subjective factor is of particular importance. This makes it necessary to build a system for the training of specialists on labor safety and sanitation.*

Another way of raising the standard of labor protection is the proper *choice of vocation*. Vocational selection is now done for only some trades in the field of transport. Its full introduction in the training and distribution of cadres requires a thorough study and analysis of the specifics of the various trades, identification of the precise qualities that a particular trade demands of the work, and a study of the individual psychological features of every worker.

VI. IMPROVEMENT OF THE SYSTEM OF PUBLIC SERVICES—AN IMPORTANT FACTOR IN RAISING GENERAL LIVING STANDARDS

1. *On a New Approach to the Development and Management of Public Services:*

Comrades, The general standard of life depends directly on the state and development of the services. Their role will be greater all the time. That is an objective, law-governed phenomenon, determined by a number of causes.

Bringing the system of services into line with the tasks of raising the general living standards requires, first of a change in the approach to determining the place, role, rates, processes and structure of services to the population.

This has made it necessary to work out, on a fundamentally new basis, the Basic Theses of the Improvement of the System of Public Services in the People's Republic of Bulgaria, which were adopted by the State Council.

How should these problems of public services be handled?

a) It is necessary to *build a single system* of public services that should cover the *whole complex of services* in the various territorial units and at the different levels.

In this connection it is essential to work out a system of norms, defining at what level, on what territory and at what a pace a particular kind of service should develop.

b) The aggregate sphere of public service should develop through the use of *modern achievements of science and technology*.

The main trend in the improvement of the system of public servicing in its main varieties of a material nature should be combination, specialization and concentration.

Along with the development of public services, conditions and possibilities should be created for some of the services to be performed by the citizens themselves through the manufacture of the necessary tools and equipment.

c) *The cultural needs of the people* will be growing very rapidly. This calls *for ever greater attention to be paid to the general development of the servicing sphere which will ensure the satisfaction of those needs.* In this connection, the question of the material base in the field of culture acquires particularly great importance. A great deal has been accomplished in Bulgaria in this respect. It is necessary, however, to take measures so that the existing material facilities in the system of public education, the higher educational establishments, the research institutes, as well as the theaters, cinemas, library clubs, cultural centers, etc. can be used in the best and most effective way. This is a priority task that should be solved as soon as possible.

Along with this, measures should be taken for the further planned and purposeful extension and improvement of the material facilities of cultural work, which should ensure full cultural services to the population.

d) A modern form of management of the unified system of public services should be evolved, skillfully combining the principle of centralism with the broad development of democratic elements.

In the building and management of the complex system of public services, the territorial principle should be adopted, taking into account the branch features in the development of the individual kinds of services.

e) The formation, development and functioning of the sphere of public services should rest on science-based dynamic norms for a given period, which should accurately reflect society's potential to satisfy the population's needs.

2. *On the Further Development of Inhabited Localities*

The system of public services can be improved only if based *on a clear-cut conception of the development of inhabited localities.* In this context, it is necessary to decide which settlements, affected by what factors, should develop faster than others, which should develop slowly, and which should be left to wither away.

We should get rid of the old notion that existing settlements should all be kept up at any cost; that every one of them should have conditions for full employment and comprehensive services.

In applying the new approach to the development of settlements, the demographic processes assume special importance, in particular the rapid population increase in big cities. This is an issue with crucial economic, social and political implications that calls for an examination at the present plenary session.

Whereas a quarter of a century ago only 25 per cent of our population lived in towns, today the urban population has come up to 54.7 per cent and, according to previsions, it may be expected to exceed 80 per cent of the total by the end of this century. Sofia has become one of the cities with more than a million inhabitants, and other Bulgarian towns have rapidly expanded, too.

For the time being at least, cities offer their inhabitants a number of advantages. This, however, is only one facet of the matter—the positive one.

We should clearly examine the other, negative facet, as well, vis.; that the *overconcentration of the population in the cities leads to a number of negative phenomena which cannot be compensated for by the positive ones.* As shown by world experience, certain of the consequences of scientific and technical progress are impairing normal life conditions in towns and creating a grave danger of spoiling man's environment.

For that reason precisely, the downward trend in the manpower employed in agriculture does not require or imply that the population thus released should congregate in the big cities, creating a series of social and economic difficulties for society. On the contrary, we should create conditions for an urban way of life in the villages in which manpower is being released from agriculture.

Our policy of developing inhabited localities should be adapted to general state interests. While taking a decision on one or another inhabited locality, we should be conscious of its importance for the national system of settlements, for the over-all socio-economic development of Bulgaria. At the same time, we should take into account the sum-total of conditions and factors determining the development of inhabited areas.

On the basis of an analysis of these and other factors, ways and means should be sought for effectively organizing the system of inhabited localities and, above all, of curbing the excessive growth of big cities. We should not forget that the hypertrophy of big cities is essentially a chain process; as the cities grow, the need for their further development grows, too. Experience has shown that the process cannot be restricted by administrative measures alone.

A new form of effective organization of the settlement network, whose advantages we are not yet sufficiently using, is *the settlement system*. In this case, the system of inhabited localities, called agglomeration, whose population is united by the community of location of employment, recreation and public services, has to be treated as a single unity.

The application of this form leads to a fuller use of the housing stock in the villages and small towns, while also creating objective conditions for better controlling the growth of big cities by administrative measures.

The over-all future development of inhabited *localities should be planned in close connection with the projects for socio-economic development and especially the spatial organization of material production.* The dialectic relationship between labor resources and production capacities places the development of the settlement system in close connection with the general scheme of territorial distribution of the productive forces. There is a similar interconnection with the system of complex services. These important conditions should find their place in the process of territorial planning, an important element of which is the question of the development of inhabited localities.

3. Creation of Modern Home Trade and Public Catering—
   an Important Trend in Service Development

The fuller satisfaction of people's needs calls for *special attention to be paid to home trade and public catering.*

At every stage of socialist construction, our Party has taken steps to develop and improve trade and public catering. On that basis, especially after the April 1956 Plenary Session of the CC, a comparatively high annual growth rate of trade was established. The trade services expanded considerably in scale. Still, trade and public catering continue to lag behind the over-all socio-economic growth rate. *The rapid modernization of home trade and public catering is not only an economic, not only a commercial issue, but also one of highly political, ideological, social and educational significance.*

We should bring home trade and public catering into line with the Party policy of over-all satisfaction of the people's needs. In order to cope with that task, we should solve several important problems.

First. Create *a comprehensive system of shopping services* so that the population can satisfy its needs of consumer goods and trade services easily at any time. This implies a good knowledge of consumer demand both on a national scale and by regions. It is high time for consumer research to be placed entirely on a scientific basis.

The survey of consumer demand from the point of view of the operative regulation of trade makes it necessary to introduce as soon as possible an automated system of controlling trade in kind and goods stocks. In this way, rapid and systematic information will be ensured about the movement of goods by shops and regions in the country, and trade will be able accurately and promptly to feed back to production information about which ranges and kinds of goods sell quickly and which find no market, so that production may provide goods that are sold on the market and not just goods in general.

Second. The material and technical base of trade services should be linked with the use of modern scientific research in the fields of economics, organization and management, technology, commodity research, etc. The main trend in that respect should be *a most effective use of the available material base,* including the necessary reorganization, regrouping and introduction of modern technologies.

The further development of the material and technical base of trade services should be placed on a normative basis and closely linked to the general scheme of the territorial development of productive forces, and to the development of settlements and the building of the over-all complex of public services.

Third. The organizational forms in the sphere of trade and public catering should be improved, and on that basis the cultural standard of *trade services should be raised to the level of the most advanced countries.*

World practice has shown that not only in industry but in the sphere of circulation, too, a policy of concentration should be followed by creating large-scale integrated warehouse facilities and building large shops that provide the population with a wide range of goods.

In the field of trade in durable goods, it is necessary to continue the policy of building large department and specialized stores, with a view to a comprehensive satisfaction of consumer needs; specialized shopping services, bringing together and connecting the purchase with the service of goods and improving the cultural standards of shop services.

The principal form of retail trade should be *self-service* so that by 1980 most of the turnover will be occurring in self-service shops.

The form of *combined and multipurpose use* of material facilities for public catering should be applied widely; for students' and working people's canteens, for cooked food to be delivered to schools, to various social events, parties, etc. A conception should be worked out for the rapid building and development of automatic shopping facilities. In the system of public catering, semi-finished foods should be used widely and shopping facilities should be combined with canteens.

The system of services in the field of public catering should be approved.

Fourth. The further rapid development of home trade and public catering calls for the introduction of radical improvements in the system of planning the goods turnover and stocks, in the links of trade with production, and in pricing, as well as in the development of an economic mechanism of trade management ensuring the marketing of goods most convenient for buyers, with the most courteous service and without any delays or bureaucratic restrictions.

Ensuring stability in supplying the population presupposes the existence of the necessary stocks of goods and a smooth flow of goods of the necessary range into the shops.

It is imperative to improve the operation of shops as a basic unity in the system of trade servicing and public catering.

Fifth. The problem of personnel in trade and public catering should be solved in a new way. The underestimation of the occupation of trade should be overcome by imparting a new content to it. The shop assistant, the public catering staff, should assist and advise the working people in meeting their needs.

Sixth. The development of trade and trade services should become a national concern involving all the people. All branches of the nation's economy should share in the responsibility.

Seventh. In working out dynamic norms, the salaries and the number of those employed in trade should be increased so as to ensure much higher cultural standards of servicing.

4. *For Improved Health Services*

An important prerequisite for raising the living standard is the constant concern of the Party and Government for promoting the nation's health. During the period of people's rule the number of beds in hospitals and sanatoria has ineased considerably, but the population's needs for hospital services have not yet been met.

The development of tehnical progress and the creation of new methods and techniques of prevention, diagnosis, treatment and rehabilitation call for *an increase in the funds spent on meeting the needs of up-to-date medical equipment, apparatus and devices.*

As for the body of *doctors,* their number and proficiency make it possible to a great extent to ensure high quality and easily available medical aid. What is needed, however, is, on the one hand, the correct distribution and, on the other, an increase in the efficiency of the work of doctors. To this end, and in order to free doctors from work that is not properly in their sphere, it is imperative for more funds to be allocated for the introduction of up-to-date equipment and the supply of a health network with sufficient para-medical personnel. Even more serious attention should be paid to a *scientific organization of labor at health establishments.*

A drastic improvement in hospital services is closely connected with a modern and scientific treatment of patients. That makes it essential to create an optimum so-called hospital-psychological climate and comfort, without which modern treatment is unthinkable.

Parallel with the improvement of free treatment, we should consider an improvement in the system of free supply of patients with medicines. In Bulgaria, medicines for hospital patients are free of charge, as well as for certain grave diseases and for patients staying at home. Ways and means of a gradual transition to a free supply of drugs for all kinds of diseases treated at home should now be considered.

5. *Main Trends in the Development of Community, Transport, Communication and Other Services*

The working people's living standards depend a great deal on the development of community, transport, communication and other kinds of services. These services, too, are lagging in their development.

What should be done to overcome the lag?

First of all, the development of community services should be speeded up even under the Sixth Five-Year plan, and should be adapted to the over-all development of the whole sphere of public services. *The construction of the material base should be placed on an industrial foundation by introducing the most modern technological devices and organization of services.* Some modern and more progressive forms, such as subscription servicing, warranty maintenance, improvement of insurance coverage of certain commodities, etc. should be applied on a wider scale.

Special attention should, as heretofore, be paid to the development of services that free women from washing, cleaning clothes, looking after the house, etc.

The problem of *public transport* has been getting more and more acute, and this makes it imperative to review the existing growth rates and to take prompt measures to increase the number of buses and trolley buses. Public transport should develop especially quickly in industrial areas, with their great congregation of industrial and office workers, and the acute need for their rapid conveyance at fixed hours of the day. The problem of public transport in Sofia should find a general solution; a start should be made in this five-year period, and this should be set as a political and economic task. The modern scientific and technical revolution and the further raising of our people's cultural standards are intimately linked to the *development of communications, and, more particularly, to the telephone services which must be more widely extended on the basis of new, modern solutions.*

6. *Introduction of Up-to-date Forms of Administration Services*

The methods and forms of administrative services existing in Bulgaria are quite outdated. Along what lines should this sphere of services be improved?

a) The system of administrative services should be simplified by re-evaluating the formalities involved so as to reduce them to a rational minimum, eliminating all the red-tape elements.

b) The order in which the various kinds of administrative services are rendered should be strictly fixed, and no state bodies should be allowed to change it for insignificant reasons and for their own convenience, to the detriment of the population's interests.

c) The compulsory formalities for the various kinds of administrative services, as well as the objectively needed changes in them, should be made known to the population in a suitable way, in advance.

d) The working hours of offices engaged in administrative services should be adapted to the citizens' free time.

e) The People's Councils, as the bodies performing the greatest number of administrative services, and the other organs of state power should streamline the various units in such a way that citizens receive the necessary services from one place, whereas all inquiries, checks, etc.; should be performed as part of their official duties by the staff of the respective office.

f) Suitable economic units should be established for comprehensive administrative services which, at the request of citizens needing them, should procure the necessary administrative services for them on their behalf and at their expense.

The modern forms of administrative services applied in advanced countries should be studied, as well as the possibilities of introducing an automated system of management in administrative services.

VII. CARE AND CONSIDERATION
  FOR THE PEOPLE ON THE PART
  OF THE ORGANS OF PUBLIC ADMINISTRATION

Comrades, when speaking of care for the people, we must take into account not only material values, their incomes and material living conditions. No less important is *the atmosphere, the social environment in which the free socialist worker creates and lives.* In this context, the problems of the further development of productive relations, of socialist democracy, of securing the proper conditions for the working people's full expression as masters of society, and of safeguarding the political and moral fate of every individual, assume particular significance.

1. *Further Refinement of Relations Between People and the Extension of Socialist Democracy*

Here we have in mind primarily the development and refinement of socialist relations in our society, a problem of fundamental importance.

The main link in the entire system of social relations under socialism, their salient trait, is the relationship of friendly cooperation and mutual assistance between producers having equal rights, united by the public character of ownership and the general objective of production: to provide ever more fully for the steadily growing material and cultural needs of the working people.

Friendly cooperation pervades every single cell of our social organism and determines the relations between people. It lies at the root of all the links of our system of public administration. It is inherent not only in the state sector, but also in the cooperative sector. The relationship of friendly cooperation and mutual assistance is also a powerful factor in the development of the world socialist system.

One of the main advantages of socialism over capitalism is that the new society provides no economic or social foundation for relations of alienation to arise in the production process. It is common knowledge that under capitalism man develops as an object of production and exploitation. Under socialism, on the contrary, exploitation has been done away with once and for all, and the working people have become the masters of production and management. Labor is not a commodity. Work is directly social in character.

At the same time, we cannot fail to take into account that remnants and traits typical of the already abolished system of alienation still linger in the individual psychology and in the consciousness of factory and office workers, in their behavior as well as in the organs of public administration.

Some contradictions and difficulties arise from all this, and they call for measures to completely eliminate the conditions that generate them.

One of the chief trends in developing and improving the system of productive and social relations should be to further *develop socialist democracy in all directions.*

What are the questions now on the agenda in this area?

a) The people should be given the greatest opportunities for more direct participation in forming conceptions and making decisions.

There is an urgent necessity to set up a system of information, from the grassroots up to the top, that will convey the people's opinions unadulterated, without sugar-coating. Only when we secure a flow of timely, all-round and authentic information about the views and sentiments of people will the Party, state and economy management organs be able to make decisions that correspond fully to the interests of the people and take their views and opinions into consideration.

b) The rates of scientific and technical progress, the new tasks linked with building mature socialism, make it incumbent on us to further develop the collective method in decision-making and to strengthen one-man management in their implementation. This is an objective necessity in the development of management and administration.

In this respect, we are faced with the task of perfecting the state-cum-public principle in the various spheres of administration. In this realm we have already accumulated certain positive experience that should be summed up.

It is no less important for us, and it is in keeping with the Leninist principle of democratic centralism, to develop to the utmost the democratic principle in the administration at all levels of our socio-economic and political life.

At the same time, the principle of one-man management should be reinforced and combined with the strict observance of obligations and rules of conduct. Failing to tighten one-man management, centralism and discipline make the correct development of collectivism and democracy an impossible task. These are interlinked processes. We should conform all our actions to this rule.

Decisions, once democratically adopted, should be carried through consistently and all the way. Our system should differ from the capitalist system not only in its democratic character, but also in its tighter organization and general discipline, founded on the ideological conviction and class consciousness of the working people. For this reason, discipline in our country evolves into a qualitatively new state, assuming the form of conscientiousness and self-discipline.

2. *Perfecting relations between Public Administration Organs and Man in our Society*

Perfecting the system of social relations shows another aspect: a correct, *socialist relationship between state organs and institutions, and the individual citizen.*

The citizen of our country communicates, and should be able to communicate, with the state and public organs and organizations as a free person enjoying full rights, as the full master of his country, of his present and future. Nobody has the right, just because of possible bungling on his part, to divert a worker from his task for no reason, to waste his time or to humiliate him through procrastination and abuse.

State and public institutions are made to serve man. We should organize them so that they adapt themselves to man and his needs, and not the other way round.

On the other hand, we must *take even bolder steps to improve the system and the ways in which people can actively take part in the work of the organs of government and administration.* The greater democratization and the successful functioning of the People's Councils depend on their ability to rely on the broad public, constantly to seek its cooperation by enlisting the support of the most active citizens. In solving problems of major importance that touch upon the interests of the population, the People's Councils should consult the inhabitants of their administrative and territorial unit. The practice of periodical reports by the People's Councils to their electorate should be perfected.

The problem of how officials behave towards the working people occupies a prominent place in the natural process of democratization. As you know, a large army of cadres loyal to the Party and the State has been created in our country. Life now dictates that the style and method of work of these cadres be radically improved and become attuned to the new tasks and conditions in our country.

In this context, we should stress the need to cultivate a number of valuable qualities in the contemporary leader, no matter what his rank or post:

a) *political qualities:*

1) to be loyal to the class and the Party;

2) to have a perfect grasp of the Party and state policy and to work for its implementation;

3) to display a creative approach to the concrete policy elaborated and pursued by the Party in his sector of work;

4) to educate the masses in a communist spirit, and to have a knack for working with them and organizing them;

5) to possess high moral virtues and to serve as personal examples;

b) *business qualities:*

1) to be able to guide and collaborate with the work force;

2) to possess the necessary training, corresponding to present-day achievements in science and technology;

3) to be familiar with production and to be capable of managing it;

4) to have a command of modern methods in making decisions, in implementing and seeing them through.

These requirements call for a radical change in the existing system of training, and especially the retraining, of executives.

We must completely stamp out practices such as promoting men on unprincipled grounds, through favoritism, string-pulling and nepotism.

The problem of reserve cadres, their selection, education and training also deserves serious consideration.

As was pointed out originally at the July Plenary Session, and later at the Tenth Party Congress, the Labor Code now in force has evidently become obsolete and is coming into contradiction with the new conditions and tasks of socialist construction and with the contemporary character of work and the consciousness of the people.

This calls for a new labor code to be prepared and adopted. Obviously, it is not a matter of amending the code now in force, but of working out a new act that will regulate labor relations among the people. The new labor code should correspond to the present stage of our development, to the new character of work and the new organization of production, to the requirements of the scientific and technical revolution and the new trends in the development of socialist democracy. It should be an instrument for the education and edification of a new man and of a communist attitude to work. The new code should settle legal labor problems not only for the industrial and office workers, but also for the cooperative farmers. This will, in principle, be a new moment in our labor legislation.

12

The Cardinal Task—
Higher Labor Productivity

Speech to the National Conference of
the Communist Party of Bulgaria, March 20, 1972

The report to the National Party Conference has been circulated and I should like to draw your attention to only some of the main aspects of the problems proposed for consideration here.

I should like to emphasize from the very outset that it is not the task of this conference to make an over-all review and strike a balance of the Party's work since its Tenth Congress. Nor do we set ourselves the task of mapping out all the main guidelines for work and all the problems facing the Party in the next period.

This will evidently be the task of the Eleventh Party Congress.

The Central Committee of the Party considers that the National Conference will best perform its purpose if it concentrates its attention and that of the whole Party on a single problem—*that of raising labor productivity*. That is why the report, copies of which have been circulated to you, is devoted to that problem alone. All the other questions that the report touches on are subordinate to that main problem.

Why did the Central Committee decide to submit the problem of labor productivity to the conference for a detailed discussion? It did so for several reasons:

First: Naturally, this is not the first time we are dealing with this matter; it has been discussed at every plenary session of the Central Committee devoted to economic matters, The degree of our economy's development, however, as well as the general world situation, now require that *we look upon the drive to raise labor productivity as a cardinal, key problem* in the fulfillment of the Sixth Five-Year Plan, in the building of a developed socialist society in the People's Republic of Bulgaria.

Taking a sober look at matters, we must unfortunately admit that we have not accomplished a breakthrough in this respect since the Tenth Party Congress. It is true that the growth rates of labor productivity in Bulgaria are among the highest in the world, but this cannot possibly satisfy us. Even with such growth rates, we can hardly hope to catch up with the most advanced socialist and capitalist countries.

Second: We now view this matter in the light of Lenin's great idea that higher labor productivity is the chief condition and the decisive factor for the complete victory of the new system.

It is only by a rapid raising of labor productivity that we shall be able to guarantee future high and stable growth rates in our economy, to increase the nation's economic potential, and to create a progressive structure of social production. Only by stepping up the growth rates of labor productivity shall we be able to augment the national income faster and hence to raise the people's material and cultural standards more rapidly.

As Marxist-Leninists we know that on the world arena the historic question "who will prevail?" will be decided ultimately in the key sphere of social life, in the field of the economy, We have every reason to state, therefore, that the drive to raise labor productivity is, in the full sense of the word, *a class struggle.*

We are quite confident that socialism will demonstrate its complete superiority over capitalism not only in the field of social relations, not only in the field of culture and ideology, not only in building a more perfect structure of the economy and of the whole society, but in the field of labor productivity as well, One proof of this is the high rates at which the socialist states are raising their labor productivity. Let us take Bulgaria, for example. Labor productivity in our nation's economy doubled in ten years from 1960 to 1970. In 1972, it was 2.5 times as high as in 1960.

The socialist states, and particularly the Soviet Union, have highly developed productive forces and a solid scientific potential. Socialist production relations offer a wide scope to the initiative of the masses, enabling them to take a most active part in the management of production and the government of the state.

All these things are an earnest of the fact that we shall prevail in this particular sphere of class struggle.

Naturally, socialism needs time to fully manifest its superiority over the capitalist system, and this applies also to the sphere of labor productivity. However, we are duty bound to do everything within our power for an early implementation of that historic task.

The third reason for raising the labor productivity question is the need to speed up the rates of completing the building of the material and technical foundations of socialism in the People's Republic of Bulgaria.

Marx's thesis about the determining role of the productive forces in the development of society is, of course, as fully valid for Bulgaria as it is for other countries. Therefore, in the Party Program adopted by the Tenth Congress, the main emphasis in the construction of a developed socialist society, and later in the transition to communism, is placed on the tasks relating to the construction of the material and technical foundations. Our achievements in developing the productive forces and in introducing the results of the scientific and technical revolution are considerable; indeed, this is especially true of the years following the April 1956 Plenary Session of the Central Committee.

Being realists, however, we take due account of the fact *that our economic policy should always be adapted to the country's specific conditions. Bulgaria has limited material, human and financial resources. That is why the material and technical foundations of*

socialism cannot be built successfully in Bulgaria unless we partici-pate most actively and on a wide scale in international socialist division of labor. This is an objective law.
Our data indicate that an increasing portion of our national in-come is generated through the participation of the country in the international division of labor. In 1973, for example, the value of foreign trade, related to the national income, was 63.5 per cent. At the end of the next five-year plan that figure is expected to be about 68 to 70 per cent.

The conclusion suggests itself, that if we want our participation in the international division of labor to be effective, our products to be competitive, and our national income from imports and exports to keep on rising, we must radically raise labor productivity and im-prove the quality of goods.

The fourth consideration prompting us to effect a dramatic in-crease in labor productivity is *the shortage of manpower in Bulgaria.* The ways of increasing it are running out. Therefore we are unable in some areas of production, to make full use of the existing production capacities.

What then is the answer?

It is a further intensive development of our economy, a rapid raising of labor productivity.

Some comrades believe that the shortage of manpower can be made up by a significant increase in the birth-rate. It is no secret that the birth-rate in Bulgaria is low. This phenomenon is charac-teristic of both the capitalist states (with the exception of Japan) and the socialist states of all countries where industrialization has reached an advanced stage.

It is quite true that the birth-rate in the world in general is on the increase. According to UN forecasts, if at present the world's popu-lation is 3,800 million by the year 2,000 it will be nearly 6,000 million. This increase, however will not be spread uniformly; it will be mainly characteristic of former colonial countries, recently liber-ated.

As you know, a campaign to raise the birth-rate is under way in Bulgaria. A number of measures have been taken along these lines and, as a result, the birth-rate has started to rise. But this is a lengthy process and more tangible results can be expected only in a few years' time. It should, however, be remembered that those born recently or in the past few years will not enter production until 15 or 20 years from now. Consequently, even a rising birth-rate cannot alleviate our present difficulties relating to manpower shortage.

Furthermore, we are witnessing a process whereby the nation is growing older—mainly due to the longer life expectancy. Whereas, before September 9, 1944, the average life expectancy in Bulgaria was about 52 years, now it is over 70 years. This is a major social gain but it means that an increasing number of people are not taking part in the reproduction process and are in need of additional care on the part of society.

At the same time, more and more people will be needed in such spheres as the services, education, science and culture.

Fifth. An exceptionally important consideration of principle, I would say, is the following: the drive to raise labor productivity rapidly stems from the nature of socialism, is dictated by the objective laws and processes operating during the stage of building a developed socialist society. The building of mature socialism is impossible without maximum time-saving, as Marx has mentioned.

Consequently, at present, the raising of labor productivity is the main link which, if we grasp it, as Lenin taught us, will enable us to pull the whole chain.

The economic, social, cultural, ideological and political tasks of the construction of a developed socialist society intersect and the interests of every man, every work force, and the personal, group and social interests meet and come to a focus.

The shorter our time for raising the level of labor productivity, the higher the rates of our socio-economic development will be and *the greater our contribution* to the victory of the socialist system in the historic duel between the two opposing social systems, socialism and capitalism.

Comrades, as you see, we are now faced with an extremely important task. This task is, however, as difficult as it is important. It will require much effort, hard work and conscientiousness. We are quite confident that this task will be solved successfully; *all the necessary domestic and international conditions are at hand.*

What are these conditions?

First. Bulgaria has solid material and technical foundations, scientific potential, managers and personnel, and an experienced Communist vanguard.

Second. We have entered a new stage of international socialist integration and, above all, of integration with the great Soviet Union.

The course adopted by the July Plenary Session of the CC of the BCP of all-round and close rapprochement between the People's Republic of Bulgaria and the Soviet Union introduces essentially new elements in the country's over-all development and calls for a new approach to the question of raising labor productivity. Integration with the Soviet Union and with the other socialist states enables us to establish a more effective structure of the economy, to build large enterprises with large serial and efficient production, with modern technologies, to solve scientific and technical problems, etc. jointly.

All this is a striking demonstration of the new character of mutual relations between the socialist states—relations of comradely cooperation and mutual assistance. *This is one of the main advantages of socialism.*

Third. The present favorable international conditions also enable us to apply a new approach to the drive to raise labor productivity. I am referring to the transition from the cold war to the establishment of the principles of peaceful coexistence. I have in mind the shift in the world balance of power in favor of socialism. I also have in mind the higher international prestige of the People's Republic of Bulgaria, which has come to be accepted and increasingly appreciated as an equal partner.

All this creates conditions for the capitalist nations to show greater readiness to intensify economic cooperation with us.

These are, comrades, some of the favorable prerequisites enabling us to go about raising labor productivity *in a new way and on a new scale.*

A circumstance of crucial importance is that, in solving this key task, we are relying and should rely most widely on the scientific and technical revolution.

At a recent symposium in Moscow, scientists from the socialist states discussed the question as to whether the scientific and technical revolution is near its end or whether it is likely to continue its dynamic course for some time to come. They did not arrive at a clear-cut answer, but one thing is clear to us—science and technology are developing so rapidly and have become such powerful factors that they should be used as fully as possible.

In our socialist conditions, *science becomes a powerful productive force.* Under socialism there is no social class antagonism. Society as a whole has a stake in providing a creative climate for the progress of science and technology, and in placing them at the people's service. The socialist production relations open up quite exceptional opportunities for the development of the scientific and technical revolution. *It is not profit, as under capitalism, but the concern for man, for satisfying his material and cultural needs, that is the main driving force in the development of science.*

In turn, the scientific and cultural revolution effects radical changes in the solution of problems in the field of the economy, in culture, in public administration, in daily life—in a word, in all spheres of social life. It is our powerful ally in the drive to build the material and technical foundations of socialism.

In imperialist countries, however, science in the hands of the monopolies leads to intensifying social stresses, to inflation, rising unemployment, etc.

Science introduces radical changes not only in public life but also in the mutual relations between man and his environment. That is why the protection of the environment has now become a world problem.

Quite a few bourgeois philosophers, sociologists and politicians are faced with the delemma—what is science, a blessing or a curse?

Until recently, bourgeois scientists and propagandists regarded the scientific and technical revolution as a magical way of surmounting the contradictions of capitalism and of establishing "class peace." Those hopes have been shattered irretrievably. Now bourgeois propaganda is resorting to a new ideological diversion. It is speculating with the adverse consequences of the scientific and technical revolution. The radio and television, the bourgeois press, often depict science and technology as a demon threatening people's lives. They are attempting to suggest that the main cause of the misery, the hunger and the poverty of millions in the capitalist

world, and of the social and class conflicts in the bourgeois countries, is not the capitalist system but the scientific and technical
revolution.

In the hands of the imperialists, science does indeed become a
means of stepping up exploitation in the interest of the monopolies,
of strengthening militarism; it turns into a sword of Damocles dang-
ling menacingly over the world.

We, under the conditions of socialism, are waging an organized
struggle against the adverse consequences of the scientific and
technical revolution, using it to augment social wealth and to ensure
man's all-round development. *We regard science as a supreme good.*

*The accelerated growth of labor productivity, and even a single
step forward in any field of social life, are inconceivable without
science, without its achievements and their speedy and effective
application in production.*

The radical changes brought by the scientific and technical revolution and its truly great advances call, however, for a new approach to solving the problem of raising labor productivity.

The scientific and technical revolution requires a new approach to
the modernization and reconstruction of enterprises and to the concentration and specialization of production:

1) it requires a new approach and new technologies in production;

2) it requires a new approach to the technology of public administration;

3) it requires new solutions of the problem of fully utilizing the
nation's raw material resources;

4) it requires a new approach in the drive to improve the quality
of production.

All this faces us with two main tasks:

First: Without wasting a moment, we should start using most fully
the scientific and technical achievements of world science and technology.

Science is international in character. It is international in the
sense that every nation, big or smell, makes its contribution to its
development and enrichment. It is international, too, in the sense
that every nation can use and apply the results of the development
of science in other countries.

It would be superfluous to emphasize to this conference how vastly important it is for a country like ours, with limited resources, to rely on the scientific achievements of the advanced states, and especially of Soviet science, on the scientific potential of the USSR. The prompt practical application of other countries' scientific achievements does not in any way and to any extent reflect on our national dignity. Only dogmatists and short-sighted people will fail to understand that it is neither within our power nor is it necessary for us to rediscover already discovered things, that any period of marking time is detrimental to socialism and to the country. Conversely, the more flexible and more ingenious we are, the better mechanism we evolve for using foreign scientific and technical achievements on a world level, the more rapidly will we raise labor productivity and the faster the socialist system will develop and become consolidated.

The second task, no less important, is for us to properly organize and control our own scientific front, so that it may make its contribution to raising labor productivity and to the building up of a developed socialist society in Bulgaria.

We expect from our scientists considerable achievements in the development of Bulgarian science. The task now is for all our institutes, both those at the Academy of Sciences and those outside the Academy, to tackle the most crucial and topical problems of production and practical work. Our scientific front, our scientific and technical intelligentsia, should now stand in the front ranks of the drive for new technologies, for new products, for higher quality, for solving the raw materials problem, for raising labor productivity. *We should reduce as much as possible the distance from the research laboratory to the factory, from the scientific invention to its application in production and in practice.* Scientific achievements should be applied in the most effective way. A statesman-like approach calls for the most rational utilization of the large funds we are allocating for research, and the potential of our scientific cadres.

Mass scientific and technical creative work and the movement of innovators and inventors should develop on an even broader scale.

What are the general conclusions that can be drawn from this examination of labor productivity and from the analysis of the conditions and methods for increasing it?

First: We can now set ourselves qualitatively new tasks, much more effective, much more productive, in the drive to raise labor productivity.

Second: We are now able to use a new approach and new ways and means of rapidly raising labor productivity.

Third: We should organically link the advantages of socialism with the scientific and technical revolution now in progress; we should use the achievements of modern science and technology to the utmost and within the shortest period of time.

Comrades, the tasks we have to solve, the ways and means by which we should achieve higher labor productivity at the present stage, are clear, In addition, we have all the necessary conditions and every opportunity to solve this key problem of our development.

What matters now is to turn this opportunity into a reality. This cannot and will not happen automatically. The conscious, organized and purposeful efforts and actions of the subjective factor are necessary. That is why our Party has always devoted special attention to the task of raising the working people's consciousness, involving the masses in the management of production and society, enhancing the role of the public organizations, strengthening the scientific character of administration, as well as advancing the prestige and the vanguard role of the communists, of the whole Party.

The subjective factor acquires very great importance at the present stage of our development. The fulfillment of the complex tasks involved in building a developed socialist society now depends even more critically on the training and conscientiousness of managers and personnel and the work forces, and on the fighting ability of the Party organizations.

Which of our problems should be given special emphasis so that the role of the subjective factor may develop even more broadly and efficiently?

First: Constant and intensive care is required by the Party committees and organizations, by the ministries, the economic and public bodies and organizations for *improving the training of managers and personnel, their conscientiousness and their sense of responsibility.* The fate of our economic plans, the drive for higher labor productivity, is primarily in the hands of our cadres.

The instruction and education, the selection and distribution of cadres, the improvement of their qualifications, are of exceptional importance now. The solution of this problem should come up to the level of the new requirements.

Second: Special care is needed for *strengthening the work force,* as an important cell of our social organism. A comradely and creative atmosphere should be developed in the work force; it should become a center of education and instruction and of a most active participation in raising labor productivity.

Third: The tightening of discipline—labor, production, plan, technological, contract and financial discipline—assumes the importance of a first priority political task now.

We have to admit that discipline now is one of our weak points. We continue to allow undue liberality and to connive at violations of discipline. If we do not accomplish a reversal in the matter of tightening discipline, if we do not step up our educational activities among the working people in a spirit of conscious discipline or, in Lenin's phrase, "self-discipline," many of the fine science-based decisions we are taking will remain dead letters.

No leniency should be allowed towards those who violate discipline, towards those who by their lack of responsibility and slovenliness foil the efforts aimed at higher labor productivity and at raising the people's material and cultural standards.

Fourth: The drive for higher labor productivity makes new, *far higher demands on all organs of public administration from top to bottom and from bottom to top.*

The role and responsibility of the Council of Ministers, of the ministries and committees, of the state corporation, the individual enterprises, and the People's Councils, should be enhanced. The rights and the competence of the state and economic bodies have now been specified. It is an achievement that the large turnover of management in the sphere of material production has now been ended. This stability paves the way for a more efficient control of the work to raise labor productivity.

In the work of the organs of public administration, the following principle should be strictly observed in the future: *the decisions should be taken by the person who is most competent and is able to carry out the decisions made and bears responsibility for its implementation.*

Fifth: Work force extention plans[1] are of tremendous importance in mobilizing the energies and the creativity of the working people *in developing socialist emulation on a new and scientific basis.*

No distortion of the work force extension plans should, however, be allowed. We should not permit them to be deprived of those positive, creative and innovative elements that are inherent in them. Work force extention plans are neither temporary nor campaign phenomena. They are and should be a powerful lever for stimulating the forces and the daring of the working people, for organizing socialist emulation, for promoting the nation-wide campaign for high labor productivity. With their help, material and cultural incentives, personal and public interests should be combined ever more skillfully.

Sixth: The strength of our Party is in its broad, strong and indestructible ties with the masses. The Party has always confidently relied on the trade unions, on the Komsomol, on the Fatherland Front, on all mass public organizations in Bulgaria. These organizations have rendered a historic service for the victory of the socialist revolution and for the building of the socialist system. At present, too, we are relying on them completely and we are convinced that they will mobilize the efforts of their members for the implementation of the major task being discussed by the conference.

We are confident that our loyal ally, *the Bulgarian Agrarian Party,* will continue to make its contribution to raising labor productivity and to the nation's socialist advancement.

Seven: Our Party, the Party committees and organizations, all communists, are *once again called upon to be in the van of the drive for higher labor productivity.* Whether we shall cope with the task assigned depends to the utmost on the work of the Party committees and organizations, of the communists, and on their devotion and consciousness.

Major responsibilities in the work of raising the consciousness of

[1] *Work force extension plans,* "counter plans" which the workers have adopted to overfulfill the centrally adopted plan of production.

communists and of all working people for their active participation in raising labor productivity will be assumed by all units and forms of Party education, of the mass information and propaganda media and of our whole ideological front.

I should like here to stress another important aspect of the task we shall be discussing at the conference. The drive for higher labor productivity, for the broadest participation of the working people in it, is at the same time a drive for the further transformation of Bulgaria into a technical and communist nation.

All of us are quite well aware that higher labor productivity cannot be achieved merely by way of introducing new equipment, by improving the working people's qualifications and their technical training, by way of a better mastery of technology. *The outcome of that drive will depend, possibly even more, on the consciousness and ideological tempering of the workers of socialism.*

The complex of tasks we must solve in order to achieve higher labor productivity than exists under capitalism cannot, therefore, be reduced to technical or "technocratic" tasks only. These tasks are to no small degree ideological. It would be a gross error to try and break this unbreakable unity between the technological and ideological aspect of the problem.

In our socialist conditions, when we speak of a "technical nation" we understand at the same time a "communist nation." And conversely, when we speak of a "communist nation" we have in mind a "technical nation." Such is the dialectics of the process of development of the nation under socialism and during the transition to communism. Would any one of us be able to imagine the Bulgarian nation becoming technical without at the same time becoming communist? Or our nation becoming communist without at the same time becoming technical?

From that point of view, too, the vast importance, not only economic but also social, cultural, political and ideological, of the nation-wide drive for higher labor productivity is readily perceived.

Comrades, in conclusion, I should like to express my confidence that the Party committees and organizations and the communists will be the heart and soul of the creative efforts aimed at raising labor productivity and implementing the general line of the Bulgarian Communist Party. Our general line is well known:

—it is a line of building and strengthening the socialist system in fraternal and indestructible unity with the Soviet Union, with all countries of the socialist community;

—it is a line of ever fuller satisfaction of the people's material and cultural needs, of man's all-round development;

—it is a line of peace, understanding and cooperation with all nations;

—it is a line of ensuring a steady material and cultural growth for our socialist country, the People Republic of Bulgaria.

In the name of that general policy, in the name of the drive for its implementation in life, the Central Committee of the Party submits the problem of raising labor productivity in Bulgaria to the National Party Conference for discussion.

Thank you for your attention.

13

Peace in the Balkans, in Europe and in the World

Speech at a mass public meeting in the Christo Botev Stadium in the city of Blagoevgrad, June 25, 1974

Dear Comrades, the annual celebrations in honor of the patron of your town and your district, Dimiter Blagoev, are a noble tradition. To pay homage to the name and lifework of Dimiter Blagoev in today's free, socialist Bulgaria is a foremost filial duty to the father of scientific socialism in our country, to the apostle of the Bulgarian party of revolutionary Marxism, to the great harbinger of our days.

To pay homage to the name and lifework of this man is a vital ideological and spiritual need for all contemporary Bulgarians, who have been born, grown up and worked with Blagoev's unshakeable faith in the justness of the communist cause.

The founder and champion of our Party was a faithful Bulgarian son who grew up in the bosom of the country and was reared in the spirit of the noblest ideas of the national liberation revolution. We cannot visualize the living image of Dimiter Blagoev without conjur-

221

ing up the memory of the bright Bulgarian youth of the village of Zagorichene in the second half of the last century. In his short autobiography, the days of Levski and Botev come back to life; it vibrates with the enthusiasm of his first teenage work. *The Wails of Bulgaria* sparkles with the tears of his teacher, Slaveikov, the Father, at the meeting with the Russian liberation troops. One can hear the whistle of bullets around the boy who, in the battle at Stara Zagora, carried bread and water to the fighting volunteers and helped the wounded. It rings with faith in the future of free Bulgaria, which the young man defended as a volunteer in the 1885 war.

If today the People's Republic of Bulgaria is an advanced socialist country, we are duty bound to appreciate the contribution of our great first teacher. The land of Rakovski and Karavelov, of Botev and Levski, of Hadji Dimiter and Stefan Karadja;[1] has become a flourishing land because giants like Dimiter Blagoev and his comrades-in-arms planted new seeds in it. From the vantage point of the 30th anniversary of our victory, we can better than ever view the Bulgarian rocks and eagles; haunts where thousands of Blagoev's heirs left their bones, for the sake of the people's socialist fulfillment.

Nothing happens by chance in history and nothing is gratuitous. While still a student at the Gabrovo secondary school, Dimiter Blagoev asked himself the question that he later put to his comrades in Petrograd, "What is the meaning of life, what is it that is worth living for?"

He found the answer to this question in the thinking of Marx and Engels and in the experience of the Russian Revolution. To his last breath, Dimiter Blagoev remained faithful to what had become the meaning and reason of his life—the fight for socialism and the goal of happiness for all.

---

[1] *Georgi Rakovski* (1821-1867), revolutionary democrat, founder of the Bulgarian national liberation movement, writer, publicist, historian; *Luben Karavelov* (1834-1879), author, publicist, a leader of the Bulgarian national liberation movement; *Hristo Botev* (1848-1876), the most popular and best known poet in Bulgaria, journalist and revolutionary democrat; one of the leaders of the national liberation movement; *Vassil Levski* (1837-1873), revolutionary democrat, a leader of the national liberation movement; *Hadji Dimiter* (1840-1868) and *Stefen Karadja* (1842-1868), guerrilla commanders of the national liberation movement.

From the thoughts and deeds that Dimiter Blagoev left behind as his heritage to us, we have learned and are learning class intransigence to the bourgeoisie and all its hirelings. Neither threats nor honeyed words could ever lead the party of Dimiter Blagoev and his followers astray from the stirring slogan, "Class against class"!

From the thoughts and deeds he left behind, we have learned and continue to learn how to subordinate our personal life, interests and will to the all-important life of the Party, to its interests and its will.

From the thoughts and deeds that Dimiter Blagoev left behind, we have learned and are learning to have faith in the powers and the historic mission of the working class.

Such behests were also left to us by Georgi Dimitrov, the first disciple and continuator of Blagoev's cause. We have never wavered, and will never waver, from the consistent creative championing of these bequests!

Our five-year plans today reflect labor heroism and the creative endeavor to procure the material and spiritual well-being of our people for the full human happiness of the present and future generations. Everything for the welfare of man, everything in the name of man!

Our immortal teacher showed us the right direction to travel to gain happiness for the whole people; and we have reached this day at the cost of countless sacrifices and difficulties. All Bulgaria, rallied around the Blagoev and Dimitrov Communist Party, is blazing new paths towards the happiness of all.

Once Engels called Dimiter Blagoev's Party the outpost of scientific communism in Southeast Europe. Today the country, in which Blagoev's Party is the leading and directing force, deservedly has won the reputation of a reliable mainstay of the socialist world, a loyal ally of Lenin's great state, a convinced fighter for peace and understanding among the peoples of the Balkan Peninsula and Europe. We can never forget that Dimiter Blagoev was the herald of this new and urgently necessary spirit of understanding among the Balkan nations—formerly suffering and exploited—and that his name has always enjoyed unquestioned prestige among all socialist, progressive and democratic peoples of the Balkans.

Irreconcilably opposed to nationalism, to chauvinism, to senseless fratricidal wars, Dimiter Blagoev and his comrades-at-arms consistently and perseveringly upheld their revolutionary Marxist, internationalist class positions. They defended these positions in the face of both the Bulgarian reactionary, treacherous bourgeoisie and the ruling reactionary cliques in the Balkan countries at the beginning of this century.

Today Marxism-Leninism is not only the dominant ideology in the People's Republic of Bulgaria; it is also a world outlook, the basis of the thoughts and feelings of the whole Bulgarian nation. The Bulgarian Communist Party is an ideologically armed and active detachment of the world communist and workers' movement. Again, we may well remember Dimiter Blagoev's behest to us: "If being a renegade is an ugly thing in itself, being a renegade from socialist convictions is much uglier!" In the minds of the fighters for socialism, peace and peaceful cooperation among nations, socialist Bulgaria and the Bulgarian Communist Party have always stood for loyalty, uncompromising ideological firmness, class solidarity and honesty. It was thus that Dimiter Blagoev educated us and the deeds of his followers shaped us; it was thus that we grew up in our own revolutionary experience.

People and Party, Party and people, in this country are indivisible. This unity is the life-giving source of all that is good in our socialist country. The ideological and political unity of Bulgarian patriots and Bulgarian Communists, of the Party and the people, of all working classes and social groups, of the representatives of every generation, is as unshakeable as a rock in the Pirin Mountains.

But we would be indulging only in propaganda and agitation for the advantages of the socialist system if everything we have referred to had not become integral to the daily life of our people. Let us take as an example your town and district. Many of us remember Gorna Djoumaya and the Gorna Djoumaya region. We remember a God-forsaken provincial area of old Bulgaria and a dead little town with run-down houses. Material and cultural poverty prevailed, harsh customs and cruel primitive exploitation. There was drudgery in the tiny fields and malnutrition; dozens of thousands were illiterate. There was overt and latent unemployment; scandalous excesses of big and small rulers. That was Gorna Djoumaya and the region of Gorna Djoumaya in the past, and such, too, was old Bulgaria.

Today we see contemporary Blagoevgrad. It grows with every

passing year into a modern socialist town with sunlit buildings, clean and attractive streets, its own white factories and cultural monuments, its bustling economic and cultural life. What has changed radically is not merely Blagoevgrad itself; the whole district is new; the whole country has been renewed. Would any of the older inhabitants of what was once Gorna Djoumaya have been able to imagine 30 years ago that some of the major centers of radio electronics, of the communications industry, of instrument manufacture, of the chemical and food industries and of power generation, would develop here? If someone had predicted this, it would have sounded vain and somewhat rash.

We are glad and proud that Blagoevgrad district, which worthily bears the name of its patron, continues to develop as one of the prosperous regions of the People's Republic of Bulgaria. Industrial output has increased seven times in the period since the April 1956 Plenary Session. As a result of concentration and intensification, the district has become a major producer of tobacco, fruit and vegetables. Your district is responsible for one-fifth of the nation's tobacco produce and one-tenth of the total exports of early tomatoes and peaches. Real incomes are growing every year; people are becoming more prosperous; a bright and well-educated younger generation is growing up; the district's cultural life is growing richer; thousands of specialists are devoting their knowledge and skill to construction.

These successes are deservedly crowning the long revolutionary struggles in this part of the country. The whole Bulgarian people gratefully remembers the heroic feat of the working people who, with the communists at their head, rose in an armed uprising in September 1923.

The whole Bulgarian people gratefully remembers the first pages in the annals of our partisan movement, which Ivan Kozarov wrote with his own blood. The whole Bulgarian people gratefully remembers the legendary partisan commander Nikola Parapounov and the thousands of patriots of this region, who gave their lives for Bulgaria's freedom and independence, for the great cause of the Bulgarian Communist Party, for socialism and communism.

Your successes were and are a brilliant confirmation of the strength of the socialist system, of the Party's general line, of the policy of the Central Committee and the government, and of the monolithic unity of the whole people in the name of welfare and prosperity.

In the last 30 years we have more than once proved that we know how to value success without shutting our eyes to difficulties, nor resting content with achievements, nor being lulled into complacency by the thought that we have used up all the objective possibilities of socialism. One should always look ahead and advance upward—there are no peaks we cannot climb!

I am, therefore, happy to inform you that on the initiative of the Party Central Committee and with the participation of the District Party Committee, a document is under preparation for the further acceleration of the socio-economic development of Blagoevgrad district. The document, to be published in a few days, makes provisions for various important undertakings in all main spheres of life and draws up the guidelines for the development of your district in the next few years.

Such decrees have been known to have had an extremely beneficial effect on the development of other regions of Bulgaria.

What are the most important points in this decree of the Central Committee and the Council of Ministers?

First, it is planned to continue the process of accelerated industrialization of the district and at the highest development rates in Bulgaria!

Radio electronics, communications equipment, instrument-making, the chemical industry, the food and tobacco industries, the light industry—these are the main branches that will continue to develop in your district. Many new plants of optimum size will be built to ensure production with world standard indices.

In the field of agriculture and forestry, the policy of production concentration and the introduction of industrial technologies and methods of work will continue. Specialization will also continue in tobacco production, field and greenhouse production, development of orchards and vineyards, dairy cattle-breeding and sheep-breeding. Irrigation and land improvement construction, too, will be developing on a larger scale.

Pasture land in the hilly and mountainous regions of the district will have to be used more thoroughly for the development of stock-breeding, since it constitutes an important reserve of which full use should be made.

The decree provides measures for the further improvement of inhabited localities and for solving more rapidly the housing problem in the towns. Measures have been mapped out for the development of transport, the road network and communication; for the development and improvement of trade, tourism and services; and for the further building and extension of schools, canteens, boarding houses and child-care establishments.

The Party Central Committee and the government have demanded of the Committee of Art and Culture and the district People's Council in Blagoevgrad to specify the projects to be built under the next five-year plan in the field of culture—priority being given to the construction of a district library and a district history museum, along with measures for the restoration and conservation of existing and newly built monuments which celebrate significant events in Bulgarian history that occurred in this area. These will be a powerful factor in the patriotic education of youth and of the whole population in Blagoevgrad district.

A comprehensive program is also to be adopted for the construction of youth and sports facilities, the development of holiday facilities, the fuller employment of labor resources—raising further the working people's living standards.

As you see, this is a document of tremendous importance for the future of the Blagoevgrad district. It takes into account the real potentialities and the needs of the district's development in the years to come; and it ensures that problems will be solved in a comprehensive way.

I am confident that all of you, the working people of Blagoevgrad district, will take this decree as a new expression of the constant concern for you on the part of the whole Party and of the whole people. We should join our efforts to create conditions for this region of Bulgaria, with its unexplored and untapped resources-—fine fertile land, an admirable patriotic population—to develop and advance economically, culturally and politically in harmony with all other parts of the country, and to make its ever growing contribution to the socialist construction of the People's Republic of Bulgaria.

These, comrades, are our views and our appraisal of the present and future of Blagoevgrad district—this beautiful corner of our country. Your successes and your future development can be appreciated when they are viewed against the background of Bulgaria's general development.

Our people will soon be celebrating the 30th anniversary of the socialist revolution. This will be a bright holiday, a holiday of pride in our achievements, a holiday celebrating our ambition to score new successes.

Casting our eyes on the past, we can say with full confidence that the last 30 years have been years of hard and constructive work, years in which the Bulgarian people have worked miracles—as both our friends and enemies agree. The three decades of free life have been decades of deep revolutionary changes in industry, agriculture, the development of science, art and culture; in the people's consciousness and way of life, and in raising their living standards.

The mean annual rates of general economic growth in Bulgaria since the Tenth Party Congress have remained among the highest not only in Europe but also throughout the world. In the three years since the Congress, the national income has increased by almost a quarter. About 95 per cent of this growth is effected through higher social labor productivity.

We are trying to develop the most advanced economic branches, products of the scientific and technical revolution with key importance for the building of the material and technical foundations of advanced socialism in Bulgaria. The whole nation is proud of the large plants in the Devnya industrial complex, of the Chemical Combine in Svishtov, of Bulgaria's first atomic power station, of the projects in the Bobov Dol energy complex, of the Rhodope hydroelectric power schemes, of the Soviet Union-Bulgaria gas pipeline, and other projects that have marked a new step in Bulgaria's industrial development and in the intensification of her economy.

Agricultural output has increased considerably, and agricultural production is increasingly being placed on an industrial basis.

We can state with satisfaction that Bulgaria has become an equal and respected partner in international economic cooperation.

Literature and art are genuinely flourishing. Socialism has opened up broad vistas for mass scientific, technical and cultural creative endeavor, for the growth and expression of talents.

People's happiness and the raising of prosperity are the content and meaning of the Party's policy and of its undeviating work and struggle for the building of socialism. The Party's policy is deeply popular in character, and therefore it has the full support of the working people in Bulgaria.

Recently, comrades, we have implemented quite extensive measures in fulfillment of the December Program for raising the people's living standards. The minimum wage and the minimum pensions of workers and peasants have been raised; the salaries of teachers, of scientific and medical workers, of artistic and creative people, of junior level production managers, etc., have been raised. Special attention has been devoted to the matter of births; maternity leave has been increased. The monthly family allowances received by cooperative farmers were made equal to those of industrial and office workers. Child-care establishments are able to take in more children.

One of our major gains is the five-day working week, which has been introduced in over 20 districts with more than 1.2 million working people. The social consumption funds have increased by more than 28 per cent. They are funds that are being used to build up a modern educational system and to improve the health services and develop culture.

But in this field again there is no room for complacency. There is a great deal more to be done. It is necessary to provide more goods of higher quality and greater variety in the shops; to considerably improve the trade services and public catering; to increase housing construction; to carry out the implementation of the Party's social program.

Our successes, comrades, are telling evidence of the viability of the socialist system and of the talent and daring of our people. These successes incarnate the great transforming power of socialist internationalism, of the fraternity, cooperation and mutual assistance of the socialist countries.

During the last few days we witnessed the celebration in Sofia of the 25th Jubilee Anniversary of the Council for Mutual Economic Assistance (CMEA), the international organization that embodies the new mutual relationships between the socialist countries in the field of economic, scientific and technical cooperation. This is a major event in the life of the world socialist community. The session in Sofia made important decisions that will further extend and deepen socialist economic integration. Thanks to the CMEA, the socialist countries that are its members are striding with joint efforts towards the common goal. Integration increases our strength tenfold; it gives us courage and confidence and enables us to cope with difficulties more easily.

The People's Republic of Bulgaria is a loyal member of the organization and an active factor for its development and perfecting. Today about 80 per cent of our foreign trade is carried out with the CMEA member states. Every year about 55 per cent of Bulgarian exports are directed to the Soviet Union, from which we get more than half of our imports. The Soviet Union provides the main part of our machines, equipment, oil, ferrous ores, coke and high-caloric coal, cellulose, wood pulp and many of the valuable prime and raw materials that we need.

Thanks to our cooperation with the socialist countries, and especially with the Soviet Union, Bulgaria has specialized in the manufacture of important machine-building products, a highly effective production in extensive series. Today, in only five days, Bulgaria produces as much machine-building output as it turned out in the whole of 1948! Socialist integration ensures a market for our output and creates conditions for high and stable rates of economic growth.

This, comrades, is true internationalism in action! The Soviet Union, the first country in the world to break the fetters of capitalism and become an invincible stronghold of socialism, helps the economic development of the other socialist countries like a brother.

We shall be eternally grateful to the Soviet people, a heroic people with whose decisive assistance we were freed from fascist slavery. Now the Soviet Union is lending us its strong hand in the building of socialism and in strengthening the economic might of our country! We are undeviatingly pursuing and will continue to pursue the course of the Party towards increasing closeness between Bulgaria and the Soviet Union. This course, which corresponds to the cherished wishes of every Bulgarian patriot, is the cornerstone of our policy, the main avenue of our development to socialism and communism.

Comrades, the stage that Bulgaria is going through now is of exceptional importance for our historical development. It is a stage in the building of a developed socialist society; a stage in which the socialist system must manifest its advantages over capitalism in every field.

Socialism has already demonstrated its superiority in the rate of economic development, in culture, in the field of democracy and in the conditions it creates for the development of the personality.

Now it is our duty to reveal fully the superiority of socialism in the field of social labor productivity as well. We can and must achieve a higher labor productivity than that of capitalism. It was not by chance that the National Party Conference placed on its agenda just one item—social labor productivity. The decisive front of the fight to see "who will prevail" on the world arena now passes through the field of social labor productivity, through the economic field. The fight for high labor productivity is a class struggle, not only an economic but also an ideological and political struggle.

Now it is necessary to adopt a new approach to the question of concentration and specialization of production, of modernization and reconstruction of fixed capital, since this is the most direct way to raise social labor productivity.

What we need now is not only individual improvements of production thechnology, not mere improvements in the work of separate machines and assemblies; we also need to introduce technologies that are new in principle, reflecting the last word in scientific and technical progress.

We should still more carefully make use of all raw materials; we should introduce a thorough, deep and complex processing of raw materials obtained in Bulgaria or imported from other countries. Bulgaria is not rich in raw materials. This fact makes it even more incumbent on us to husband them properly and use them in the most effective way.

Success in our work depends to the greatest extent on its correct organization, on the timely control of what is being done and what should be done, on the establishment of strong and conscientious discipline.

You know how sharply the National Party Conference posed the problem of discipline. The task now is to effect a turning point in tightening discipline, doing away with all manifestations of improper laxness and carelessness.

Recently the press published a special decision of the State Council on acts and phenomena that undermine socialist discipline and are incompatible with socialist morality and with the nature of the socialist system. We must confess that weaknesses in discipline are now the Achilles' heel of our work and struggle in implementing plans, raising labor productivity and bringing up the quality of output to a world standard.

Comrades, no indulgence should be allowed to those who break planning, technological, contract, finance and labor discipline or to any violation of discipline in our society. Every violation of discipline inflicts harm on the national economy and at the same time damages the interests of the working people themselves. All work forces are vitally interested in the strict observance of discipline; all of you, workers from town and village, are vitally interested in it.

The struggle for high socialist discipline should become the personal concern of every Bulgarian patriot, of every working man and woman in Bulgaria.

Production and discipline, discipline and production—this is the keyword now!

Labor productivity is the key task, on the fulfillment of which the fate of our plans hinges, the fate of the December Program for raising the people's living standards. Higher labor productivity would mean more factories, more farming machines, more schools and more social welfare measures.

What are our most urgent tasks today?

More efforts are needed to implement the work force extension plans in all fields of material production. The fight for the implementation of the plans should be waged in every enterprise, in every workshop, in every agro-industrial complex, in every block, on every stock-breeding farm—with the personal interest and high responsibility of every manager, staff member and worker.

It is necessary to provide exemplary organization for gathering in the harvest in time and without loss, and to ensure that the maximum possible areas are sown to second crops.

I should like to inform you that at present the Central Committee of the Party and the government are working hard on the plan for the period to come—1976-1980. The guiding principle in drawing up the Seventh Five-Year Plan is to create new conditions for realizing the main objective of our general line: the ever fuller, comprehensive and harmonious satisfaction of the growing needs of the working people. This calls for sustaining the high rates of economic development.

In the next five-year period we shall continue developing and improving the material and technical foundation of advanced socialism, modernizing and reconstructing important projects, and introducing progressive changes in the branch structure of production to make it even more productive and efficient. Stock-breeding should reach such a level of development as to ensure the necessary amounts of meat, milk and other animal products, in accordance with scientific nutrition standards. More measures will be taken in fulfillment of the December Program for raising the people's living standards.

There is no doubt that the Seventh Five-Year Plan, which will enhance the economic might of Bulgaria and intensify the integration processes with the Soviet Union and the other socialist countries, will stimulate our people to creative work for building the developed socialist society in the People's Republic of Bulgaria.

Comrades, one need not be a communist nor even be sympathetic to socialism to realize that when a country like Bulgaria sets itself such goals, it relies on peace and peaceful cooperation. The socialist system is the first social system in mankind's millenial history that implements in practice the principles of real humanism.

What did our fathers and mothers talk about in the twenties and thirties? They talked about wars and privation, about anonymous graves in the remote corners of the Balkan Peninsula, about the number of widows and orphans, about commissariats and coupons, about disablement pensions and unemployment.

What do we often talk about today when we recall the past of fighting against capitalism and fascism, especially the years of nazi invasion? We talk about prisons and concentration camps, about blood-soaked uprisings and partisan battles, about executions and hangings, about black squads and fascist bashibozouks[2], who carried our comrades' heads impaled on posts around village squares.

---

[2] *bashibozouks,* irregular Turkish troops, notorious for their brutal violence against the Bulgarian guerrilla fighters who fought the Turkish Ottoman tyranny.

We have every reason to declare categorically: we do not want sufferings and sacrifices for ourselves, for our children and grandchildren! Everything we have done in the 30 years since the victory could have been done only in conditions of peace. All our plans for the future can be translated into reality in a peaceful setting only. May those who are of the same age as our freedom—the thirty-year-olds and their children—know about war only from schoolbooks and their memories!

There is no man or woman of our times who does not enjoy the almost three decades of peace. There is no man or woman of our times who does not recognize that the great credit for the historic preservation of peace is attributable to socialism. The policy of strengthening peace and reducing the danger of nuclear war, consistently and patiently pursued by the socialist countries, headed by the most powerful of them, the Soviet Union, has proved fruitful. For the first time in human history there has appeared a factor for peace and cooperation such as the community of the socialist countries, with their concerted policy of influencing the international situation.

The People's Republic of Bulgaria is a socialist state and its foreign policy is coordinated with the foreign policies of the community of socialist nations. Its policies embrace constructive discussion and purposeful effort to resolve the most urgent and acute international problems in Europe and the world. It is a class, socialist, truly internationalist policy that corresponds to the interests of all revolutionary forces and to the longings of all peoples.

The peace program proclaimed by the Twenty-Fourth Congress of the CPSU is our program, too. It has already produced visible results for all people. The flames of the still smouldering war-fires in Asia and the Middle East have been brought under control; considerable progress has been achieved in the efforts to make Europe a zone of lasting peace and cooperation; a serious turn for the better has been accomplished in the relations between the Soviet Union and the United States of America; the process of détente and the relaxation of international tensions is making headway.

Joint efforts are now needed to bring about a successful outcome of the European conference aimed at strengthening peace and security in Europe. To this end, its concluding stage should be held at the summit level.

The front of the fight for peace and peaceful cooperation has cut across all continents of the planet, all large and small countries, the minds and hearts of the representatives of all peoples. As on any front, one should fight on this front to win final victory—a victory in the name of the happiness and welfare of all mankind.

"The fight for the triumph of realism, for the triumph of reason in international relations," Comrade Leonid Brezhnev declared in his last speech, "does not promise to be an easy one at all. Every line on the way to lasting peace is captured by fighting for it, in acute clashes with the most reactionary imperialist circles and their helpers. In practically all bourgeois countries, the fight goes on between the representatives of the aggressive forces and the champions of realism. No matter what serious forms this conflict might take, we are sure of one thing: the fugure does not belong to the champions of the 'cold war,' it does not belong to those who would like to precipitate the peoples into the abyss of war."[3]

Our Party, our state and our people share these thoughts completely and with a deep inner conviction.

The People's Republic of Bulgaria is a socialist country in the heart of the Balkan Peninsula, which has been the shared homeland of all the Balkan states for many centuries. When we talk about making Europe a zone of lasting peace and useful cooperation, we have in mind, above all, our share and our responsibility in solving that problem in the Balkans.

The present set-up in our peninsula provides all the necessary prerequisites for understanding, security and cooperation along every line in the political, economic, scientific, technical and cultural life of our peoples. A common Balkan proverb says that man lives not with his brother but with his neighbor. History has placed us next to each other as neighbors to live in peace and understanding. It has deprived us of the right to choose other neighbors.

You who live next to our frontier with the Socialist Federative

---

[3] *L.I. Brezhnev*, Everything for the People's Benefit, speech before the Baumansky constituency of Moscow, June 14, 1974.

Republic of Yugoslavia must be best aware of the historic need of the policy pursued by our country.

Loyal to the principles of proletarian internationalism and to the behests of Dimiter Blagoev and Georgi Dimitrov, our Party has always consistently worked for extending and deepening cooperation with the League of Yugoslav Communists and with the Socialist Federative Republic of Yugoslavia.

This Bulgarian policy fully corresponds to the spirit of the common historical destiny and fraternal friendship between our people and the Yugoslav people, between Bulgarian and Yugoslav communists. Having sprung up many decades ago from the first seeds of socialist ideas in the Balkans, this friendship developed in the joint struggle of our peoples against capitalism and fascism. It was even more firmly established during the period of socialist construction in the two countries.

The communists and working people in the People's Republic of Bulgaria follow with interest the socialist construction in neighboring Yugoslavia, and we sincerely rejoice at the achievements in their socio-political, economic and cultural life, and acclaim the efforts to consolidate and further enhance the role of the League of Yugoslav Communists.

Our relations are gaining a wider basis with the visits of Party and state leaders, with the cooperation between socio-political, youth, trade union, cultural and other organizations of the two countries. The traditional rallies on the Bulgaro-Yugoslav frontier where our people meet as brothers and fighters for our common socialist cause, make a contribution to mutual acquaintance and understanding that is not insignificant.

We share the belief of your district Party Committee that the Blagoevgrad district, as well as all other districts along the Yugoslav frontier, should be a strong link of friendship between our two countries.

A guarantee of the progress of relations between the People's Republic of Bulgaria and the Socialist Federative Republic of Yugoslavia is our common goal in the construction of socialism. This goal enables us to approach the problems of our mutual relations from socialist, class, genuine internationalist positions and to solve them

in the interest of our own people, in the interest of Balkan cooperation and in the interest of peace in Europe and the world.

We have frank and close relations with our other socialist neighbor, the Socialist Republic of Romania. We find ways to achieve
unity of action in solving the most important problems of mutual
interest; we cooperate advantageously; we work jointly with a sense
of responsibility as Balkan socialist states.

With our non-socialist Balkan neighbors—the Republic of Turkey
and the Republic of Greece, we are maintaining good neighborly
bilateral relations—political, economic and cultural. We are
gratified to say that we are meeting with understanding on many of
the most urgent issues in implementing the principles of peaceful
coexistence, good will and mutual advantage.

As you can see, therefore, the Balkan Peninsula has long ceased
to be one of Europe's slums where anything might happen and
where it was always essential to keep a foreign police force to maintain order. The Balkan states are able to solve their own Balkan
problems and to increase more and more their real contribution to
solving the crucial problems of our days in Europe and the world.
The limit of our possibilities in this respect is far from attained, and
it is our common duty to make constant efforts for the better future
of the Balkan Peninsula, in which the only masters are the Balkan
peoples themselves.

Comrades, celebrations like today's move us because they recap-
ture for us memories of the past, fill us with pride in the present and
faith in the future.

With the work of Dimiter Blagoev and Georgi Dimitrov, we feel
we have given something to the world. The realization of the importance of their contribution to the development of the workers'
socialist movement in the Balkans and in the world adds to our
sense of duty to our contemporaries. If today the communist movement is the mightiest force in the world fight for socialism and
peace, for national and social freedom, for the happiness and well-
being of mankind, it is our prime duty to do our utmost to promote
its strength and cohesion, to further the world historic role of its
invincible mainstay—the Soviet Union and the Communist Party of
the Soviet Union.

I urge you, dear comrades of Blagoevgrad and Blagoevgrad district, workers and farmers, boys and girls, communists and organized agrarians, men and women patriots, to creative work for the flowering of our dear country!

Once again I greet you most cordially on behalf of the Central Committee of our Blagoev-Dimitrov Party.

With all my heart and soul I wish you fresh successes in your work and happiness in your homes!

May the working days of our shock-work year, the 30th Anniversary Year, be bright, sunny and full of joy!

Long live and prosper the People's Republic of Bulgaria!

Glory to the universally recognized leader and organizer of the people—the Bulgarian Communist Party!

Long live communism!